Mothering in Marginalized Contexts

Funded by the Government of Canada
Financé par la gouvernement du Canada | Canada

Demeter Press
140 Holland Street West
P. O. Box 13022
Bradford, ON L3Z 2Y5
Tel: (905) 775-9089
Email: info@demeterpress.org
Website: www.demeterpress.org

Demeter Press logo based on the sculpture "Demeter" by Maria-Luise Bodirsky <www.keramik-atelier.bodirsky.de>

Front cover design: Richard Suykens, Spy Design, www.spydesigns.ca

Printed and Bound in Canada

Library and Archives Canada Cataloguing in Publication

McDonald-Harker, Caroline, 1978-, author
Mothering in marginalized contexts : narratives of women who mother in and through domestic violence / Caroline McDonald-Harker.

Includes bibliographical references.
ISBN 978-1-77258-011-2 (paperback)

1. Family violence. 2. Mothers--Abuse of. 3. Women--Abuse of. 4. Wife
abuse. 5. Motherhood. I. Title.

HV6626.M42 2016 362.82'920852 C2016-900332-9

Mothering in Marginalized Contexts

Narratives of Women Who Mother in and through Domestic Violence

Caroline McDonald-Harker, Ph.D.

DEMETER

DEMETER PRESS

This book is dedicated to the mothers who inspire me in motherhood: the twenty-nine abused women who were part of this study and shared their stories of mothering in situations of domestic violence; Dr. Andrea O'Reilly, the founding mother of motherhood-mothering studies; my mother, Denise Renaud McDonald; my sisters, Angeline McDonald Campeau and Christine McDonald Peterson; and my sister-in-law, Marissa Saigeon McDonald.

TABLE OF CONTENTS

Acknowledgments
ix

Preface
The Journey of *Mothering in Marginalized Contexts*
xi

Introduction
The Dominant Ideology of Intensive Motherhood, the Discourse of the "Good Mother" and the "Bad Mother," and Mothering in the Context of Domestic Violence
1

1.
Mothering in the Social Context of Domestic Violence: What We Know and Don't Know
24

2.
Women's Narratives and Experiences of Mothering in Domestic Violence: From Their Voices
46

3.
Abused Women's Knowledge and Understandings of the Dominant Ideology and Discourse of Motherhood
97

4.
Abused Women's Subjective Constructions of their Mothering Identities: The Influence of the Dominant Ideology of Intensive Motherhood and the Discourse of the "Good Mother" Versus "Bad Mother"
157

5.
Abused Women's Mothering Identities: Intersections of Gender, Race, and Social Class
226

Conclusion
Finding Empowerment through the Storms of Motherhood and Domestic Violence
254

Works Cited
263

ACKNOWLEDGEMENTS

I would like to thank the twenty-nine abused women participants who were part of this study and who willingly and courageously shared their stories of struggle, suffering, and sorrow. These women's personal stories help render more visible the individual voices, experiences, and lived realities of women who mother in the social context of domestic violence. Particular thanks to the abused women's shelters in Calgary, Alberta, and surrounding areas who supported me in my research by helping me recruit participants for this study and by allowing me to conduct the interviews on site at their respective shelter.

I am deeply grateful to Dr. Andrea O'Reilly, whose pioneering work in motherhood-mothering studies has inspired my own scholarly research and writing in this area as well as my personal role, identity, and practice as a mother. She is the perfect example of an empowered mother and someone whom I greatly admire, respect, and hold in the highest regard. Words cannot express how thankful I am for her mentorship, support, and kindness. Also, many thanks to Demeter Press and the publishing team.

My sincere appreciation goes to a number of colleagues and friends who endlessly support me in my pursuits—Dr. Joanne Minaker, Dr. Dale Ballucci, Dr. Timothy Haney, and Julie Bourbonnais White. Their friendship, encouragement, and guidance have been invaluable in my growth as a scholar and a person.

I wish to acknowledge and thank my family for their unconditional love and support throughout the process of writing this book. With love to my parents, Michael McDonald and Denise

Renaud McDonald. They taught me to work hard, never give up, and pursue my hopes and dreams in life. I am particularly grateful to them for teaching me how to mother with love, care, and confidence. Many thanks to my parents-in-law, Orin Harker and Valerie Frodsham Harker, for their guidance. I am beholden to Valerie for helping me with the preface by putting into words my personal journey and experience of writing this book. Much appreciation to my siblings, Angeline McDonald Campeau, Christine McDonald Peterson, and Jonathan McDonald. They have always taken an interest in my work and have encouraged me along the way. Above all, I would like to thank my spouse, Benjamin Harker, for his unwavering love, respect, and devotion as well as our three wonderful children. My son, Camden, and my two daughters, Cadrien and Caesalen, have given me the wonderful opportunity of being a mother and experiencing motherhood.

PREFACE

The Journey of Mothering in Marginalized Contexts

THERE HAVE BEEN MOMENTS in my life when, in the midst of circumstances outside the margins of conformity, a particular insight showed up and could not be ignored. An awareness emerged that demanded changes in perceptions. Focus and direction shifted and were never the same again. These are known as watershed moments—critical turning points. We all have them, as individuals and as groups. Countries are affected, institutions are reorganized, and individuals are transformed as a result of watershed moments. I have had a few, but among the most remarkable watershed moments of my life were the revelations that came to me during a qualitative research study that I conducted for my PhD research. While conducting this study, I sat with and interviewed twenty-nine women who had experienced severe abuse at the hands of their intimate male partners and were living with their children in abused women's shelters in Calgary, Alberta.

Despite being criticized, vilified, and stigmatized as "bad mothers" for having lived and mothered in domestic abuse relationships, these abused women victims found ways to exercise agency, resistance, and empowerment in both their and their children's lives. This book is based on the profound narratives, experiences, and lived realities of these women who mothered in and through domestic violence.

My journey and purpose in writing this book began well ahead of this experience. After my undergraduate degree and throughout my master's degree in sociology, I worked as a counsellor at an abused women's emergency shelter. I was a single student and needed to pay for my education. This appeared to be an opportunity that would provide income and, at the same time, give me insights into my area of study. Despite my many years in university studying and training to be a sociologist, nothing prepared me for what I encountered when I began working at the shelter. Severely abused and seeking admission to the shelter, countless women with children "in tow" would arrive daily. The physical, psychological, and emotional conditions these women were in when they arrived, the abusive situations they had escaped, and the experiences of violence they shared with me, were inconceivable. On particularly challenging days, it was almost more than I could bear. At the end of a shift, I would sit in my car in the parking lot and try to process the horror. Sometimes I would cry. During the sixteen months that I worked there, I developed an intense compassion for the female sufferers of domestic violence. These women and this kind of suffering felt senseless—horrendous. It was not anything I had ever dealt with or experienced, and I wanted to understand. I wanted to help. I wanted to contribute to advocate for change. This was the beginning of a consuming exploration of domestic violence and its ensuing challenges to women and mothering.

Not surprisingly, I decided to study domestic violence for my master's research, which investigated substance use as a coping mechanism in the lives of abused women. After my master's degree, I began working on my PhD degree in sociology. Towards the end of my first year in the program, I met and married my spouse. Being married and in a PhD program gave rise to a variety of well-meaning advice and direction. Loved ones, friends, esteemed advisers freely opined—some even harangued on the wisdom (or lack thereof) of trying to juggle marriage and a demanding educational pursuit. I heard it all: "There's a time and a place for marriage and family, and graduate school is not one of them"; "Don't lose your focus, you need to stay dedicated to your studies or you will never finish your PhD"; "You're not planning on children now that you are married are you?" The message was loud and clear: "Female graduate students are rarely taken seriously once they are married," let alone "once they have children." It was alarming. In graduate school, I even had friends who had made the decision to never have children, choosing instead a life of academe because of the perceived incompatibility of having or doing both. But I had always wanted to be married, and I had always aspired to be a mother.

I continued to work away in my PhD program. But during this time, another challenge presented itself. For many years, I had struggled with a serious health condition. My doctors, contrary to some of my academic "advisors," recommended that I think about having children sooner rather than later. I was told that my window for conception might be smaller than I realized and that there was a strong possibility that waiting would close the door on pregnancy, motherhood, and family. I took this advice seriously and managed to become pregnant at the end of my second year in the program, not without struggle however. The thrill of this realization was followed almost immediately with the fallout of my condition. I wasn't just married. I was married and "with child." The voices from the ranks of the educators in the ivory tower began to resound in my own mind. I felt an ambivalence that was extremely uncomfortable. I had worked so hard to come this far and I wondered if my competency would be challenged or if my commitment would be called into question. I actually felt shamed by my pregnant condition. I worried that I would be criticized for a lack of academic focus. So I did everything possible to minimize the news. That fall and winter—thanks to cold weather, baggy sweaters, and mostly working from home—I hid the reality of my pregnant condition until I was thirty-four weeks along.

But there was more than simply the outward appearance of my pregnant body and the fear of criticism. I was also faced with having to embrace my new role as both a graduate student and a mother. Graduate school was rigorous enough on its own. I began asking myself many questions. How was I going to balance being both a student and a mother? Would motherhood and all the challenges and demands of raising and caring for a baby turn me into a "bad" student? On the other hand, was keeping up with the standards of the "good" student that I had established going to turn me into a "bad" mother? How could I mother a new baby and still successfully work towards completing my PhD? Mothering felt messy, opposing, dividing, and difficult. The strain pulled and pushed at me.

It was during the first few months of my pregnancy, in the midst of so much inner conflict, that I began the process of selecting the topic for my PhD research. I spent months pouring through academic books and journals, making lists, and thinking critically about various potential topics. Nothing seemed cogent, nothing felt compelling. I was still struggling with the fact that I was about to become a mother, so a lot of the conversations in my head reflected concerns and fears about finishing my program, which began to inform my topic choices. Certainly, there were other women who were pregnant or who had children and who had successfully accomplished something rigorous. How did they navigate it? How did they feel? What were their experiences? It was at that moment that I realized I had been face to face with an enormous group of women whose lives could fill volumes with exactly the kind of stories and answers that seemed so relevant to me at that time. I thought of the many mothers that I had encountered who were admitted into the shelter where I worked. I reflected on their struggles to cope, to accept change, to instigate steps for establishing a new life for themselves and their children, a life that was free of violence. I wondered where they found the courage and the strength to change their worlds, to stand up and leave abusive homes, and to care for their children in such desperate and difficult situations. I remembered so many of the women and their efforts to help their children adjust after having fled from abuse—to cope with lives that had been shattered by this abuse. All of this advocating was juxtaposed onto their own suffering. It was amazing that they would still embrace motherhood when it was most inconvenient and when their own lives were in a state of disarray.

These mothers—their strength, fortitude, and conviction in their mothering, despite the abusive context in which they found themselves—began to have an impact on my own subjective identity as a mother. How did I feel about motherhood? How did I view myself as a mother? How did I define my mothering? The circumstances that I was trying to navigate were minimal in comparison with the women in shelters, but my memories of them began to intrigue me. Nothing I knew was as brutal, but I felt a firm connection. What had seemed atrocious and troubling years before was now becoming illuminating. On a cold November afternoon in the beginning of the third year of my PhD program, fully pregnant, I sat in front of my computer at home and began to formulate my PhD research study. I was excited. I wanted to know more about the mothers in shelters, their backgrounds, their struggles, their triumphs, their determination, and the ways that they navigated their mothering. It would take months to put together the research proposal, but something significant was taking shape. This was about to become a consuming, affirming, and never to be forgotten chapter in my life. This exploration gave me new insight into motherhood and mothering.

I recruited and interviewed the twenty-nine women participants for the study from nine different abused women's shelters in Calgary, Alberta, and surrounding areas from January to April 2009. As I conducted in-depth face-to-face interviews with these mothers, I learned a great deal about the narratives, experiences, and lived realities of abused women who mother in and through domestic violence. Rich, yet wrenching, these were the stories of courageous women and their children who had found themselves in the disappointing circumstances of life in an abused women's shelter. These narratives revealed the numerous stigmas, oppressions, and struggles that they had experienced. They had suffered at the hands of someone who had at one time been a chosen intimate partner, but then threatened, battered, and injured them until they had to flee in fear with their children. The resulting fight for survival was more than just needing a place to live. These victimized women were ravaged by their abuse, challenged by a lack of means, and in most cases, left with the sole and overwhelming responsibility of caring for their children. In addition to every other disappointment, these women were also undermined by a society that vilifies its victims, particularly in situations of domestic violence. They were faced with the added burden of agencies that questioned, scrutinized, and criticized their mothering capabilities and, in many cases, attempted to remove them from their mothering responsibilities, fragmenting their families to an even greater extent. Labels of incompetency were freely applied to these mothers with broad brushstrokes.

Listening to these women's stories was sobering. It was disconcerting to observe the trend of a patriarchal society that removes the accountability from the men who inflict the abuse in the first place, and it was disappointing to see that, instead, the suspicion was laid on mothers who now had to prove their innocence of wrongdoing and suspected "bad mothering." These women's mothering capabilities were all too commonly called into question. Directly and indirectly they were repeatedly faced with queries such as the following: what kind of a mother are you? How have you allowed yourself and your children to live in an abusive situation? Can you protect your children? Can you even take care of your children? Will you abuse your children like your partner abused you? Yet these were resourceful women who had left their homes, after deliberating, organizing, and overcoming forces that would have kept them and their children in situations of abuse. These were women who had gone to great lengths to protect and care for their children. They sometimes remained in abusive relationships, at risk of further abuse, so that they could wait for "the right moment"—a safe time to leave and with a safe place to go with their children. These were women whose circumstances may not have been a perfect reflection of the idealized "gold standard" of mothering, but they nevertheless had made courageous choices and adaptations in challenging and oppressive social contexts. Where is the logic and the justice in concluding that instead of empowering these brave and determined mothers and helping them on their way, it would be better to hold them culpable and, in many cases, to take away their children and to place them in the homes and in the hands of strangers?

Despite these struggles, these women's narratives revealed powerful, unique, and completely individual approaches to motherhood and mothering—ones that had grown out of their challenging situations. Out of their oppressive and stigmatized circumstances, and with limited resources, these mothers formed unique brands of mother care and mother identity. Because they loved and wanted to protect their children and because they themselves wanted to survive, these mothers refused to give up on motherhood. Instead, they found new ways of defining meanings of motherhood, practices of mothering, and mother identities—ones that were empowering. They believed in themselves and they believed they were good mothers. They looked at what their children needed and then drew from what they had to offer to find effective ways of defining and carrying out the practice of mothering. These mothers had learned something that often evades more fortunate mothers—those with the advantage of raising their children in the calm, safe, and supportive conditions of privilege. The experiences of these mothers are reflected in the following quote by one of the participants in the study named Carly, a thirty-year-old mother of two children who experienced verbal, psychological, and financial abuse from her previous male partner for over a year.

> *Because of the abuse I'm very hard on myself.... But my kids are my biggest strength. You know what, it's terrible and it's unfortunate. I mean, it's no way to deal with anything, but I'll tell you, I honestly don't think I'd be here today.... I really don't. I think that I would've taken my own life. I was so down and it was really hard for a while.... Some people just have a crappy life. I got dealt one of them ... I'm extremely fortunate ... I got two beautiful babies ... being with my boys and just doing something together, whether it be just sitting here talking ... or building a snow man, you know. As many mishaps and misfortunate things that have happened to me, I'm here for my babies ... I'm a good mother ... I'm a strong mother, too. I'm very strong at being a mother because of my [children].*

Carly describes how her children were her biggest strength, gave her hope, and helped her to see that she was and is a "good mother," despite the abusive circumstances that she lived and mothered in. Carly and the other women's narratives were a revelation to me. I was awestruck by the depth of their determination, the strength of their resistance, and their resolve to affect change. Something about the struggle, something about mothering in circumstances so far from ideal, took these women to a straightforward and more informed and more useful understanding of motherhood, mothering practices, and mother identity.

Indeed, my years of struggle as a PhD student—where I balanced the demands of graduate school while giving birth to and raising not only one but three children—and still my struggles today as a tenure-track professor—where I balance the strenuous demands of academe while raising my now four-, seven-, and ten-year-old children—have been a major motivation and driver for writing this book. This book examines the narratives, experiences, and lived realities of abused women—mothers who are stigmatized, criticized, and vilified for failing to meet dominant ideologies of what a "good mother" is or should be because they have lived and mothered in domestic violence relationships. This book gives a voice to the twenty-nine abused women participants who were part of this research study and to abused women, more generally, who have been marginalized, kept on the periphery, and largely excluded from discussions about mothering in situations of domestic violence. Only when we give abused mothers a voice are we able to begin to understand their unique mothering positions, understandings, identities, and practices, which have been silenced and neglected for far too long. Indeed, from the inception of my own motherhood, followed by my years of research as a maternal scholar and even now upon the completion of this book, I have felt and continue to feel compelled to provide a voice against the judgment of mothers, to end the oppressive and restrictive bifurcation of mothers into categories of either "good" or "bad" mothers, to re-envision a more inclusive understanding of mothering, and to empower all mothers, regardless of differences in their lives and social circumstances. This has been my watershed moment, and it is my hope that this book is a step in that direction.

INTRODUCTION

The Dominant Ideology of Intensive Motherhood, the Discourse of the "Good Mother" and the "Bad Mother," and Mothering in the Context of Domestic Violence

TODAY, IN NORTH AMERICAN CULTURE and beyond, when we hear the word "mother," it often evokes a specific image in our mind. Aside from the commonly held understanding that a mother is a woman who has child(ren), mothers are assumed to intrinsically possess a specific set of characteristics—they are loving, caring, nurturing, and devoted. Mothers are also expected to carry out their mothering in specific spaces and places—in a heterosexual and married relationship, within a male breadwinner and female caregiver model, and in a safe and private household. There are even specific sets of criteria against which women's mothering is assessed and measured. Today's current standards of mothering, which are highly idealized, go beyond expectations that mothers merely bear and care for children (which itself requires substantial work) and require that mothers also dedicate and acquiesce their entire physical, psychological, emotional, and intellectual well-being to not only be *perfect* mothers but also raise *perfect* children (Hays; Douglas and Michaels; Ennis). Modern motherhood is thus influenced and shaped by a dominant ideology motherhood, specifically one that emphasizes intensive mothering. The ideology of intensive motherhood is a current "system of ideas" about motherhood that emphasizes and requires a rigorous, exhaustive, and demanding type of mothering.[1] According to Sharon Hays "intensive mothering" is a "gendered model that advises mothers to expend a tremendous amount of time, energy, and money in raising their children" (x). In this sense, mothering is more than just being loving, caring, nurturing, and devoted. It is also being selfless, sacrificial, and ever present; it is having endless energy, giving all of one's time to children, putting children before any other need, person, or commitment (including oneself); and it is listening to expert advice and being responsible for everything that happens in children's lives. This "type" of mothering is what is constructed, defined, and portrayed as "good mothering" and reflects a privileged Eurocentric, heterosexual, white, and middle or upper-class perspective of mothering and childrearing.

In a media-laden era of radio, television, movies, books, magazines, and more recently internet and social network sites such as Pinterest, mommy blogs, Facebook, Instagram, and Twitter, mothers more than ever before are bombarded with specific images of what constitutes "good mothering" and against which they are measured—extravagant children's birthday parties, handmade children's crafts, healthy homemade children's snacks and meals, creative and fun-filled children's playdates, celebrity-fashioned clothing for children, magazine worthy children's bedrooms, "Fit-Mama" and baby yoga classes, "Stars and Strollers" mommy and baby movie viewing, and "Parent-Child Mother Goose" rhyme, songs, and stories programs, to name just a few. Indeed, this model of motherhood puts flawless, esteemed, and admired mothers from past television shows—such as Lucy Ricardo from the 1950s' "I Love Lucy," Carol Brady from the 1960s' "Brady Bunch," Caroline Ingalls from the 1970s' "Little House on the Prairie," and Clair Huxtable from the 1980s' "The Cosby Show"—to shame. It is not hard to see that the expectations put on mothers over the years have drastically increased and intensified since the 1950s. Motherhood, therefore, is a culturally constructed practice that is shaped, altered, and transformed with time, place, space, and social conditions (O'Reilly, *Rocking the Cradle*).

IDEOLOGIES OF MOTHERHOOD—PAST AND PRESENT

The mothering standards that women are held to have been continuously redesigned in response to changing societal factors such as norms, values, politics, laws, and economics, to name a few. This is clearly seen in the way that constructions about ideal motherhood have changed and shifted historically. In the 1960s' post-war era, when men returned from the war and women were encouraged to abandon their wartime employment and return back to the home so that men could take up these jobs, "custodial mothering" emerged as the dominant form of mothering (O'Reilly, *Rocking the Cradle*). Custodial mothering defined and promoted mothering in the following ways: 1) mothering is natural to women; 2) mothers are the central caregiver of their biological children; and 3) children require full-time mothering. Good mothering during this time was constructed as women returning and remaining in the home full time to raise their children as a way to "effect social reorganization" in this post-war period and to "redesign feminine gender behavior and roles (O'Reilly, *Rocking the Cradle* 38). Although custodial mothering mandated full-time mothering, the "emphasis was on the physical proximity of mother and child—i.e., the mother was to be 'at home' with the children, with little said on the mother needing to be continually attuned to the psychological, emotional or cognitive needs of her children" (O'Reilly, *Rocking the Cradle* 40). Back then children played outside with little to no supervision and headed home when the streetlights came on. This was the "children should be seen but not heard style of mothering" (O'Reilly, *Rocking the Cradle* 40).

In the 1980s, "intensive mothering" began to emerge as the dominant mode of mothering and is today, in a more heightened form, the prevailing standard of mothering against which mothers' lives are regulated and judged (O'Reilly, *Mother Matters*). Intensive mothering requires more than mere physical proximity between mothers and their children, as in the case of custodial mothering. Instead, mothers are "expected to spend 'quality time' with their children" where "they are told to play with their children, read to them, and take classes with them" (O'Reilly, *Rocking the Cradle* 40). Intensive mothering, as defined by Andrea O'Reilly, delineates and promotes mothering in the following eight ways: 1) children can only be properly cared for by their biological mother; 2) mothering must be provided 24/7; 3) mothers must always put their children's needs before their own; 4) mothers must turn to experts for instruction; 5) mothers must be fully satisfied, fulfilled, completed, and composed in motherhood; 6) mothers must lavish excessive amounts of time, energy, and money on the rearing of their children; 7) mothers have full responsibility but no power from which to mother; and 8) "motherwork," (childrearing specifically) is regarded as a personal, private undertaking with no political import (*Mother Matters*; *What Do Mothers Need*). Today, mothers are expected to be not only in close proximity to children but to supervise, entertain, and endlessly engage with children in a multitude of activities from playing, reading, and taking classes with them (O'Reilly, *Rocking the Cradle*). There has been a shift from a family-centred to, what Hays describes as, a child-centred lifestyle. Good mothering is thus "intensive mothering." This is, I argue, the children should be seen, heard, *and* "prodigized" style of mothering.

The forces of neoliberalism, emerging in the mid–1980s and increasing in the 1990s, added to the intensive mothering discourse by situating children as social capital to be invested in (Vandenbeld). Mothers are increasingly "investing" in their children to give them an educational and competitive advantage by enrolling them in organized extracurricular activities, such as art classes, dance classes, piano lessons, math and reading programs, second language courses, and sports such as, basketball, golf, soccer, and hockey. These extracurricular activities require a significant amount of time commitment not only from children but also from mothers, as they are the ones who largely shoulder the burden of bringing children to and from these activities. Moreover, these activities are financially expensive (usually costing several hundred to even thousand dollars per activity) and involve not only registration costs but also the costs of training, buying equipment and uniforms, fundraising, and transportation. More and more, mothers are enrolling their children in these "enriching" activities, or what Hillary Levey Friedman refers to as "competitive kid capital," whether or not the mothers can afford to, because they fear their children will fall behind (Palladino; O'Reilly, *Rocking the Cradle*). Even mothers in lower social classes, despite their financial inability to provide such activities for their children, still view them as desirable and beneficial to children (Hays; Takševa, "The Commercialization of Motherhood and Mothering"). When mothers, despite their social class, are willing to spend whatever it takes on their children because they believe such an investment is essential, this "impacts the baseline of what constitutes socially appropriate norms of childrearing" (Palladino 288).

O'Reilly points out how the influences of neoliberalism and intensive mothering have created a significant challenge for twenty-first motherhood, as mothers today are expected to do more but with fewer resources (*Mother Outlaws*). Mothers are left with an expectation to invest in their children but have few economic opportunities as well as little social and family support to do so. As Hays correctly states, "In a society where over half of all mothers with young children are now working outside the home, one might wonder why our culture pressures women to dedicate so much of themselves to child rearing" (x)—more so now than what was expected in the custodial mothering era when mothers actually had more time to devote to childrearing. The emergence of intensive mothering parallels the increasing presence and participation of women in today's paid labour force (O'Reilly, *Mother Outlaws*). In fact, women who work outside the home are just as likely, if not more likely, to embrace the tenets of intensive mothering as a way to make the time that they have with their children count because they have their own income and can determine how to spend it (Hays; O'Reilly, *Rocking the Cradle*). Not surprisingly, mothering standards have historically been redesigned to put more demands and expectations on mothers at the very time when they are beginning to progress and to feel confident about themselves as women and in their mothering roles and practices.

The pressures to conform to the current ideology of intensive motherhood come from multiple sources; it is considered the legitimate standard to which all mothers should aspire to, attain, and be compared and assessed against. This mothering ideal comes not only from media but also from the policies, practices, and instructions of formal institutions such as teachers' recommendations in the educational system; doctors' and nurses' advice in the healthcare system; social workers', counselors', and psychologists' recommendations in social service agencies; and political leaders' and policy writers' messages from government. Intensive mothering as the ideal also comes from interpersonal associations and interactions, such as input and advice from family, friends, co-workers, other mothers, and even strangers (Green 24). The ideology of intensive motherhood has become so culturally entrenched that it now represents the "face" of motherhood.

Mothers are encouraged to engage in intensive mothering based on the assumption that it will make them a "good mother" and enable them to effectively raise their children. But does intensive mothering actually benefit mothers and children? Is it helping mothers raise children to be confident instead of insecure, independent rather than dependent, responsible rather than unaccountable, self-sufficient rather than indulged? Interestingly, to date, the research does not bear this out. The research does, however, show that mothers today are experiencing unprecedented levels of stress, anxiety, depression, exhaustion, depletion, and guilt (Rullo and Musatti; Rizzo, Schiffrin, and Liss; Wall). As Horwitz asserts:

> There are many factors such as temperament, level of ability, presence or absence of extended family, media, school experience, societal messages about a variety of issues, life experiences, and social supports that influence our children's development. However, mothers believe that if they engage in intensive mothering they can protect their children from all these influence…. Mothers buy into the belief that they can raise the perfect child if they follow the "right" practices, which also suggests that if the child does not turn out perfect, they are at fault. Mothering intensively may not prevent these children from struggling later in life or protect them from other influences that may lead to later problems. But mothering intensively is depleting and hurting mothers, so no one wins. (28)

Intensive mothering, therefore, is actually limiting, impairing, and oppressing mothers by promoting an ideal that is impossible to achieve (Horwitz). There is no question that mothers play a vital and important role in the lives of their children, but expectations that mothers must focus exclusively on the needs of their children at the expense of everything else, including themselves, to the point of exhaustion and depletion really benefit no one (Ennis). Not all mothers fit the definition of intensive mothering and not all women can or want to intensively mother. But the important point is that children have never required this style of mothering. If this is so, why is intensive mothering nonetheless held up as the ideal way to mother?

CURRENT DISCOURSES OF THE "GOOD MOTHER" VERSUS THE "BAD MOTHER"

The ideology of intensive motherhood exerts a powerful influence within our society. Not only is it portrayed and reinforced in numerous social institutions, cultural practices, and social interactions but it is also acquired and reproduced through discourse—language, statements, terms, and classifications that define how women must mother. Today mothers are compared, categorized, and defined in two diametrically opposed ways—they are either a "good mother" or a "bad mother." Mothers who adhere and live up to the standards of intensive mothering are considered to be "good mothers," and mothers who do not are deemed to be "bad mothers." Every day mothers are faced with and judged according to these overarching and opposing discursive classifications. Mothers, therefore, are constantly engaging in an inner monologue with themselves, in which they question if they are living up to the standards of intensive mothering in order to be characterized as a "good mother" for fear of being labeled the dreaded "bad mother." Ask any mother, and she will tell you that racing through her mind on any given day are endless questions: did I spend enough time with my children? Was I there for my children when they needed me? Did I help my children the way they needed to be helped? Did I teach my children what they needed to know? Did I give my children everything they needed? This gives new meaning to the term "helicopter" parenting or in this case, what I refer to as "helicopter mothering," where mothers are increasingly not only hovering over their children and intensively mothering them but also hovering over themselves to verify and ensure that they are indeed intensively mothering for the "benefit" of their children.

While the ideology of intensive motherhood sets up beliefs systems that inform and persuade mothers to engage in intensive mothering, the discourse of the "good mother" versus the "bad mother" provides the language that pressures and coerces mothers to actually engage in intensively mothering their children. When a mother is incapable of attaining the standards of intensive mothering, which are impossible to achieve, she faces blame, shame, and being labeled a "bad mother." The message is clear—*she* is a failure. Mothers, then, are set up to face guilt instead of appreciation, judgment instead of support, criticism instead of respect, and failure instead of success. We live in a culture that "assigns mothers all the responsibility for mothering, but gives them no real power from which to mother" (O'Reilly, *Mother Outlaws* 11). It is no surprise then that many mothers at one point or another experience extreme stress, worry, self-doubt, inadequacy, and guilt, even when their children's needs are met. However, intensive mothering is not natural, normal, and inevitable; rather, it is a social construction based on highly idealized criteria that are unrealistic and impossible to achieve. As a society, we often assume and believe that intensive mothering is desirable, achievable, and even necessary, not because it actually is but because it is so pervasive and culturally entrenched that "like air" it is "unnoticeable" and invisible (Thurer xv). Consequently, within our society, we often do not question the dominant standards of "good mothering" that mothers are held to and judged against. The "good mother" versus the "bad mother" dichotomy serves to "control, police, and sanction the actions and activities of mothers who are expected to meet or conform to dominant standards of motherhood" (Crawford 11). As Douglas and Michaels rightly put it "everyone watches us, we watch ourselves and other mothers, and we watch ourselves watching ourselves" (6). Under the "gaze of others," as Ruddick called it, many mothers "relinquish authority to others, lose confidence in their own values" ("Maternal Thinking," 111). This heightened surveillance—which others do to mothers, mothers do to themselves, and mothers do to other mothers—ensures that all mothers are following the standards of intensive mothering. This scrutiny moves the focus away from questioning the existence, perpetuation, and reinforcement of these socially constructed and idealized mothering standards in the first place and results in the stigmatization of mothers who do not conform to these "good mothering" practices. Women are disempowered in their mothering experience when the focus is on their deficiencies rather than their strengths and contributions.

MOTHERING IN CIRCUMSTANCES OF DOMESTIC VIOLENCE—CONFORMING TO OR CONTRAVENING STANDARDS OF "GOOD MOTHERING"?

A disconnect exists between the idealized standards of mothering and the reality of the diverse social positions, locations, and circumstances in which women carry out their mothering. Nonetheless, mothers are not given liberty to mother in ways that they consider fitting and functional for themselves and their children but are pressured to mother within these socially prescribed ideals, which are privileged, restrictive, and exclusionary (Green, *Feminist Mothers*). Consequently, some mothers are perceived, labeled, and portrayed as "bad mothers" because they mother outside the boundaries of "good mothering," including the following examples: teen mothers, mothers who give their child up for adoption, disabled mothers, working mothers, mothers who have a nanny, mothers who drink or use drugs, and incarcerated mothers. This is even more so the case for mothers living in marginalized circumstances based on marital status, sexual orientation, race, ethnicity, and social class, including the following examples: single mothers, lesbian mothers, mothers of colour, and low-income mothers. By singling them out and constructing them as "bad mothers," the current ideology of intensive motherhood acts as an institutionalized form of domination and oppression against mothers who do not, cannot, or will not mother in this way. This social construction of the seemingly normal and inevitable discursive classification of women as "good mothers" or "bad mothers" sets up norms for women to meet that have little to do with the real lives of women.

THE SOCIAL CONSTRUCT OF ABUSED MOTHERS AS "BAD MOTHERS"

In recent years, mothers who are victims of domestic violence are one group of mothers who have become especially stigmatized, criticized, and vilified for mothering outside the boundaries of "good mothering" because they have lived in circumstances of abuse. Many abused mothers come to the attention of legal and extra-legal state agencies (such as the criminal justice system, abused women's shelters, child protection services etc.), indirectly through their involvement as "victims." Yet despite being the victims, abused mothers are often perceived and characterized as "bad mothers" because their ability to shelter, care for, protect, and provide a safe and secure environment for their children is called into question and deemed deficient. When abused women are believed to be "failing" as mothers, they are held accountable through extensive scrutiny, monitoring, governance, and control (McDonald-Harker; Nixon; Wilson). In this sense, victimization and mothering are often perceived as contradictory. That is, mothering in the context of domestic violence is constructed as a particular kind of deviant mothering that offends sensibilities about how a "good mother" ought to be (McDonald-Harker; Lapierre, "Striving to Be 'Good' Mothers"). In fact, one of the participants in this study named Eden[2] spoke about the complexity of being not only an abused woman but also a mother and about the daily stigmatization and judgment that women like her face from having mothered in an abusive social context. She stated:

> *I think abused mothers are very, um, what is that word I'm looking for, they're really, misunderstood! Like people think they know who abused mothers are, you know, they think they're bad either way.... So I think when you're abused, a lot of the times they expect you to prove yourself because they probably think "Oh she's had a bad past or she was probably bad before, she probably drank, did drugs," whatever.... They expect them [abused mothers] to work extra hard. They expect them to prove to everyone that, you know, they're not a bad person and they're not doing drugs or alcohol. But yeah, that exactly, they expect them to prove to everyone that they can have a good life too.... But being abused has taught me that there's all different kinds of forms of ways of mothering and raising a child.... I'm not perfect, I know that, but I think I'm a good mom. We're in a bad situation now,*

> *but I value myself as a strong woman because I've been through so much.*

There are several thousands of other women in Canada, just like Eden, who are victims and who mother every single day in abusive situations. Placing all of the responsibility on mothers obscures the gender inequalities that underlie domestic violence relationships—whereby males are the perpetrators and females are the victims—and removes responsibility from the men-fathers who inflict the abuse. Nonetheless, the focus still remains on the failures of the abused mother and on the precarious situation in which *she* has put herself and her children (McDonald-Harker; Radford and Hester, "Overcoming Mother Blaming"). As Radford and Hester argue, blaming women for their own victimization and undermining their mothering play a key role in locking them into abusive relationships and exacerbating the damage done by domestic violence ("Overcoming Mother Blaming"). Yet our knowledge about mothering in the context of domestic violence is relatively recent, limited in scope, and tends to focus on domestic violence and motherhood-mothering as separate topics of inquiry rather than as interrelated, which they certainly are.

THE RECOGNITION OF DOMESTIC VIOLENCE AS A SOCIAL PROBLEM IN THE 1960S AND 1970S

To date, there is limited knowledge and understanding about the multiple, varied, and subjective experiences of women who mother in the marginalized circumstances of domestic violence. In the last fifty years, the public, academic, and policy attention paid to the social problem of violence against women has increased considerably. Violence against women is recognized today as a serious violation of human rights and is a major issue on the international human rights agenda. According to Article One of The United Nations Declaration on Violence Against Women, violence against women is an act of gender-based violence that results, or is likely to result, in physical, sexual, or psychological harm or suffering to women, including threats of such acts, coercion, or arbitrary deprivation of liberty, whether occurring in public or in private life (United

Nations). This widely accepted definition refers to the gender-based roots of violence, and recognizes that violence against women is one of the crucial social mechanisms by which women are forced into a subordinate position. It broadens the definition of violence by including both the physical and psychological harm done towards women, and it includes acts in both private and public life. Domestic violence is one aspect of violence against women, and specifically refers to physical, sexual, psychological, emotional, financial, or verbal abuse perpetrated by an intimate partner (Jasinski 5). The language used to refer to violence against women varies and includes the following terms: "domestic violence," "partner abuse," "domestic abuse," "spousal abuse," "intimate partner violence," "woman abuse" and "wife abuse" (Radford). Although anyone can experience domestic violence at the hands of an intimate partner, "women are most frequently the victims of domestic violence," and "suffer the most persistent abuse and the most severe injuries" (Radford and Hester, "Introduction" 8).

In the late 1960s and early 1970s, the topic of domestic violence emerged as an important and central topic of public and academic attention and inquiry. The impetus for much of the growth in interest in domestic violence was the pioneering work of several feminist scholars and activists who focused attention on what they correctly viewed as a neglected area of study (Johnson xi). As such, when the topic of domestic violence emerged at this time it was not because the condition was new; rather, it took claims-making activities to define this condition as a social problem and to convince the general public that the behaviours now called "domestic violence" were morally intolerable and that women now called "abused women" deserved and required public sympathy and safety. Feminists argued that domestic violence provided a powerful illustration of the systematic oppression of women in the context of male domination (Dobash and Dobash, *Violence against Wives*).

Efforts to politicize the problem of domestic violence and to aid female victims had two focuses. The first emphasis was to challenge the dominant view of the family as a place of safety and stability by drawing attention to the potential for violence and danger. Feminists argued that the distinction between the private and the public spheres perpetuated the oppression of women by protecting the heinous acts of men in the home from social or legislative or sanctions. The second emphasis was the creation of women's shelters as transitional institutions—the bridge between home and the larger society. Feminists argued that women would remain trapped in violent homes unless they and their children could go to a safe place for a short period of time during an emergency or a crisis. As such, there was a push to mobilize resources to create an alternative to violence (Schechter). Abused women's shelters were among the first services targeted to address the needs of abused women. The first shelters for abused women in Canada were established in 1973 and included Transition House in Vancouver B.C., Ishtar in Langley, B.C., Oasis House (now Calgary Women's Emergency Shelter) in Calgary, Alberta, Saskatoon's Interval House in Saskatoon, Saskatchewan, and Interval House in Toronto, Ontario (Gilman 10-11; Hebert and Foley; MacLeod; Walker).

From the time the first abused women's shelters opened, feminist activists, scholars, shelter workers, and abused women have been vocal in their demands for research on domestic violence, which led to the development of a large body of feminist literature on domestic violence. The literature largely examines domestic violence according to two main conceptualizations—domestic violence as a gendered social problem and as resulting from a patriarchal social structure. On the one hand, the literature focuses on how males are the primary perpetrators of violence and women are the primary victims of this violence (Kurz; Berk et al.; Dobash and Dobash *Violence Against Wives*; Pleck et al.; Russell; Walker, L.). This literature places the issue of gendered power at the centre of analysis and is concerned with men's violence against women. On the other hand, the literature focuses on how male abuse results from historic and current power differentials that keep men dominant and women subordinate, primarily through the use of control, including psychological, emotional, physical, and sexual abuse (Bograde; Bowker; Dobash and Dobash; Dobash and Dobash; and Lenton). This literature attributes male dominance, and the abuse used to sustain it, to male socialization. It is the acceptance, reproduction, and institutionalization of male abuse in everyday life that perpetuates women's subordination. The patriarchal ideology of the family, for example, institutionalizes the subordination and control of women by men through the structure of male-female roles. Male partners who abuse female partners do so in order to maintain their dominant position and the subordinate position of females in relationships.

Recently, the literature has begun to move beyond an exploration of domestic violence as solely a gendered social problem and as resulting from patriarchal social structure, to one that focuses on differences among women's experiences of abuse, women's subjectivities as socially constructed, shifting and conflicting, and discourses as shaping and constructing women's subjectivities (Browne; Ferraro and Johnson; Hyden). This shift in the literature comes from recognition that the etymology of domestic violence has reflected a white, middle-class feminist focus on challenging patriarchy within the household and has ignored social dimensions other than gender inequality as key explanatory factors of domestic violence. Overall, however, the feminist literature on domestic violence does not specifically consider mothering as an important aspect of the varied, heterogeneous, multiple facets of abused women's lives.

THE EMERGENCE OF MOTHERHOOD AND MOTHERING AS A TOPIC OF STUDY IN THE 1980S AND 1990S

The topic of motherhood and mothering has only more recently emerged as an important and central topic of academic attention and inquiry. Beginning in the 1980s, feminist scholars began to see the necessity of feminist consciousness to create a rewarding and disciplined expression of conscience through mothering and to develop a theory of mothering. Early feminist work focused attention on the subjugation of women. Feminist scholars rejected motherhood, as it equated the responsibility of motherhood with oppression (Featherstone; Firestone; Knowles and Cole). This work upheld that "women's self-determination depended on women's ability to control their reproduction," which created a distinction between "woman" and "mother" that had benefited women (Chase and Rogers 6). Later feminist work focused attention on differences between men and women. Feminist scholars embraced motherhood, as they equated women's procreative potential with moral superiority over men (Featherstone and Trinder 153). Some of this work "elevated all women's potential for motherhood to an essential, unifying principle" (Chase and Rogers 14). Other work rejected this totalizing approach to motherhood and sought to draw attention to the value of motherhood without idealizing it (Chase and Rogers 15).

Both the early and later feminist scholarship opened up conceptualizations of women's lives in relation to motherhood and mothering, which led to the development of a large body of feminist literature on motherhood-mothering beginning in the 1990s. The literature largely examines motherhood-mothering along two broad tracks. One track has a universalistic focus and consists of efforts to develop a model of mothering that offers breadth and universality and delineates commonalities in women's mothering experiences. This literature emphasizes that although mothers differ culturally and individually, they share, by definition and condition, a set of activities (Ruddick). That is, they engage in maternal practice: the nurturing, protecting, and training of their children (Ladd-Taylor; Leonard).

The other and more recent track has a particularized focus and consists of efforts to develop a model of mothering that draws attention to variations and diversity in women's mothering. This literature emphasizes differences among the meanings and experiences of mothers; mothers' subjectivities as diverse and multiple; mothering as mediated by experiences of race, class, sexuality, age and ability; and connections between ideology, experience, and agency in the lives of mothers (Baca, "Adaptation and Continuity," "Family, Feminism, and Race"; Collins, "Black Feminist Thought," "Shifting the Center"; Cossman; Croghan and Miell; Garey; Glenn et al.; Gordon; Hays; Little; Luxton; Mauthner; McMahon; Ranson; Seagram and Daniluk; Stack and Burton). This shift in the literature is due to recognition of the complexity of factors that influence women's experiences of motherhood and mothering. Particular attention is paid to the current ideology of mothering, how it creates compelling but unrealistic standards for women, how it is so pervasive and taken for granted that women themselves are often harshly self-critical, how it operates as a regulatory mechanism, and how some mothers are more regulated by the ideology of mothering than other mothers. In this sense, there are socio-historical, cultural, and economic contexts that shape, in various ways, the activities and understandings of mothers. Overall, the feminist motherhood-mothering literature begins to point to the complexity of factors that influence women's experiences of motherhood. However, it does not specifically consider domestic violence as one of the diverse social contexts in which women perform and experience mothering.

TOWARDS A GREATER UNDERSTANDING—BRIDGING THE GAP BETWEEN THE SEPARATE FOCUSES ON DOMESTIC VIOLENCE AND MOTHERHOOD-MOTHERING

Although in recent years there have been burgeoning research and literature in both the areas of domestic violence and motherhood-mothering, there is surprisingly little overlap between these two bodies of work in the social sciences. Feminist scholars in the area of domestic violence have largely neglected to take into consideration the recent contributions of those who theorize and study motherhood-mothering. Likewise, feminist motherhood-mothering scholars have not, to date, extensively studied mothering in the context of domestic violence. The lack of research that specifically focuses on and examines abused women's mothering experiences continues to persist despite long-standing research findings that indicate the following: women with children are up to three times more likely to experience domestic violence than are childless women; women's responses to violence, women's help seeking choices, and women's experiences with domestic violence interventions are shaped by a diversity of factors, particularly their status or role as mothers; and mothers accompanied by their children make up a large number of residents in women's shelters (Edelson, Mbilinyi, and Shetty; Holden and Ritchie; Holden et al.; Levendosky and Graham-Bermann; Mirlees-Black). For example, Statistics Canada's only violence against women survey from 1993, which examined the safety of women both inside and outside the home, found that 2.6 million (29 percent) of women who had ever been married or who had lived with a man in a common-law relationship experienced at least one episode of violence by a husband or live-in partner

("The Violence against Women Survey"). Moreover, Statistics Canada's 2009 General Social Survey estimated that approximately 606,600 Canadian women (6 percent) currently or previously in a common-law or marriage relationship had experienced spousal violence in the previous five years. In terms of the most serious types of violence reported, 34 percent of women reported being beaten, choked, or threatened with a gun or knife by an intimate male partner. In addition, 42 percent of women reported being injured in the previous five years, 33 percent reported that they feared for their life, and 40 percent reported that they took time off from their everyday activities because of the violence

Furthermore, Statistics Canada's latest Transition Home Survey for 2011-2012 found that between April 1, 2011, and March 31, 2012, there were 98,699 women and children admitted to the 601 abused women's shelters across Canada (of which 62,594 were women and 36,105 were children). In Alberta alone, there were 13,991 women and children admitted to the 53 abused women's shelters in this province (of which 7,388 were women and 6,603 were children) ("Transition Home Survey").

To date, only a small body of literature on mothering exists in the context of domestic violence, and it is largely from a quantitative, clinical, psychological, and social work perspective. This literature primarily focuses on two main areas: the effects of domestic violence on women and the effects of domestic violence on children (Austin, Lawrence, and Foy; Cascardi and O'Leary; Follingstad et al.). However, there is no research, to my knowledge, that examines mothering in the context of domestic violence from a feminist sociological perspective. This absence raises a number of important questions: how much is known about abused women's personal mothering experiences? How much is known about abused women's subjective mothering identities? How much is known about the role that dominant ideologies of mothering as well as intersections of gender, race, and social class play in shaping abused women's mothering experiences and identities? Unfortunately the answer is not very much at all. As Radford and Hester indicate, "despite almost thirty years of research into and activism against violence against women, little has been written about mothering in the context of abuse," particularly "from the viewpoint of women's experiences" ("Overcoming Mother Blaming" 135). Little, therefore, is known about abused women's mothering experiences from their own voices, perspectives, and subjectivities. When mothers experience domestic violence they are cast to the margins, and when their personal mothering experiences are overlooked, ignored, or disregarded, they are even further marginalized.

THE RESEARCH STUDY: THE BASIS OF THIS BOOK

This book provides a rare and in-depth feminist sociological examination of the individual narratives, experiences, and lived realities of abused women—a group of mothers who are stigmatized, criticized, and vilified for failing to meet dominant ideologies of what a "good mother" is or should be, because they have lived and mothered in domestic violence relationships. This book highlights the ways that women who mother in the social context of domestic violence experience the dominant ideology of intensive mothering, negotiate the resulting discourses of the "good" and the "bad" mother, and ultimately find ways to empower themselves despite the constraints of their situations.

This book is based on a qualitative research study of twenty-nine abused mothers residing in nine different abused women's shelters in Calgary, Alberta and surrounding areas. Face-to-face in-depth interviews were conducted from January to April 2009 with women who experienced abuse from an intimate male partner and who were also mothers of one child or more.[3] The interviews, which ranged in length from 1.5 to 3.5 hours were transcribed, coded, and analyzed from May 2009 to June 2011. This research study explores the following three main research areas: 1) abused women's perceptions of the current standards and expectations of mothering that mothers (particularly abused mothers) are held to; 2) the ways that abused women view and construct themselves as mothers and what discourses they draw from, resist, and negotiate in constructing their mothering identities; and 3) how intersections of the abusive social context, gender, race, and social class shape abused women's constructions of their mothering identities.

The findings of the study indicate that the large majority of the abused mother participants articulated, then challenged, and resisted the constricting and oppressive nature of the ideology of intensive motherhood and the associated discourses of the "good mother" and "bad mother." These mothers found ways to empower themselves in their subjective constructions of their mothering identities, despite the idealized mothering standards to which they are held and judged. Thus, the mothers in this study engaged in what O'Reilly refers to as "empowered mothering," which consists of engaging in agency, authority, autonomy, and authenticity in their everyday lives. These mothers did so by constructing valued, fortified, and empowering identities for themselves as mothers in the face of the ideology of intensive motherhood that delegitimizes and subjugates them. In defining themselves as mothers, they resisted the intensive mothering ideals in three main ways: 1) by negotiating the existing "good mother" and "bad mother" discourses; 2) by drawing on the "good mother" discourse and then redefining what a "good mother" to have more inclusive boundaries; and 3) by rejecting both the "good mother" and "bad mother" discourses and replacing them with their own experientially based alternative mothering discourses. Many of the abused mother participants stated that although they are often portrayed and viewed by others as "bad mothers," they do not view themselves as "bad mothers" but as "good mothers," "strong mothers," "super woman/hero mothers," or "warrior mothers" for example. These mothers' assertions that they are not in fact "bad mothers" was something they believed and articulated over and over. In fact, many of the mothers stated that their mothering is one of the few things they know that they have done right in their lives.

The findings also indicate that the abused mother participants who were among the most marginalized—specifically, those who were single, poor, and non-white—were more likely to resist the ideology of intensive motherhood in constructing their subjective mothering identities, despite being in the most oppressive social milieus. These mothers engaged in "motherwork for identity" for their own identities as mothers by resisting not only dominant discourses of race, class, and gender but also dominant discourses of mothering (Collins, "Shifting the Centre"). These marginalized mothers may not have had gender, social class, and racial privilege, but they sought to create subjective autonomous identities for themselves as mothers instead of submitting to identifying themselves as members of a stigmatized group of "bad mothers." In this sense, the abused mother participants struggled and fought for the right to their own self-definition as mothers in the face of much oppression and adversity.

Overall, the findings of the study reveal that abused mothers are not passive victims who merely accept and internalize the ideology of intensive motherhood that casts them in a negative light; rather, they are active agents who question these idealized standards as being restrictive and unachievable; who view their mothering in a positive light, even though they live and mother in social milieus deemed outside the boundaries of acceptable mothering; and who maintain that they are indeed worthy mothers, despite their stigmatized status.

This book points to how mothers—even in the most marginalized, subjugated, and oppressive of circumstances—find ways to exercise agency, resistance, and empowerment in and through their mothering. Mothering in marginalized conditions of abuse allows these women to turn off the voices of criticism and denigration perpetuated by intensive mothering ideals and call forth from within themselves their own voices—ones that are empowering. This book calls into question the false notion that there is only one standard, one definition, and one social location in which effective mothering is performed. The voices of the abused women in the study add yet another critique to the dominant discourse of intensive mothering. Indeed, this book is a voice against the judgment of mothers, a call to end the oppressive and restrictive bifurcation of mothers into categories of either "good" or "bad" mothers, and an attempt to re-envision a more inclusive understanding of mothering. This book then is a step towards the empowerment of all mothers, regardless of differences in their lives and social circumstances.

ORGANIZATION OF BOOK

This book is organized into five chapters. Chapter one provides a comprehensive overview of the limited research that has examined mothering in the social context of domestic violence. In this chapter, I discuss the overall findings of this research as well as the gaps of knowledge about abused women's mothering experiences. This chapter provides an important background for understanding the ways that abused women's mothering has thus far been framed, examined, and understood. Such knowledge is necessary for understanding the social context in which these women carry out and experience mothering in their everyday lives from their own voices.

Chapter two introduces the twenty women who took part in the study in order to make visible their voices, accounts, and lived experiences. The first part of this chapter provides a collective synopsis of the women's abuse experiences and socio-demographic characteristics. The second part of this chapter presents the individual narrative profiles of a select number of abused women in order to preserve the authenticity and integrity of their experiences from their own accounts.

Chapters three through five provide the detailed findings of the study. Chapter three presents the women's cultural knowledge about motherhood. In this chapter, I discuss the specific ways that the abused mothers in the study articulate, understand, and experience the dominant ideologies and discourses of mothering and the consequences it has on their lives. This chapter provides important insight into the ways that the women in the study view, define, and experience motherhood and mothering.

Chapter four presents the specific ways that the abused mothers in the study view and construct themselves as mothers. In this chapter, I discuss the dominant ideology and discourse of mothering that the women in the study draw from, resist, and negotiate in constructing their mothering identities.

Chapter five discusses the role that social location plays in shaping and influencing abused women's mothering identities. In this chapter, I discuss the various ways that gender, race, and social class intersect to influence whether the women in the study draw from, negotiate, or resist the discourse of intensive mothering in constructing their mothering identities.

Finally, in the conclusion, I summarize some of the key findings of the study and then expound on the implications that these findings have for wider understandings of mothers, motherhood, mothering, and theories-practices of maternal empowerment.

WHO THIS BOOK IS FOR

This book was written for family law, criminal justice providers, child protection and social welfare practitioners, child, youth, and family services, domestic violence shelters and services, health services, social services, and policymakers who work with individuals affected by domestic violence, particularly mothers and their children. This book is also for educators both inside and outside of academe, students, and frontline service providers as well as for mothers themselves who have experienced domestic violence. This book offers the opportunity to critically reflect on our current understandings, policies, and practices of addressing domestic violence, particularly in relation to mothers and their children with an eye towards improvement.

It is my hope that this book provides a window into the ways that women experience mothering in circumstances of domestic violence based on their own voices, experiences, and lived realities. This book offers a voice against the judgment of not only abused mothers but all mothers, encourages an end to the oppressive and restrictive bifurcation of mothers into categories of either "good" or "bad" mothers, contributes to re-envisioning a more inclusive understanding of mothering, and commences a process towards empowering all mothers and their children, regardless of differences in their lives and social circumstances. This book also contributes to envisioning ways of making motherhood and mothering more empowering as institution, practice, and identity.

ENDNOTES

[1]This ideology of intensive motherhood is also referred to as the "institution of motherhood" (Rich), "myths of motherhood" (Thurer), "patriarchal motherhood" (O'Reilly "Outlawing Motherhood"; O'Reilly, *Mother Outlaws*), the "new momism" (Douglas and Michaels), and the "dominant discourse of motherhood" (Horwitz).
[2]All names of study participants have been replaced with pseudonyms.

[3]Although this study focuses on the experiences of this particular group of women, there are numerous mothers who experience abuse in non-heterosexual and non-intimate relationships as well as numerous women who experience abuse who are not mothers.

1.
MOTHERING IN THE SOCIAL CONTEXT OF DOMESTIC VIOLENCE

What We Know and Don't Know

THERE'S TOO MANY PEOPLE out there that are reading textbooks that don't know what's going on [in abused women's lives], that have never experienced [abuse], and that have never taken the five minutes that it might take to know about somebody that has experienced [abuse], or somebody that has gone through these things, you know. That's where we need to find out what to do, and society doesn't do that. To me, it's just a bunch of people fresh out of college that have done nothing but read a couple of textbooks from like 1972.... You have to be strong to be a mother, it's a difficult job, but it's also a rewarding job. But when you're abused, it takes away from who you are, and it brings you down. You're totally beat down and to put those pieces back together on top of being a mother and doing what's right for your kids, and who's to say what's right, every situation is different. You're coming from a negative situation and trying to better yourself, and you're lost, and it's almost like you just want somebody to hold you and lift you up and let you fly away. Still, abused mothers are looked down upon. But it's easy to sit on the outside and look in and give advice. But actions do speak so much louder than words, and forever in a day they will. There needs to be more out there for abused mothers, finding out what's really going on, going to the core of the problem, not just trying to scrape the peeling off the apple because there's still so much more. I'd rather soothe my own soul by

> *knowing something that's real. It doesn't take having kids to understand. It just takes being a person and knowing that the other person is a person, too. I am a person, please don't make me feel like a lower-class citizen because I'm not.... A lot of times it makes me believe I'm not a good mother, you know, for that temporary, brief moment, it makes me feel like a bad mother... just for the simple fact that you're broken down ... something's been taken from you and you've been made to feel that you're not worthy, you know. That's a very, very crappy feeling.... But I'm not a bad mother, I'm a good mother.* (Quotation from Carly, a thirty-one-year-old mother of two children who experienced verbal, psychological, and financial abuse from her previous male partner for one year)

Carly was one of the first few women whom I interviewed as part of the study. There was much frustration in her voice as she spoke about the lack of knowledge and understanding about what it is like for women who mother in situations of domestic violence. As I sat across from her in the living room of her small one-bedroom apartment in a second-stage shelter in downtown Calgary, she began our interview by telling me, "I thought a long time about meeting with you." When I asked her why she was initially reluctant to contact me, she replied that she was so used to people not listening to women who had experienced domestic violence—as evidenced by the books that are currently available on the topic—that she wondered if it would even be worth her time to share her story. Added to that was her concern that most of the knowledge about abused women's mothering induces blame rather than support for mothers, which then casts them as "bad mothers," something she herself had felt and experienced. Constructing abused mothers as "bad mothers" for having mothered in abusive relationships reifies the belief that only one place and space in which to mother exists, and does not allow for understandings of mothering outside of these parameters, such as in situations of domestic violence. After much thought, Carly decided that she wanted to share her story with me, even if it ended up helping only one person. She explained: "I think what you're doing is great, and I hope it's going to help women out there, society and everything else because there's too much bullcrap out there." Carly's comment about the disconnection between the current knowledge about women's mothering and their actual lives and experiences is something that I heard over and over again from the women in the study; such a gap also highlights our limited understanding about mothering in circumstances of domestic violence.

Since the early 1990s, women and children advocates, clinicians, and researchers have increasingly become concerned about the prevalence of abuse experienced by women with children. Concerns about women's mothering have frequently been raised alongside concerns about children living in situations of domestic violence, although the focus has been on the latter. As such, much of the focus and attention has specifically been on the impact that domestic violence has on women's mothering, and, in turn, the impact that their mothering has on their children. Domestic violence has, therefore, been perceived and framed as a child welfare matter, regardless of whether children have witnessed or experienced abuse themselves. A focus on domestic violence as a child welfare issue has led to the development of a small but growing body of scholarly research on mothering in the context of domestic violence, mostly from a quantitative, clinical, psychological, and social work perspective. This scholarly research focuses on three main areas: 1) the impact of domestic violence on mothering practices with their children; 2) the impact of domestic violence on mother-child relationships; and to a lesser extent 3) the impact of protective interventions on mothering. Much of the early research examines abused women's mothering deficits, their alleged negative and ineffective mothering abilities. However, some recent research calls into question the assumption that abuse universally impairs women's mothering, and, instead, focuses on women's mothering strengths and their positive and effective mothering abilities.

As Lapierre correctly points out, the literature's primary "focus on children means that women have been relegated to the periphery, to be solely considered in relation to their children, and there appears to be no commitment to the development of a holistic understanding of abused women's complex experiences as mothers" ("Mothering in the Context of Domestic Violence" 456). Added to this is the fact that much of the literature uses gender-blind terms such as "parents" or "parenting" instead of "mothers" and "mothering." These gender-blind terms are particularly problematic in situations of domestic violence because it is often the mothers who flee with their children from these violent relationships, who are the primary caregivers for their children, and who ultimately are held to different social standards and expectations compared to the fathers. Focusing on and referring to the "parenting" that women engage in reinforces the invisibility of their unique role as mothers and takes the focus away from their individual voices and experiences of mothering. In light of the existing body of research, what is known specifically about mothering in the social context of domestic violence? As the above quote from Carly illustrates, and as will be discussed in this chapter, there is still much that is *not* known, particularly from a feminist sociological perspective, about abused women's narratives, experiences, and lived realities based on their own voices.

In this chapter, I provide a comprehensive overview of the research that has thus far been conducted, the overall findings, the gaps in the literature, and the implications that these gaps have for our overall understanding of mothering in the social context of domestic violence. This chapter provides an important background for understanding the ways that abused women's mothering has thus far been framed, examined, and understood in scholarly work and how this framing shapes the ways that abused mothers are constructed and portrayed in wider society. Such knowledge is necessary to understand the social context in which the abused women in the study carry out and experience mothering in their everyday lives, which is the focus of this book.

DOMESTIC VIOLENCE AND MOTHERING PRACTICES

A large part of the existing literature on mothering in the context of domestic violence focuses on the impact that experiencing abuse has on mothering practices. This research mostly examines abused women's parenting behaviour, parenting stress, disciplinary methods used with children, abilities to parent their children, and parent-child interactions. On the one hand, some of this research suggests that domestic violence has a negative influence on aspects of abused women's mothering practices. On the other hand, some of this research suggests that domestic violence often has no effect, or even a positive influence, on their overall mothering practices (Buchbinder; Hazen et al; Holden and Ritchie; Holden et al; Letourneau, Fedick, and Willms; Levendosky and Graham-Bermann, "The Moderating Effects of Parenting Stress"; Lapierre, "More Responsibilities, Less Control," "Striving to Be 'Good' Mothers"; Levendosky, Lynch, and Graham-Bermann; Moore and Peppler; Morrel et al.; Peled and Gil; Sullivan et al.).

Much of the early literature finds that the hardships of domestic violence adversely affect women's capabilities as mothers. Some of this research indicates that experiencing domestic violence has a less than positive influence on mothering practices because abused women engage in harsh and, even at times, aggressive disciplinary practices that involve the use of physical and verbal punishments. Moore and Peppler compared the mothering practices of abused and non-abused mothers and found that abused mothers were no more punitive and verbally aggressive with their children but were more physically aggressive with their children compared to non-abused mothers (166). They also found that abused mothers who were verbally aggressive with their children were more likely to report higher levels of behaviour problems in their children (178). This implies that women who experience domestic violence may become "too exhausted, distressed, and distracted to provide their children with the necessary attention, discipline, and affection" (Moore and Peppler 179). As a result, verbal aggression directed towards children may augment or exacerbate children's pre-existing emotional susceptibility brought about by witnessing interparental violence (179). This research is useful as it begins to examine mothering in the social context of domestic violence. However, it does not exclusively examine the abuse experiences of these 113 abused mothers in their study but rather examines their experiences alongside homeless mothers' (n=82), married mothers' (n=100), and single mothers' (n=82) experiences. Furthermore, the research does not give primacy to abused mothers' individual voices, as their mothering experiences are based on both their subjective reports and their children's reports.

Another study conducted by Morrel et al. also compared abused mothers to non-abused mothers and, specifically, examined the long-term impact of domestic violence on the mothering practices of 206 women, their children, and their children's teachers. They focused on the mechanism linking maternal history of victimization to their disciplinary practices, and to their children's behaviour problems, social competence, and intelligence. Overall, they found that in comparison to non-abused women, abused women in their study were 1) more likely to report externalizing and internalizing behaviour in their children; 2) equally likely to have behaviour problems, to be socially incompetent, and to have lower levels of cognitive development; and 3) more likely to engage in harsh disciplinary practices, such as using verbal aggression to discipline their children, leading to behaviour problems in their children (Morrel et al. 29). Although this research points to some evidence of diminished parenting among abused mothers, abused mothers' individual voices are not considered in their own right but rather are adjacent to the voices of other individuals, such as their children's, and their children's teachers.

Other research indicates that abused mothers experience higher levels of parenting stress, causing children to exhibit behavioural problems. Levendosky and Graham-Bermann ("The Moderating Effects of Parenting Stress") studied 60 sheltered abused women and 61 non-sheltered women and their children aged 7 to 12 from urban communities in order to examine the effects of domestic violence on their experiences of parenting stress well as the effects of this parenting stress on children's adjustment (387-389, 394). They found that in comparison to non-abused women, abused women experienced higher levels of parenting stress and that children whose mothers experienced higher levels of parenting stress exhibited more internalizing, externalizing, and total behaviour problems (392-393). This implies that the children of women who feel stressed by their parenting responsibilities in the face of domestic violence suffer more emotional and behavioural impact (393). In this regard, "increased parenting stress" may cause "mothers to react to their children's behaviours in less effective ways, which leads to more internalizing and externalizing behaviour problems" (393). This research begins to direct greater attention to abused mothers' unique experiences from their viewpoint but mostly examines their perceptions of how their mothering affects their children. In this regard, abused women are considered only in relation to their children.

Limited research finds that abused mothers exhibit coercive parenting strategies when dealing with their children's problematic behaviour, which negatively affects their ability to respond to their children. Hazen et al.'s study is the only one that focuses exclusively on abused mothers' individual voices. This study, which was based on secondary data analysis, consisted of 2,020 abused women who had children between the ages of 4 and 14 years. They examined the influence of abused women's experiences of intimate partner violence, incidents of depression, and parenting practices on their children's behaviour. They found that 1) severe intimate partner violence experienced by abused women was associated with child behaviour problems; and that 2) abused women's strict parenting practices moderated this relation between severe intimate partner violence and child behaviour problems (99). This research suggests that abused mothers may have difficulty dealing with children who display behavioural and emotional difficulties and may react by using coercive parenting strategies (106). Although this research is unique in that it focuses on abused mothers' own views and experiences, it is based on secondary data analysis and still considers abused women solely in relation to their children.

Despite this literature, sufficient evidence does not exist to conclude that experiencing domestic violence has a less than positive influence on mothering practices. In fact, some literature counters these findings and, instead, suggests that experiencing domestic violence often has no influence, and, in some cases, even has a positive influence on mothering practices, as mothers tend engage in efforts to compensate for the abuse and to protect their children from the abuse. Some research shows that even though experiencing domestic violence directly affects abused women's well-being, it does not necessarily translate into negative mothering practices. Both Holden and Ritchie's research from 1991 and Holden et al.'s research from 1997 exemplifies this shift in capturing the complexities of mothering in the context of domestic violence. Both of these studies call into question the emphasis on abused women's mothering deficiencies and point to the fact that although experiencing domestic violence may affect abused women's well-being, it may not necessarily affect their mothering. For example, Holden and Ritchie's study compared 37 abused women and their children between the ages of 2 and 8 years from an abused women's shelter to 37 non-abused women and their children between the ages of 2 and 8 years. They examined relations between marital discord, parental behaviour, and child behaviour and found that in comparison to non-abused women, abused women reported that 1) their children had more internalizing behaviour problems, more difficult temperaments, and more aggressive behaviour; and 2) they themselves had high levels of childrearing stress and inconsistency in their childrearing behaviour (311). However despite the fact that stress was associated with child behaviour problems, there were no differences in the quality of childrearing between abused and non-abused mothers. This research suggests no differences between abused and non-abused mothers in either their use of negative parenting practices such as verbal and physical aggression, or their use of positive parenting practices such as reasoning and physical affection. In this sense, experiencing domestic violence does not negatively affect women's mothering practices.

Holden et al.'s later study provides a more in-depth examination of the impact of domestic violence on women's mothering practices. They examined parenting behaviour, behavioural intentions, and childrearing beliefs (297). Overall, they found that even though abused women reported higher levels of mothering stress and depression, abused women were no more aggressive, no more punitive, no less affectionate, no less proactive, and no less capable of providing structure to their children than were non-abused women (p.325). In fact, abused women's higher levels of mothering stress and depression significantly decreased six months after the end of the violent relationship (325). This research suggests there is no evidence of diminished parenting among abused mothers in comparison to non-abused mothers.

Both of these studies direct greater attention to abused mothers' unique experiences because they shift the focus from only examining abused mothers' deficiencies to also examining abused mothers' strengths. However, similar to the research discussed above, this research compares abused and non-abused mothers, bases abused women's mothering experiences not only on their subjective reports but on the reports and/or observations of others, and considers abused women mostly in relation to their children.

Other research reveals that experiencing domestic violence has a positive influence on mothering practices because abused women show greater positive discipline and warm and nurturing behaviour towards their children. Letourneau, Fedick, and Willms' study provides a greater focus on abused mothers' individual voices about their mothering experiences, particularly their coping strategies. Although their study also compares abused and non-abused mothers, it differs in that it examines women's mothering experiences based solely on their subjective reports. They drew their sample from five cycles of the Statistic Canada's National Longitudinal Survey of Children and Youth by Statistics Canada from 1994 to 2003 and included 3,245 mothers in the sample for analysis, 208 whose children were exposed to domestic violence and 3,037 whose children were not exposed to domestic violence. They examined the relationship between exposure to family violence and parenting behaviour and found that in comparison to non-abused women, abused women showed greater positive discipline and warm and nurturing behaviour toward their children. As the authors state, "mothers of children exposed to domestic violence may indeed compensate for exposure to violence in their parenting interactions with their children" (649). This research is useful as it focuses on abused mothers' own viewpoints about their coping strategies. Nonetheless this research, which is based on secondary data analysis, compares abused and non-abused mothers, considers abused women's coping strategies solely in relation to their children, and provides a somewhat limited understanding of how abused women view, understand, and carry out their mothering in their own lives. Consequently, abused women's viewpoints about other aspects of their mothering are overlooked.

Some research even demonstrates that abused mothers are available to their children, closely supervise their children, and use non-corporal punishment with their children, which further supports that experiencing domestic violence has multiple positive impacts on mothering practices. Sullivan et al.'s study from the year 2000 focuses solely on the mothering experiences of abused women and examines their emotional availability to children, the discipline strategies they use/ with their children, and how parenting stress affects their disciplinary practices. This study involved 80 abused women and their children who were between the ages of 7 and 11 years from domestic violence shelter programs, a community-based family service organization, and a Social Services department, and focused on reports from both abused mothers and their children (51, 56). They found that mothers were available to their children; they closely supervised their children, enjoyed being parents, and were more likely to use non-corporal punishment with their children than corporal punishment. This research suggests that experiencing abuse does not directly affect mothers' level of parenting stress or their use of discipline with their children (p. 51). However, this research also considers aspects of abused women's mothering solely in relation to their children. Consequently, it provides a somewhat limited understanding of how abused women view, understand, and carry out their mothering in their own lives. Abused women's viewpoints about their own subjective meanings of mothering are not given importance.

Other research supports the assertion that experiencing domestic violence has a positive influence on mothering practices, as it finds that abused mothers are more likely to demonstrate an increased sensitivity to their children's feelings, empathy for and protectiveness of their children, and awareness of how their behaviour may affect their children. Two specific studies focus solely on abused women's mothering experiences and individual voices and examine abused women's subjective meanings of mothering in the context of domestic violence. Unlike all of the studies discussed above, which utilize a quantitative methodology, these two studies utilize use a qualitative methodology. The first study conducted by Levendosky, Lynch, and Graham-Berman in 2000 consisted of semi-structured interviews with 61 abused women residing in abused women's shelters and 34 abused women residing in the community (251). They examined the effects of domestic violence on how women parent their children, on women's abilities to parent their children, and on what type of parents they are (252). They found that most abused women believed that their parenting was both negatively and positively affected by their partners' violence (247). Many of the abused women in this study felt that experiencing abuse, on the one hand, took a toll on their on their emotional energy, affected the time they were able to devote to their children, and, at times, resulted in anger towards their children. But, on the other hand, they felt that experiencing abuse also led to increased sensitivity to their children's feelings, resulted in empathy for and protectiveness of their children, and made them more aware of how their behaviour may affect their children. This research suggests that abused women are not helpless victims who are focused solely on their abusive partner's needs but rather are active agents who mobilize their resources to respond to the violence on behalf of their children (247).

The second study conducted by Buchbinder consisted of semi-structured in-depth interviews with 20 abused women who sought help from a domestic violence intervention unit. Buchbinder examined abused women's perceptions of how their past experiences of child abuse and their current experiences of domestic violence affect their motherhood (309). This study found that abused women 1) made the conscious decision to use the memories of their negative feelings in their family of origin as a driving force to be different as mothers themselves (p.311); and 2) faced their past by avoiding violent behaviour with their own children. In this sense, abused women were committed to not repeating the cycle of violence in their own lives (315). This research suggests that abused women construct a basic mission in their life that structures the core meaning of their motherhood—to repair the negative experiences of emotional and physical distress in order to build a positive and safe emotional reality for their children (Buchbinder). Both of these studies focus on abused mothers' viewpoints about various aspects and meanings of their mothering and motherhood. However, these studies examine abused women's views of how they carry out their mothering and not their views of themselves as mothers. Consequently, these studies do not move beyond examinations that provide a general and partial understanding of the complex experiences of mothering in the context of domestic violence.

Little research focuses on abused women's perceptions of their mothering practices. But that which exists indicates that abused women separate their victimization experiences from their mothering and actively strive to prevent the impact that abuse has had on them from affecting their mothering practices and their children. Peled and Gil, who utilize a qualitative methodology, conducted interviews with 15 mothers who used the services of domestic violence prevention centres. They specifically examined abused women's overall perceptions of their mothering and its relation to their children. They found that the abused mothers main struggle was "to create a buffer between the children's world and the violent world" in order to prevent the abuse from "affecting their functioning as mothers" (457). When they spoke about the violence, they spoke about it as separate from their children, and when they spoke about their children, they spoke about them as separate from the violence. This research suggests that such a split narrative in the study is "an indication of our failure as a society to allow mothers to acknowledge and examine their less-than-perfect experiences of mothering, feel normal and reinforced in doing so, and receive the support they need in their efforts to grant their children and themselves a good-enough mothering experience" (Peled and Gill 457). This research is useful as it begins to point to how abused mothers' victimization experiences are separate from their mothering practices and, therefore, do not negatively impact their ability to care for their children. However, this research does not directly ask the women their perceptions of the current mothering standards that they feel they are held to or if and how this may affect their mothering. Consequently, this lack of knowledge allows the dominant ideology of motherhood to remain invisible in the lives of abused mothers.

One qualitative study conducted by Lapierre ("Striving to Be 'Good' Mothers") examines abused women's perceptions of their mothering but in relation to their mothering difficulties and challenges. This study utilized data collected from focus groups and face-to-face interviews with 26 women residing in shelters and found that domestic violence created complications for women and their mothering because the abusive male partner often attempted to target their "mothering and mother-child relationships as part of their violent strategies" (346). Consequently, women experienced an increased sense of responsibility regarding their children and a loss of control over their mothering. Lapierre also found that all of the participants expressed a strong desire to be "good mothers" and to be seen as such by adopting "good mothering" strategies, such as putting their children first and protecting and caring for their children. This research suggests that despite the difficult circumstances that domestic violence creates, women typically strive to be effective mothers both during and after abuse (353). This research is useful as it points to the dominant ideology of motherhood that many mothers, particularly abused mothers, are held to and judged by, even in research. In this study, the women neither directly stated that they attempted to be nor did they view themselves as "good mothers" but rather spoke about positive mothering strategies that they had adopted in their lives, which the researchers then deemed as "good mothering." This, therefore, holds abused mothers to dominant ideologies of what a good mothers is or should be—what constitutes "good mothering"—and applies a value judgment to their mothering.

This research on the whole shows that abused women's individual voices are overwhelmingly missing. This neglect is in large part because many of these research studies utilize quantitative research methods, such as standardized questionnaires, which do not allow for the production of individual narratives. As a result, the complexities of mothering in the context of domestic violence are rendered invisible. Most of the research focuses on asking women about their mothering exclusively in relation to their children and not in their own right as individuals. Likewise, much of the research does not ask women directly but makes inferences about their knowledge, views, and understandings of their mothering by holding them to the standards of "good mothering." It is important to focus on women's subjective accounts of how they view, understand, and carry out their mothering in their own lives in order to develop a clear and holistic understanding of the complex experiences of mothering in the context of domestic violence. Neglecting to focus on abused mothers' individual voices makes it impossible to understand their unique circumstances and the constraints under which they perform their mothering.

DOMESTIC VIOLENCE AND MOTHER-CHILD RELATIONSHIPS

The literature on mothering in the social context of domestic violence focuses, to a lesser extent, on the impact that experiencing abuse has on mother-child relationships. This research mostly examines the psychological, emotional, and social characteristics of mother-child relationships, mother-child attachment, responsiveness between mothers and their children, communication between mothers and their children, and the quality of mother-child relationships. On the one hand, some of this research suggests that domestic violence has detrimental effects on mother-child relationships yet, on the other hand, some of this research suggests that mother-child relationships successfully endure during and after abuse, particularly when mothers and their children receive social support (Abrahams; Jarvis et al.; Levendosky and Graham-Bermann; Levendosky et al.; McCloskey, Figueredo, and Koss; Mullender; Zeanah et al.).

Some of the literature indicates that domestic violence harms and damages mother-child relationships. This research suggests that experiencing domestic violence has damaging effects on mother-child relationships because mothers have disordered attachments with their children. Zeanah et al. examined the impact of domestic violence on mother-child relationships by comparing a total of 72 abused and non-abused mothers and their 15-month-old infants from a prenatal clinic and pediatric clinic of a tertiary referral centre. Through observations of the interactions between mothers and their children in two laboratory procedures and interviews with mothers and children in their homes, they found that in comparison to non-abused mothers, abused mothers who experienced more serious partner violence were more likely to have infants with disorganized attachments to them (Zeanah et al. 71). This suggests that abused mothers may maltreat their children, elicit fear in their children, and project their unresolved trauma and mourning on their children (83). This research is useful because it begins to examine more specific and concrete aspects of abused women's mothering experiences—their mother-child relationships. However, this study does not take into consideration how abused women are more strongly held to socially constructed standards of mothering than non-abused mothers, because they are mothering in an abusive context and are deemed in need of constant surveillance and correction.

Other research claims that experiencing domestic violence strains mother-child relationships, as it leads to mothers having difficulty communicating with their children. Mullender et al. conducted a qualitative study in which they interviewed 24 abused women and their 54 children as well as 14 domestic violence professionals. They found that the violence affected abused women's parenting and that the violent incidents and the anxiety of being constantly "on guard" meant that they were exhausted and had limited energy to devote to their children (159). They also found that women's mothering was orientated not around what they felt and believed was good for children, but around efforts to limit further harm to themselves or their children (164). This research suggests that the needs and perceptions of women and children in situations of domestic violence may be incompatible and lead to difficulties in communication between women and their children (167). Although this research directs greater attention to the specific challenges that abused women uniquely face in their mother-child relationships, it continues to overlook how societal expectations of how mothers "should be," what mothers "should do," and where mothers "should perform their mothering," affect abused women's mothering experiences.

Some research supports the assertion that experiencing domestic violence impairs mother-child relationships, as it finds that abused mothers express less maternal warmth towards their children. Two studies evaluate abused women's mothering according to socially constructed standards of mothering, specifically that mothers should always put their children's needs before their own. Both of these studies focus only on abused mothers. The first study conducted by Levendosky and Graham-Bermann consisted of observations of 95 abused women and their school-aged children, some of whom were living in local domestic violence shelters, and examined parenting behaviour (82). They found that abused women's experience of psychological and physical abuse led to less maternal warmth (90), which suggests that the experience of chronic abuse may deplete abused women of the ability to give emotional support to others, including their children.

The second study conducted by McCloskey et al. (1995) differs in that it consisted of interviews rather than observations with abused women. The researchers interviewed 365 abused mothers and their children between the ages of 6 and 12 from abused women's shelters and the community. They examined positive aspects of mother-child relationships, including warmth, kindness, and expressed affection, and found that abused women expressed less maternal warmth and that even when abused women did express more maternal warmth, it failed to buffer children from the harmful psychological consequences of family violence (1258). This research suggests that in situations of domestic violence, the more affirming feature of abused women's mother-child relationships are "unlikely to help" (1258).

Both of these studies are useful, as they begin to direct greater attention to the societal mothering standards by explicitly evaluating the ways that abused women conform to a specific list of what is deemed as effective mothering. However, they do not question the specific list of mothering standards but rather evaluate and judge abused women's mothering according to these standards by investigating whether they, in fact, measure up to them. Consequently, these studies, like Lapierre's study discussed above, unintentionally reveal the dominant ideology of motherhood that abused women are judged against, but they do not critically examine how it is imposed on abused women or the impact that it has on abused women's subjective views of themselves as mothers, on their children, and on their relationships with their children.

Limited research focuses on abused women's subjective views of themselves and their children, particularly as they relate to standards of mothering. This research provides important insight into mothers' own perceptions of their relationships with their children. Abrahams conducted interviews with abused mothers about their views on their mothering capabilities and their mother-child relationships. In the interviews, the mothers reported a loss in self-confidence in their mothering; moreover, they said that they were emotionally drained and had little to give their children and that they took out their frustrations on their children and experienced an emotional distance between themselves and their children (29-30). This research suggests that the numbing aspects of the trauma of domestic violence can lead to mothers being emotionally distant towards their children and directs greater attention to abused women's subjective views of themselves as mother. However, the study does not examine how the standards of mothering are social constructions set out by the dominant ideology of motherhood and how these standards are imposed differently on women. As such, this research does not provide an understanding of the complex ways that the dominant ideology of motherhood shapes abused women's mothering subjective experiences and views of themselves as mothers.

Contrary to the literature discussed above, a growing body of literature is emerging that suggests that not enough evidence exists to conclude that domestic violence is detrimental for all mother-child relationships. This recent literature points to the fact that mother-child relationships often successfully endure through abuse, particularly when mothers receive external social support. Some research demonstrates that abused women are responsive to their children, even in the midst of coping with abuse. Levendosky et al. examined the impact of domestic violence on mother-child relationships by utilizing both observational and self-reported data from 103 abused mothers and their preschool-aged children involved with several school, family, social service, and domestic violence agencies and programs. They found that although abused mothers who were depressed and traumatized by the abuse had lower parenting effectiveness and more insecure attachment to their children, those who were not depressed and not traumatized by the abuse appeared to be compensating for the abuse by becoming more effective and responsive to their children (275). This research shows that "domestic violence may indeed have a positive effect on mother-child attachment. This supports the idea that many women in domestic violence situations are often coping very well with the violence and are not suffering from 'learned helplessness'" (Levendosky et al. 285). This research is useful as it begins to call into question the previous studies that focused on and portrayed abused mothers as "bad mothers" for failing to conform to dominant ideology of motherhood and illustrates that abused women do attempt to compensate for the abuse by forging stronger relationships with their children. However, this research does not examine what abused women think about dominant standards of mothering. In this sense, there is a lack of understanding about abused women's subjective perceptions of the standards of mothering and whether or not they exercise agency in the face of these standards of mothering.

Other research demonstrates that despite experiencing domestic violence, many women adopt positive parenting strategies and have high-quality and supportive relationships with their children. Jarvis et al. studied the mother-child relationships of 30 abused mothers and their children between the ages of 6 to 12 years residing in domestic violence emergency shelters. They conducted individual interviews and psychometric assessments with women and their children approximately 3 weeks after they entered the domestic violence emergency shelter and found that abused mothers had "supportive maternal relationship" with their children, which served to "buffer against adverse psychological consequences" (391). This research shows how abused women are active subjects who attempt to compensate for the abuse by forging stronger relationships with their children, even in times of extreme crisis. However, this research does not examine whether or not abused women also exercise this same agency when it comes to the standards of mothering that are imposed on them. As such, this research continues to overlook how dominant standards of mothering affect abused women's mothering experiences and how abused women may also be active subjects who question the dominant ideology of motherhood.

Overall, this literature fails to situate and examine abused women's mothering experiences in relation to the dominant ideology of motherhood, which dictates specific standards that mothers must follow and is the model against which all mothering practices are measured (Horwitz). This is in large part because these research studies do not critically examine how this dominant ideology of motherhood and its related standards are social constructions that are imposed on women. Consequently, abused mothers are measured against a set of mothering expectations that sets them up for failure. In order to develop a comprehensive and inclusive understanding of women's experiences of mothering in the context of domestic violence, it is necessary to also focus on the power structures, hegemonic narratives, and pervasive messages that frame and shape their experiences.

DOMESTIC VIOLENCE PROTECTIVE INTERVENTIONS AND ABUSED WOMEN'S MOTHERING

A limited amount of the literature on mothering in the social context of domestic violence focuses on the impact of domestic violence protective interventions on abused women's parenting. This research is useful as it gives explicit attention to abused mothers' subjectivity and, therefore, begins to focus on their experiences in abusive situations. However, this literature consists of only two qualitative research studies, both of which were conducted by Krane and Davies. Overall, this research suggests that domestic violence protective interventions, particularly abused women's shelters, do not effectively recognize and address abused women's mothering needs because they lack efforts to assist abused mothers.

In their first study ("Sisterhood Is Not Enough"), Krane and Davies conducted participant observations and interviews with 5 shelter staff and 12 former shelter residents over a 4 year period in an abused women's shelter in a large Canadian city (173). They examined the practices of abused women's shelters and gave particular attention to the extent to which issues of mothering were addressed (167). They found that abused women who were mothers had different interests and needs but that these differences were not taken into consideration in abused women's shelters (181). They also found that interventions in abused women's shelters expected women residents to pursue their individual needs, heal themselves, develop autonomy, establish their right to independence, and ultimately choose to live violence-free and separate from their abusive male partners (186). Such an intervention model denied various and, at times, competing and complex facets of women's lives, particularly in relation to mothering, and, therefore, failed to also meet the interests and needs of women with children (186). This research shows that the social category "woman" continues to be treated as if fixed, homogeneous, and one-dimensional in abused women's shelters (186). Other facets of abused women's social location, such as their mothering status, race, religion, and so forth, are neither featured nor understood, which risks efforts to end the violence in their lives (187).

Building on the findings of this first study, Krane and Davies conducted a second study ("Mothering under Difficult Circumstances") to examine how shelter staff understand and address the particular challenges that abused mothers face. They conducted participant observations of staff and residents as well as interviews with 11 shelter staff in an abused women's shelter. They found that there was an overall invisibility of mothering in shelters and that when mothering was rendered visible, it was subject to idealized constructions and scrutinized through a lens that was highly sensitive to abuse of power and control (32-34). The message given to abused mothers was that good mothers should always be available and their children's needs should always come first, no matter what had happened to them (33). At the same time a contradictory message was also conveyed to abused mothers: to confront the violence in their lives they needed to think about themselves, choose themselves, or put themselves first (33). This research concludes that abused women must view themselves as separate from their mothering roles and responsibilities, while, at the same time, they must be held responsible for adequately caring, nurturing, and protecting their children.

Both of these studies are useful as they begin to examine, to a limited extent, abused women's subjective mothering experiences and identities in relation to the dominant ideology of motherhood. However, these studies obscure the variability of abused women's individual mothering experiences by focusing solely on how domestic violence protective interventions, and not membership in different social groups, frame abused women's mothering. Consequently, these studies do not provide an understanding of the complex ways in which gender, race, and class intersect to shape abused women's mothering experiences.

CONCLUSION

The existing literature on mothering in the context of domestic violence has undeniably directed greater attention to the prevalence of abuse experienced by women with children. However, it has many limitations. First, the literature is mostly based on quantitative, clinical, psychological, and social work perspectives. Therefore, the findings are often not based on claims made by abused mothers themselves but rather deduced from claims made by others about their mothering, such as by their children, shelter staff, child protection staff, teachers, legislative reviews, and researchers' observations. As such, little is known about abused women's various, diverse, and multiple discursive constructions of their mothering experiences. This limitation raises a number of questions: how do abused women subjectively perceive their mothering? Are abused women's subjective perceptions of their mothering experiences similar and/or different? It is necessary to move beyond this current research, which does not provide or contribute to a conceptual space in which the challenges, struggles, and individual approaches to mothering in circumstances of abuse can be freely discussed. Putting abused women's experiential knowledge of their mothering at the forefront to make their subjectivity visible is paramount.

Second, the literature does not consider the role, influence, and effects that the dominant ideology of motherhood has on the lives and experiences of abused women— specifically their knowledge of this ideology, how they personally view themselves in light of this ideology, and whether or not they accept, reject, or negotiate this ideology in their own personal lives. Most of the literature simply holds abused women to the dominant ideology of intensive motherhood and takes for granted and reifies current mothering discourses by evaluating and judging them according to the socially constructed categories of the "good mother" and the "bad mother." Little is known, therefore, about abused women's use of agency in their everyday lives, regardless of the context of abuse in which they find themselves. This limitation raises a number of important questions: what role does the ideology of motherhood play in the lives of abused mothers? How are abused mothers' lives, experiences, and identities shaped by the ideology of motherhood? It is important to move beyond this current research because it does not highlight the influence that historically specific systems of meaning have on abused mothers. Directing attention to the ways that abused women's experiential knowledge of their mothering is framed to better understand their experiences remains vital.

Third, the literature does not give attention to how individual social contexts intersect to influence the mothering experience. Most of the literature focuses solely on how domestic violence itself, and not how membership in different social groups, frames abused women's mothering. Missing from this research is how abused women's mothering is constructed, performed, and experienced through often subordinated positions within gender, race, and class relations. As such, little is known about the specific and divergent contexts in which abused women carry out and experience their mothering. This limitation raises the following questions: how are abused women's mothering experiences shaped by gender, race, and social class? How do various elements of individual social context intersect to influence abused women's mothering experiences? The research must move beyond this current approach, which does not emphasize the importance of the various and diverse aspects of abused women's lives. Exploring variations in abused women's experiential knowledge of their mothering is central to understanding their lived realities.

Given the limited manner in which abused women's mothering has thus far been framed, examined, and understood in scholarly work, a full picture of how women mother in and through domestic violence remains hidden. There are many questions that remained unanswered. To truly understand mothering in situations of domestic violence, abused women's own experiential knowledge must be the focus—this book is a step in that direction.

This book will now move to explore alternative narratives about abused women's mothering experiences—narratives that are based on abused mothers' own voices, meanings, understandings, and experiences; narratives that take into consideration the power and influence of dominant ideologies of mothering in abused mothers' lives and that recognize the diverse aspects of their individual lives as they relate to gender, race, and social class. The following chapter introduces the women in the study who shared their stories about how they subjectively view, understand, and experience mothering in the context of domestic violence.

2.
WOMEN'S NARRATIVES AND EXPERIENCES OF MOTHERING IN DOMESTIC VIOLENCE

From Their Voices

I'M NOT A POOR ME PERSON.... *I don't lie about who I am, and where I've come from.... I'm like, this is who I am, and this is where I was, and this is what I've done. There's some people that are like, oh well that's really cool that you're doing something else you know. And other people are like, yeah, so anyways, um, it's time to go, you know. I mean I've had a few confrontations, you know there were people at the bus stop by shelter where I was staying that I saw every morning, and they said good morning to me, till they saw where [my kids and I] came out of. The day where they saw where I came out of, I went to the bus stop, and they just kind of looked at me and turned away, like they didn't want any part of me. I'm like, did I change? But because they didn't know where I was from, and as soon as they found that out, they're like, oh well, you know, we're going stay away from that person, you know. Just like the neighbours in all the places that I lived in where I was abused.... I had people above me, beside, below me, but not once did anybody call, knock and say oh are you okay, or, call the police, or anything like that right. They're just like, let's turn up the TV, you know.... There's more than once that I kind of felt judged just for being, you know, a mom from domestic violence. The expectation is that that the woman is going to be a loser... she's just, you know, she's one of those people right.... So, I think ... society has almost come to accept that, you*

> *know, and they're just those people, right.* (Quotation from Kate, a thirty-six-year-old mother of three children who experienced verbal, psychological, and physical abuse from her previous male partner for six years)

When Kate shared this experience with me during our interview, she became emotional. As I sat next to her on the sofa in the living room of the home that she had recently started renting after leaving the shelter, she proceeded to tell me about multiple other times when people ignored her, dismissed her, or tried to avoid her when they found out that she had experienced abuse or when she spoke about her abuse experiences. As Kate describes in the quote above, abused mothers are often judged and believed to be "a loser" and "one of those people" for having been in an abusive relationship. Kate's comment about the reluctance of others to acknowledge and hear about women's experiences of abuse—particularly when they are mothers—is something that many of the women in this study state over and over again. This silence points to the limited opportunities that abused mothers are given to speak about their own lives and, consequently, to our limited understanding about their experiential knowledge. Holding abused women responsible for mothering in abusive situations shifts the blame away from their abuser, delegitimizes their experiences, and portrays them as a non-credible source to speak about their mothering.

As discussed in the previous chapter, the scholarly literature that has emerged since the 1990s has mostly focused on the impact of domestic violence on women's mothering and how, in turn, their mothering affects their children (Sullivan et al.). In fact, much of the literature has been based on claims made not by the abused mothers themselves but rather by others, such as their children, shelter staff, child protection staff, teachers, legislative reviews, and researchers. Consequently, abused women's individual voices, experiences, and lived realities have largely been circumvented and disregarded in both their personal lives and their encounters with others. To date no research, to my knowledge, specifically explores abused women's narratives about their subjective meanings, understandings, and experiences of mothering, particularly in relation to dominant mothering ideologies and discourses. This gap in the literature is problematic because it prevents us from having a larger picture of how women mother in and through domestic violence, one which is based on their own perspectives. It is now time to expand our discussion and understanding to include abused women's voices about their mothering experiences in ways that put their experiential knowledge at the forefront and that provides a conceptual space that makes their subjectivity visible.

In this chapter, I introduce the twenty-nine abused women who were part of the study in order to make visible their voices, accounts, and lived experiences and to bring us closer to genuinely understanding their experiences. I begin by providing a collective synopsis of the women's abuse experiences and socio-demographic characteristics in order to give a "face" to the women participants. I then present the individual narrative profiles of a select number of women participants to provide a portrait of what it is like for women to live and mother in circumstances of domestic violence—something that is often not exposed, revealed, and depicted in its raw form or from the voices of the women themselves. Individual narrative profiles are useful, as they preserve the authenticity and integrity of individuals' experiences. Given the scope of this book, I could not present all twenty-nine of the women's stories. I deliberated a lot over how many and which of the stories I would present. I felt that each and every one of the women had a unique and significant story to tell as well as notable and valuable insights to share. In the end, I decided to present seven women's stories. These seven women that I selected are most representative of the women as a collective. This chapter provides an introduction to the women in the study, their social locations, and their experiences of abuse and serves as a stepping-stone to the next three chapters, which specifically discuss the women participants' experiences of mothering in abusive situations.

THE WOMEN IN THE STUDY

The process of interviewing twenty-nine women residing in nine different abused women's shelters in Calgary, Alberta and surrounding areas for this study was often difficult and even painful for the women participants. These face-to-face in-depth interviews ranged in length from one and a half to three and a half hours; most were approximately two and a half hours. All of the women talked about how their abuse experiences brought back hurtful memories, which were more recent for some than for others. Consequently, it was often challenging for the women to discuss their abuse experiences. Many of the women became very emotional during the interviews when they recounted the atrocities done to them and to their children and how they had to mother within this abusive context. This recounting often resulted in many of the women crying and, on occasion, being unable to speak. During these times, I comforted the women by patting them on the back and on the knee or by giving them a hug. At times, we took a break, went to get a drink, or just chatted about more general things, such as the weather, what their plans were for later that day, their hobbies, etc. Then we would resume the interview.

The interview process was painful not only for the women participants but also for me as a researcher. During the interviews, I was often shocked, devastated, deeply saddened, and even angered by the terrible experiences of abuse that the women had gone through. However, I knew I had to remain composed and in control if I was to be effective in listening to and understanding their stories. This was something that I had over time learned, practised, and become proficient at doing in my role as a counsellor when I worked at an abused women's shelter several years prior. As such, my experience as a counsellor helped me in my role as a researcher when I was faced with the difficulty of hearing the cruelties that had been done to these women and their children and how it affected their mothering. It was only when the interviews were done and I was alone in the private space of my vehicle driving home that I would breakdown and all of my emotions of grief and sorrow were released. (It was very reminiscent of my experience years prior when I worked as a counsellor at a women's shelter in Ontario and would sit in my vehicle after my shift and try to process the horrible stories of abuse that the women had shared with me.) I recall this happening time and time again. I felt an immense sense of concern and compassion for these women. After all, I had just spent several hours face-to-face getting to know these women, talking with them, and hearing their most intimate personal life stories. We had connected in some inexplicable way. I'm not sure why. Perhaps it was because I was a woman just like them or because I too shared the role of mother with them or because these women had opened themselves up and shared their most deep and intimate personal experiences and emotions with me, ones that were profoundly hurtful for them. Thinking about these women gave me the strength and perseverance to carry on with the study, day after day.

Hearing the women's stories of abuse was also at times disturbing and distressing and had effects on me as a researcher that lasted long after the interview process. During the four months that I conducted the interviews and for about a month after finishing them, I often had nightmares. I would dream about the experiences of abuse that the women had gone through with exact and vivid details, but in my dream, I was the one being abused by their abuser, not the woman who had recounted the story to me. During and even long after the interviews, I felt the weight of the injustices and cruelties that were done to these women and their children by their abusive partners. In fact, throughout the whole research process—when I would recount the women's stories in my mind after the interviews, when I was transcribing word for word the interviews with the women, and when I was writing and quoting the women in the results sections of this research—I distinctly remembered the look in the women's eyes when they originally related their experiences to me. As such, I experienced these women's pain and hurt time and time again as I conducted this research. To this day, I still frequently think about these women. I do not think I will ever stop thinking about them. Sometimes, I see someone that looks like them, and then their story comes to my mind all over again. I had not fully anticipated the emotional ramifications of this research. However, these women's stories often drove the study because I felt an immense need and sense of responsibility to give a voice to these abused women and to shed greater light on the experiences of mothering in the context of domestic violence. It is my hope that this chapter, in addition to the subsequent chapters in this book, accomplishes this.

The women participants in this study occupied various social locations. Below, I discuss the women's overall abuse experiences and socio-demographic characteristics in order to present these women and their circumstances.

All of the women in this study experienced abuse from their current intimate male partner. Interestingly, more than half of the women (fifteen out of twenty-nine women) experienced abuse not only from one partner but from multiple partners over the course of their life. This synopsis focuses on the women participants' experiences in their current abusive relationship. The women's experiences of abuse ranged from emotional, psychological, financial, verbal, physical, and sexual forms of abuse. The most common forms of abuse that the women reported experiencing were physical, verbal, and psychological abuse. Of the twenty-nine women, twenty-two women reported experiencing physical abuse, twenty-two women reported experiencing verbal abuse, and fifteen women reported experiencing psychological abuse. The least common forms of abuse that the women experienced were emotional, financial and sexual abuse. Of the twenty-nine women, fourteen of the women reported experiencing emotional abuse, ten of the women reported experiencing financial abuse, and three of the women reported experiencing sexual abuse. All of the women but one mentioned experiencing multiple forms of abuse at the same time. Of the twenty-nine women, twenty-four women reported concurrently experiencing three or more forms of abuse, whereas only five of the women reported concurrently experiencing less than three forms of abuse.

At the time of the interviews, the majority of the women (twenty-two out of twenty-nine women) were residing in abused women's shelters in Calgary, Alberta. Of the twenty-two women residing in shelters, twelve women were residing in emergency shelters and ten women were residing in second-stage shelters. Only a small minority of the women had exited the shelter and were residing in their own home (seven out of twenty-nine women).

The women as a group were relatively young. The average age was thirty-seven years. The women's ages ranged between twenty-four and sixty six years. Of the twenty-nine women, twenty women were between the ages of twenty-four and thirty seven years of age, and only nine women were between the ages of thirty-seven and sixty-six years of age.

In terms of race, the women were a relatively representative group. Of the twenty-nine women, fifteen women were Aboriginal (more than half), nine women were Caucasian, one woman was Arab, one woman was Filipino, one woman was Black, and one woman was South Asian. Of these twenty-nine women, six women were landed immigrants. These women immigrated to Canada from Lebanon, the Philippines, Somalia, India, Hungary, and England.

The women's educational backgrounds varied. Most of the women had a high school education and above. Of the twenty-nine women, three women had bachelor degrees from university (one of these women had two bachelor degrees); two women had college diplomas; two women had some college credits; three women had a technical certificate; ten women had a high school diploma; six women had some high school experience; and two women had only completed elementary school. One woman had not completed elementary school.

Most of the women stated that they had worked either full time or part time at one time in their lives. However, at the time of the interviews, a large majority of the women (twenty-seven out of twenty-nine women) were currently unemployed and receiving social assistance. Of these twenty-seven women who were unemployed, many stated that they were looking for employment, and two had recently found new employment. Also, some of these unemployed women were considering returning to school: one had been attending school full time. Only a small minority of the women (two out of twenty-nine women) were employed at the time of the interviews. Of these two employed women, one was working full time and the other was working part time.

In terms of their current relationships, the majority of the women (twenty-two out of twenty-nine women) were living with their abusive male partner in either a common-law or a marriage relationship. Of these twenty-nine women, twelve women were in common-law relationships, ten women were in marriage relationships, and seven women were in dating relationships.

The average length of the women's relationships was 6.59 years. The length of the women's relationships with their abusive male partners varied from eight weeks to thirty-seven years. Among the women who were in common-law relationships, the average length of the relationship was 5.65 years. Among the women who were in marriage relationships, the average length of the relationship was 11.25 years. Finally, among the women who were in dating relationships, the average length of the relationship was 1.02 years.

All of the women in this study had children. The average number of children that the women had was 2.79 children. The number of children that the women had ranged from one to seven children. Most of the women (twenty-three out of twenty-nine women) had two or more children. The women's children ranged between the ages of three months and forty years.

Out of the twenty-nine women, eight women had lost a child—four of these women miscarried (one woman miscarried nine times, another woman miscarried two times, and the other two women only miscarried once), and three of these women lost a child after birth due to complications (mercury intoxication, congenital heart failure, prematurity). One woman both miscarried (three times) and lost a child after birth due to Sudden Infant Death Syndrome.

Despite the women's various social locations, their race and social class was representative of the shelter population. In terms of their race, half of the women were Aboriginal, which is representative of the population residing in abused women's shelters in Alberta. Alberta has the third largest Aboriginal population in Canada, leads the Canadian provinces in domestic assault, and is second in domestic-homicide. In fact, Aboriginal women are three times more likely than non-Aboriginal women to be victims of domestic violence, and more Aboriginal women experience serious forms of abuse than non-Aboriginal women (Lamberthus). Many factors have been identified as the root causes of abuse among Aboriginals. These include the impact of colonization and residential schools and the resulting effects this has had on Aboriginals, such as loss of identity and way of life, disintegration of family structures, the use of substance as a coping mechanism, low levels of education, and poverty (The Public Health Agency of Canada). Consequently, there is a high proportion of Aboriginal women residing in domestic violence shelters in Alberta.

In terms of the women's social class, the majority of the women were currently unemployed and receiving social assistance, which is also representative of the population residing in abused women's shelters. As such, the women participants shared a condition of economic insecurity and material deprivation. In Alberta, like in most other provinces in Canada, the majority of the abused women residing in domestic violence shelters live below the poverty line and, therefore, are among the most marginalized and in urgent need of assistance, as they have little or no income (Krane and Davies 417). Many of the factors involved in abused women's poverty that have been identified include issues of control, manipulation, and monitoring by abusive male partners as well as issues of lack of positive self-esteem, self-worth, and self-confidence, which has resulted in abused women not pursuing and having a strong educational background to equip themselves for skilled employment. For many abused women, their poverty creates a double disadvantage: the abuse leaves them fearful and ashamed while a lack of money leaves them with few resources for ending the abuse (Jaffe, Zerwer, and Poisson 12-13).

The women's structural conditions discussed above shaped their mothering experiences. The dominant ideologies of mothering are more likely to blame certain women on the basis of their social locations, particularly abused, single, non-white, and poor women. In this sense, abused, single, non-white, and poor women are seen as pathological or deviant and, hence, are viewed as deviating from "good mothering." As such, despite differences among the abused women participants, a "similar process of social construction vilifies" many of them based on their social location (Chase and Rogers 31). Consequently, the women's mothering experiences provide contextualized accounts that need to be understood within the broader context of intersections among their social locations and the resulting positions of oppression they occupy. This intersectionality of gender, race, and social class (which will be further discussed in chapter six) has real-life consequences for many abused women and, therefore, is important to consider and understand when examining mothering experiences.

THE VOICES OF THE WOMEN—THE EXPERIENTIAL EXPERTS

Despite their various social locations, the women's experiences of abuse influenced and shaped their experiences, not only as women but also as mothers. Below, I present the individual narrative profiles of seven abused women in order to make visible their voices and experiences.

ALIYA

Aliya is a Caucasian woman of Polish descent in her early twenties, born in Alberta. At the time of the interview, Aliya was residing in an abused women's emergency shelter in southeast Calgary, Alberta. Aliya is the mother of a two-year-old boy from her relationship with her current abusive partner. Aliya's son was residing with her at the shelter.

Aliya grew up in a European Catholic family. Her parents divorced when she was two years old. Both Aliya's father and mother were physically abusive towards her. Aliya also lived for some time with her grandparents, who were also physically abusive towards her. According to Aliya, her parents and grandparents were physically abusive because it is a "cultural" and "generational thing." Aliya completed grade eleven, but then left high school to work full time.

Aliya met her partner, who is Italian, when she was working as a waitress at a restaurant, and shortly after, they began dating. Aliya's partner has two sons from a previous marriage and is in contact with them. Shortly after meeting her partner, Aliya was forced to quit her job because her partner did not want her to work; she is currently unemployed. After dating her partner for a year, Aliya found out that she was pregnant. Aliya never lived with her partner but rather was forced to live in one of her partner's condominiums with his best friend, who later became the godfather of their child. Aliya's partner would come and visit her and their son at the condominium each day. Her partner thought that it was best that they live separately as he was not ready to introduce Aliya and their son to his two older sons who frequently visited him in his home. Aliya was in a dating relationship with her partner for three and a half years but left him eight months prior to our interview. She tried leaving her partner one other time, but she ended up returning because he was constantly "stalking" her and was tired of "running and hiding." When Aliya decided to leave her partner the second time, she wanted to ensure that she would not be constantly running and hiding from him. As such, she contacted child welfare in Calgary, Alberta, and they helped safely escort her and her son from her home to an abused women's shelter in northeast Calgary. Aliya then moved to a second-stage abused women's shelter and then finally moved to the abused women's emergency shelter where she was currently residing at the time of the interview.

Throughout their relationship, Aliya's partner was emotionally, psychologically, financially, verbally, and physically abusive. The abuse began shortly after Aliya found out that she was pregnant:

> *Things were great, and then as soon as I found out I was pregnant I started to notice little things happening, and then it got worse.... It started off as verbal abuse, then a little bit of physical abuse, and then when I was six months pregnant, um, it really became emotional, verbal, financial, and physical abuse.... There were times where I felt he was stressing me out just so I would miscarry. When I was pregnant, he hit me a bunch of times in my chest, and I said, "I'm pregnant what are you doing?" He said, "It doesn't matter it's not mine," and he knew I hadn't slept with anybody else. And then he threatened to kill me and put me six feet underground. I said, "How can you say that when I'm pregnant?" and he just didn't care. This one night he told me that he was going to take me out for dinner, so I was really excited cause I'd been cooped up in the apartment for weeks on end, and um, he came and he goes, "Well I'm going out and you're staying here." So I got really upset, and I decided to walk to the 7/11 and grab a Slurpee. When I came back, he was gone, and I had a feeling as to where he was. So I walked all the way down to this pub that I knew he was at [clears throat]. When I walked in the door, his friends were all sitting at one side of the bar all together, and he was standing at the bar with a woman. He's twenty years older than me, and he was sitting with a woman who was like ten years older than him, and her arms were all over him, and I walked up and I was just six months pregnant, and I'm like crushed and*

> *I'm like, "What are you doing?" And he's like "Just calm down, just calm down." I'm pregnant, I'm emotional, and this woman she's like, "Oh hi, who are you?" She tried to shake my hand, I slapped her hand away, and I slapped him across the face and then he grabbed me and he's like, "Don't embarrass me." And I was like, "Don't embarrass you?" and I slapped him, and he threw me on the bar in front of everybody and started to strangle me, and it took three men to pull him off me.... Another time, his friend came and told me that he was cheating on me.... He then twisted it around and said I was cheating on him. I said, "But I just caught you!" [laughs]. Like everything he would do, he would put it on me.*

The emotional, psychological, financial, verbal, and especially physical abuse became more continuous, frequent, and severe after Aliya gave birth to their son:

> *After I had the baby, it escalated to a thousand times worse and it was constant. I wasn't allowed to leave the house most of the time unless he knew where I was. Uh, when he didn't know where I was, he was constantly calling. I mean I would be at a friend's house, and she would tell me, "You know, he's outside watching," and I wouldn't know, and I'd be like, "No, no he's not," and she'd be like, "Yeah he is, I saw him," I mean, anytime I'd get money, I'd have to give him half of it. Just you know trying to tell me what I can and can't wear. I remember after I had the baby, the baby was about six months old, and I wanted to go out with a girlfriend of mine, and I wasn't wearing anything that would be considered, you know, slutty or promiscuous. I had a skirt on, but it came down to here [points to knees], my shirt came to here [points to collar bone]. There was no cleavage or anything, and he told me I looked like a prostitute. But usually it was like shaking me, grabbing me by my wrists a lot, and he strangled me a lot.... And it was to the point where I was passing out, and I thought I was going to die. I did! I literally thought my*

> *last words were going to be, "Please, I didn't do anything wrong!" There were times we'd be in the middle of, pardon me, but in the middle of making love, and he'd start strangling me and telling me if I ever cheated on him, he'd kill me. One time, he hit me so bad in my kidneys that my kidneys are now permanently deformed.*

The main reason Aliya decided to finally leave her partner was for the sake of her son. Since he was an infant, Aliya's son witnessed the abuse despite Aliya's pleas and efforts to convince her partner not to abuse her in front of their child. As Aliya's son became older and more aware, she realized that she had to leave:

> *He threatened on his oldest son's life he was going to kill me. The older my son was getting the more my son was understanding. When his dad would hit me, my son would go hit his dad and say, "Stop, stop, stop!" and that was when my son was only a year and a half. That used to be really hard for me to talk about. Now it's, okay, but it used to be really hard to talk about, and I used to just burst out crying.... I used to say to him [partner], "You're teaching him it's okay to hit and that's not okay." I didn't want my son to also grow up thinking that it's okay to hit women.... One day, my son was so mad at his dad after watching [the abuse] that he just kept hitting his dad in the face over and over and over again. I said I can't do this to my kid anymore.... That's all there is to it, I got to get outta here!*

Experiencing abuse has been very difficult, painful, and frustrating for Aliya both as a woman and a mother. Aliya often felt emotionally, mentally, and physically worn down from the abuse and would struggle to hide her pain from her son. The only times Aliya felt a sense of joy, peace, and comfort were the times she was alone with her son. Being a mother gave Aliya the courage to go on:

> *All the time it was like, I know I'm not doing anything wrong. But of course deep down inside you always feel*

> *like you are because you're always walking on eggshells.... When I was still there I was having a really hard time waking up. I just wanted to sleep all the time.... When I was awake, I just wanted to sit there and cry, and I couldn't do that in front of my son because I had him to take care of him.... My brain was not in the right spot. I couldn't focus. I was like a zombie, a walking zombie, and my son knew that I was there, but really I wasn't there. My head was gone.... One of the things that used to help me was taking my son, setting up the bed with the TV and we'd just cuddle all day and watch cartoons or something like that. But at the same time that's all I could do, because I couldn't play with him, and I wasn't allowed to go outside. That was the only time I felt good. His dad was usually not home at those times, so that was our special time together. It was our bonding time, and it was the time where, okay your dad's gone so I can breathe right now, so because I can breathe, I'm just going to take this time to just hold you and keep you.... My son's my life. He's like my soul, you know. When I'm really upset I can look at him and calm myself down. It just feels warm.*

Since she left her partner, Aliya has been in counselling and has been attempting to obtain full custody of her son with no visitation rights from her partner.

COREEN

Coreen is an Aboriginal woman in her late thirties who was born in Alberta. At the time of the interview, Coreen was residing in an abused women's emergency shelter in southwest Calgary, Alberta. Coreen is the mother of five children—a twenty-one-year-old girl from a relationship with her first partner who was not abusive, a nineteen-year-old and a seventeen-year-old boy from her relationship with her second partner who was abusive, and finally a sixteen-year-old girl and an eleven-year-old boy from her relationship with her third partner who was not abusive. Coreen also had a son with her first partner, but he died three months after he was born. At the time of the interview, Coreen was with her fourth partner who was abusive. Coreen does not have any children with this current abusive partner. None of Coreen's children were residing with her at the shelter at the time of the interview. Her twenty-one-year old daughter, her nineteen-year-old son, and her seventeen-year-old son were all living on their own; and her sixteen-year-old daughter and eleven-year-old son were living with her second partner. Coreen also has three grandchildren.

Coreen experienced many tribulations in her life. She grew up in a foster home and was physically and sexually abused by her foster father. Coreen's foster father was a priest in a residential school, and, therefore, no one believed her when she sought help. As such, Coreen ran away from her foster home when she was fourteen years old. Despite living on her own, Coreen managed to complete high school.

Prior to meeting her current partner, Coreen was in three other common-law relationships, two of which were abusive. Coreen met her first partner when she was fourteen years old. She was in a common-law relationship with this partner for seven years. This partner was not abusive. Shortly after they met, Coreen became pregnant and moved with this partner to a home on a reservation in Alberta. Coreen and her partner were very poor, and in order to survive, they ate fish from a nearby creek on the reservation where they lived. When she was pregnant, Coreen was often very sick but did not know why. When her first child was born, he was also very sick. As such, the hospital ran tests and found out that Coreen's baby boy had mercury poisoning. Three months later, he died. Coreen continued to be sick and ended up in the hospital, where doctors ran tests on Coreen and found out that she too had mercury poisoning. After an investigation, the hospital discovered that the fish Coreen ate throughout her pregnancy was contaminated with mercury. Coreen and her partner suspected something was wrong with the fish because when they would cut it open, they could see "a yellowish colour and a rainbow on the meat" of the fish. However, they "didn't think anything" of it and "just ate" the fish because they were "so hungry and there was nothing else to eat."

Four years later, Coreen and her partner had another child, which is her eldest daughter. When her daughter was three and a half years old, Coreen's partner committed suicide by "shooting himself in the head with a gun" in front of her and her daughter. Before shooting himself, Coreen's partner threatened to take her and their daughter with him as he said "If I go, you're coming with me. I'm not leaving you behind." Coreen's daughter was "screaming" and Coreen herself was screaming and "begging" her partner not to kill her and their daughter. The next thing she knew, her partner "turned the gun and shot himself, and everything went all over." After Coreen called the police, they arrived and then made Coreen and her daughter sit there in the house next to the deceased body for six hours while they questioned Coreen because they thought that she was the one who had killed her partner. Coreen's daughter kept saying, "My daddy, my daddy, my daddy did it," in her mother's defense. Coreen's daughter "still remembers" and still "suffers" from this traumatizing incident today. Coreen still has nightmares today about this incident because she still remembers the smell that lingered after her partner shot himself. Coreen and her daughter never received counselling after witnessing this incident; instead, they just tried to "block it out" of their minds.

A few years later, Coreen met her second partner. She was in a common-law relationship with this partner for two and a half years and had two children with him. This partner was psychologically and physically abusive. The abuse occurred throughout the entire relationship, except for when Coreen was pregnant. After being with her partner for some time, Coreen became an alcoholic because she "couldn't stand feeling the beatings anymore," and when she was "drunk," she "didn't feel them." As a result, Coreen lost her children to child welfare for a short time. Coreen finally decided to leave her partner because he was unfaithful; she personally found him with another woman. When Coreen left her partner, she got custody of her children again and then moved to Vancouver, B.C., to stay at an abused women's shelter.

Coreen's third partner was not abusive. She was in a common-law relationship with this partner for three years and had her two youngest children with him. Coreen is still in contact with this partner, and they have a good relationship.

Many years later, Coreen met her current partner, who is Aboriginal. Coreen was in a common-law relationship with her current partner for four years but left him three weeks prior to our interview. Coreen tried leaving two other times, but she ended up returning because she "didn't have anywhere else to go." The first time she left her partner was for two months; the second time was for one week, before returning both times. When Coreen met her partner, she was working full time at a convenience store. However, shortly after meeting her partner, Coreen was forced to quit her job because she was moved to a night shift with a male co-worker, and her partner did not want her working with another man. Coreen is currently unemployed.

Throughout their relationship, Coreen's partner was emotionally, psychologically, verbally, and physically abusive. The abuse began a year into their relationship:

> *A year after I started staying with him it started.... He's been in jail like three times because of me, cuz I've charged him for assault.... The first time I had bite marks on me, I had uh, two black eyes, and he hit me over the head with a bar. He uttered death threats in front of the cops [clears throat], then he got put in jail for five and a half months on remand. We weren't allowed to have contact with each other. So I moved back home, and then the police were looking for me. But I kept avoiding them cuz I didn't want to go to court, and then the crown prosecutor went to see him in jail and said, "We need to find her, we need her testimony, we have the pictures of what you've done to her." The judge was just like, "Whoa!" [clears throat]. Then the judge told him, "I have to let you out cuz you've already done time served and we can't find her to testify. But if I ever see you in my courtroom again with pictures like this ... and with assault charges this bad you won't be doing just federal time, you'll be doing pen time." The second time he got charged for assault and he got put in jail for two weeks. Um, those charges actually ended up getting dropped. He was chocking me, punching me, and burning me.... I had a black eye, and I had cigarette burns*

on my legs.... It took six police to break into my house to get him away from me. He wouldn't open the door, so they had to break the door down. We got evicted actually because of that incident, cuz there were too many cop cars there, and the landlord happened to be there when it was happening and he said, "You have a twenty four hour eviction, I can't handle this" [clears throat]. So yeah, so he went to jail. I went to another shelter, and then I wasn't going to go back but his family really harassed me into going back. The third time he attacked me right outside a coffee shop, like on the C-train [light rail transit system in Calgary] path and across from the cops he attacked me. Six cops came running out and they had to pull him off me cuz he had me by my hair and the people on the C-train station were just like, "Ahh," but nobody helped me. Like nobody jumped in to help me, just the cops did. Everybody just kind of stood around and walked away.... He was really mean. He would say like I'm useless, you know, like [clears throat] I'm fat, you know, nobody's going to want me cuz of my kids, if I ever leave he's going to wreck my looks so bad that nobody will want me, stuff like that. He'd wreck my stuff like my hairdryer, my curling iron, and my makeup. If I was going to leave him he'd wreck my underwear and my bras. I don't know why, but he would always do that! Like he'd cut them up, and burn them or throw them in the garbage. And like if I had a nice jacket and I looked nice, he wouldn't like it. I had a fringe jacket, buckskin my mom gave me for my birthday. It was really nice, and he yanked most of the fringes off cuz he didn't want me to wear it. So, stuff like that he did. My mom bought me a hairdryer and a curling cuz I never used to fix up, cuz I wasn't allowed. He wouldn't allow me to. He was very jealous of me. And so she told me like, "I'm not used to seeing you look so drab. Like you always fixed yourself up and you always looked good." So she bought me a curling iron and a hairdryer set from Conair. And he wrecked them. HHe cut the cords when I left him the first time, and I was like, "Uh!" I didn't want to tell my mom that [clears throat], so I thought I'll just try and find the exact same set [laughs] in case she asks me what happened to them.

Coreen decided to finally leave her partner because she could no longer endure the abuse:

I left him because, um, I just couldn't take it. Especially like hating myself and not liking who I am because of what he was telling me. I was just sick of it! I'm too old to go through this!

Experiencing abuse has diminished Coreen's self-confidence, not only as a woman but also as a mother. However, watching her children grow into adults and seeing the good that she has taught them, the love that they have for her as their mother, and their determination to end the cycle of violence in their own personal lives has been a source of hope, comfort, and encouragement for Coreen:

It [abuse] has really affected me.... My self-esteem really went down and even my kids noticed. They'd be like, "Mom, you're not even fixing up, like the only time you fix up is when he's not around." And like people, you know my friends, they'd say, "You're so different when you're with him, like you don't even talk, you don't even say hi, and you're just really quiet. But then when you're not with him you're like 'Oh, hi, what's up?'"...So, lots of times I felt like committing suicide because that's the only way I could get out of it, just leave him forever. And um [clears throat], I really just didn't like the way it made me feel.... It made me really depressed a lot, like I didn't want to go out of my house cuz of the things he would tell me.... It takes my focus away from what I need to do cuz I'm trying to survive and I'm trying to get through, and then everything else goes on hold ... like when I'm not there all the time for my kids when I need to be. I'm having my own issues, and yet they're having issues just as bad and

I can't deal with them. When they really need me I'm not there.... But watching my children become adults, especially watching my boys, makes me really proud.... My son told me, "You know mom," he said, "I really get mad at Kara," that's his wife, "I really get mad at her and sometimes I get really frustrated and I want to hit her. But you know what stops me? I see your face. I don't see her face, I see my mom, and I just can't." I said to him, "Really?" And he said, "Yeah." And even like my youngest son, my seventeen-year-old son, he said, "That's exactly the same for me. I just think, you know, if my mom's getting hit I can't hit." ... So, when I see my kids and the way they are with others, I think I did something right!

Since she left her partner, Coreen has been looking into returning to school and regaining custody of her children.

APRIL

April is a Caucasian woman in her late twenties. She was born in Ontario but moved to Alberta with her family when she was three years old. At the time of the interview, April was residing in an abused women's second-stage shelter in southwest Calgary, Alberta. April is the mother of two children—a seven-year-old daughter from her relationship with a previous partner who was not abusive and a two-year-old daughter from her relationship with her current partner who is abusive. Both of April's children were residing with her in the shelter at the time of the interview.

Like Coreen, April has faced many trials in her life. Growing up, April's father was emotionally and sexually abusive towards her mother and was physically abusive towards her and her sister. After several years of marriage, April's parents finally divorced when she was just eleven years old because her mother found out that her father was unfaithful. In fact, April was the one who personally discovered her father with another woman, which was very difficult for her. April did not speak with her father for many years. However, just four years ago, April and her sister confronted their father about his abusive and unfaithful behaviour, and he apologized. Today, April has a relatively good relationship with her father; she also has a stepbrother (from her father's previous marriage) whom she has never met. April's troubles continued to mount when she was a teenager, as she and another girl were sexually assaulted at a party by a young male teenager whom they did not know:

> *I was young ... and we went to a party, and [pause] I was raped.... I pressed charges, and the charges got dropped cuz I was drinking at his house and partying.... So because I was drinking and partying with him that gave him permission to assault me and the other girl that was there.... They had pictures of the tie marks and the bruises and the choke marks. But because I was drunk ... and because the other girl wouldn't testify to prove that he had done it to the both of us, there was no case.... She was too chicken to follow through with it.... So, he got off.*

April struggled significantly as a result of this experience. She attempted to commit suicide, and when she was not successful, she turned to alcohol and drugs to ease the incessant pain and suffering she felt day after day.

April completed high school and worked at a fast food restaurant until she had her first child a few years later with a partner she dated for over a year. She has not worked since. After her first child, April continued to use alcohol and drugs until her family intervened, took her daughter, and then entered her into an alcohol and drug treatment program. April has now been sober for three and a half years.

April met her current partner who is abusive through a mutual friend, and after dating for a few months, they moved in together. April's partner also has a child with a previous partner—a twelve-year-old son whom he is not in contact with. After dating her partner for a year, April found out that she was pregnant. The most difficult trial April experienced in her life was losing her mother on the very same day she gave birth to her second child. At the time, April's mother was in the hospital and was very ill; she then died of a stroke only thirty minutes before April gave birth to her baby:

> *I had the baby at four thirty in the morning and my mom died at four o'clock in the morning, and they [hospital staff] didn't tell me until about five thirty in the morning that she had passed. I kept saying to the hospital I was in, "Phone the other hospital and tell them to tell my mom I had the baby," and they kept saying, "No, no, no, no, your mom's sleeping, your mom's sleeping," and they all knew that she had suffered a stroke. I just feel like I didn't bond with the baby like I should have because of the emotional stress that I was going through.... Ever since she passed, it's not been the same.... I find myself crying a lot, and I really wish my mom was here.*

April was in a common-law relationship with her partner for three years but left him approximately one month prior to our interview. A year into their relationship, April wanted to leave her partner but did not because she felt she had "nobody" and "nowhere to go," and so "had to stay." Had April known about abused women's shelters back then, she would have left her partner right away.

Throughout their relationship April's partner was emotionally, psychologically, financially, verbally, and physically abusive. As with Aliya, the abuse began shortly after April found out that she was pregnant:

> *We were together six months when I found out I was pregnant. Then it started right away and lasted up until I left.... When I got pregnant he didn't want the baby. He wanted me to terminate the pregnancy, and I told him I would terminate him before I terminated the pregnancy. So, then he was like, "Oh, okay, well I'll be the father of the year," and blah, blah, blah. And then he would never touch me when I was pregnant. You know, most men hold the belly, and they love it, and they kiss it. He wouldn't. He didn't touch me once when I was pregnant.... He made gestures about my weight ... he called me a bitch and a slut ... he financially abused me, he moved me to a small town where I could not get back and forth to Calgary to*

> *my family. Uh, he would not allow me to get a job. I was not allowed to go out with my friends, I wasn't allowed to be friends with men, I wasn't even allowed to walk down the street with the kids unless he knew where I was going at all times, which I didn't know was abuse until two weeks ago [laughs] ... I had to ask him for money. I had to explain and show receipts, you know. I couldn't even go to the store and buy diapers without having him check the bank statements and bring the receipts home. Even my feminine products, I'd have to ask him and then he'd go to the store and buy them instead of me going to the store and buying them [coughs] ... I was independent, I had my whole life, and then one slip up, and I was dependent on him, and I had nothing.*

The emotional, psychological, financial, and verbal abuse continued after April gave birth to their daughter. Once their daughter was born, April's partner became even more emotionally abusive and also began to be physically abusive:

> *He cheated on me all the time and then he would keep doing it. I'd want to be intimate, and he'd rather be with magazines instead of me and watch dirty movies instead of being with me. So I guess that was my emotional abuse.... He cheated on me with a prostitute; he cheated on me with another girl when the baby was only three months old.... He threw me once against the wall. That was because I caught him cheating on me. I slapped him, and then he threw me, and I went flying against the wall. Then she came out [the woman he was cheating with], and I left with the kids.*

April decided to finally leave her partner, not only because of the myriad of abuse she was personally experiencing but more importantly because of the sexual abuse she suspected her children were experiencing from him. Given that April herself had been sexually assaulted as a teenager, she knew firsthand what it is like to be sexually assaulted:

Well the reason I left is very different from the abuse that I went through. I left him because I found out that he had sexually molested his youngest sister when they were kids. And it wasn't, you know, he was five and she was three, or he was eight and she was three. It was he was sixteen and she was six! And to me, he knew what he was doing was wrong; he knew that it was bad! ... His sister told me Christmas day ... cuz she was drunk, and so she spilled her guts. When I confronted him he admitted to it, and he wouldn't give me details, and he wouldn't go to counselling. So I packed my daughters up and left for their safety cuz I wouldn't have forgiven myself if something happened to them and I knew ... I'd blame myself more if they came to me and told me daddy's touching me, and I could have prevented that.... There were, not signs that he had done it, but signs of him being uncomfortable, like he would not run the bath for my older daughter [his step daughter]. You know, my younger daughter [his biological daughter] would be in her diapers, so my older daughter would want to be in her underwear and he'd get really uncomfortable. And so those I think might have been my signs, but I just didn't catch on. I figured he was her [oldest daughter's] stepdad, it wasn't his baby, so yeah. Now that I think about it, they were my signs, and I just didn't catch them in time.... We're going to see CASA, *which is Canadian Children Against Sexual Abuse, and they'll role play with my older daughter without directly saying did this happen to you.... I was sexually assaulted as a teenager, and I know how it felt at sixteen to go through that. So to watch them go through it, I won't! I won't! And I watch a lot of shows about sexual abuse, and I won't put them through that. I want them to have a good life.*

April's partner continued to abuse her emotionally, psychologically, and verbally even after she left him:

He's threatened to kill himself. Like I have the messages saved on my phone: "If I can't have the kids, I'd rather be dead, and I'm going to take them to court with me." He and his family were still abusing me on Facebook. I had to delete them and block them, and make it so that people can't go into my profile unless I'm friends with them. Like it's just terrible!

Experiencing abuse has changed April. She often feels confused and hurt. But what has been most difficult for April is dealing with her personal pain as a victim of abuse while still carrying out her everyday duties and role as a mother. Although April has many bad days, she also has many good days where she experiences happy and precious moments with her children. It is these good days with her children that carry her through the deepest and darkest of moments that she experiences while trying to heal from the abuse:

Well I'm not the person I was. I was very independent, and now I'm weak. I don't know where I'm going from here. I might go back to school, but just everything hit me all at once. I find myself crying a lot.... It's really hard to not show your feelings and try to be the mother that you are supposed to be. So trying to do bed time and bath time, and laughing and joking, when all you want to do is go to your room and cry your eyes out cuz your stuck, you have nowhere to go, and it's just a horrible situation.... They go to bed at seven so I break down when they go to sleep.... Some days are really, really good, and some days, I get really edged.... It's, it's, it's a struggle! Every day is a struggle! For the last seven years it's been a struggle.... I love taking them to the park ... or colouring ... or reading with them. My favourite part is reading, cuz they get so excited and then they fall asleep in my arms. That's my favourite part—the joys ... I think it [being abused] made me more [pause], protective of them [children] and more suckering [nurturing] to them, cuz I see how much pain that they're in, and I see how sad they are a lot of the times, and I just want to make them not hurt. So when they're crying, I try to [pause], you know, give them something

> *else to take their minds off of it. So it's made me more in tune with their feelings.*

Since April left her partner, she has been fighting in court to have his supervised visits with the children revoked.

KYLIE

Kylie is an Aboriginal woman in her late twenties who was born in Alberta. At the time of the interview, Kylie was residing in an abused women's second-stage shelter in southwest Calgary, Alberta. Kylie is the mother of three children—an eleven-year-old and a nine-year-old son from her relationship with her first partner who was abusive and a four-year-old daughter from her relationship with her second partner who was not abusive. Kylie does not have any children with her current partner, who is also abusive. All three of Kylie's children were residing with her at the shelter.

Kylie grew up in a very abusive home. Kylie's father was physically abusive towards her mother and even attempted to kill her by stabbing her with a knife. As such, Kylie's mother left her father when Kylie and her younger brother were very young. Kylie grew up feeling much anger, resentment, and disrespect towards her father. She did not have contact with her father until she was sixteen, and since then, she has only had contact with him on one other occasion.

Kylie did not complete high school when she was an adolescent. However, when she was a young adult, Kylie returned to school to do upgrading in order to obtain her high school diploma. Kylie then went to college and obtained a business diploma. After graduating, Kylie worked full time for over a year and a half for a local company. She started off as a receptionist and then promoted to office manager; she was about to be promoted to accounting manager. However, Kylie had to quit her job because she no longer had child care for her children. Kylie removed her children from the daycare she was sending them to because her son came home with "marks on the back of his neck" from one of the daycare workers. Kylie called child welfare and social services to report the incident. She is currently unemployed.

Prior to meeting her current abusive partner, Kylie was in two other common-law relationships, of which only the first was abusive. Kylie met her first partner, who is Aboriginal, when she was fifteen years old and, shortly thereafter, moved in with him. Kylie's partner was seven years older than she was, and, therefore, her mother greatly disapproved of their relationship. Kylie's partner also had five children from four different previous relationships. Kylie was in a common-law relationship with this partner for six years and had her two eldest sons with him. This partner was psychologically and physically abusive. The abuse began shortly after Kylie moved in with her partner and endured the whole time they were together, including when Kylie was pregnant. When Kylie was pregnant with their second child, her partner was so physically abusive that she "almost lost the baby." Kylie had to "go through ultrasounds every week just to see if the baby was going to make it" and the baby finally "did make it." Kylie stated that she "almost called the baby Lucky."

After three years, Kylie decided to leave her partner because she could no longer withstand the abuse. She moved into an apartment with her two children. However, Kylie's partner, who was in a "fit of rage" because she left him, broke into her apartment in "the middle of the night" and physically assaulted her in front of the two young children, who were thirteen months and thirty six months old at the time. Kylie became unconscious, so her partner called 911. When the ambulance and police arrived, Kylie's partner tried telling them that Kylie fell down the stairs. However, Kylie asserted that the police were sure that was not the case, and they arrested him immediately. Kylie was then taken to the hospital and her children were taken to her mother's. Kylie's partner "smashed up" her "face so badly" with his "bare fists" that she needed to have facial reconstructive surgery where titanium plates were inserted above one of her eyes, on her cheekbone and on her jaw. When Kylie and her mother returned to her apartment to gather all of her belongings, they found the socks that her partner had put on his hands prior to beating her, which were covered in blood. They also found a knife in the basement next to the window her partner had smashed to break into her apartment. Kylie believed that her partner had planned to kill her. At that moment, Kylie vowed never to return to her partner. Kylie's partner was sentenced to six years in prison for the assault.

Kylie's second partner, who is Aboriginal, was not abusive. She was in a common-law relationship with this partner for a few years and had her younger daughter with him. Kylie is still in contact with this partner, and they have a very good relationship.

Kylie met her current partner, who is Aboriginal, through friends. They moved in together after dating for a few months. Kylie was in a dating relationship with this partner for only three months and left her partner approximately five months prior to our interview. Throughout their relationship, Kylie's partner was psychologically, verbally, and physically abusive. The abuse began right after they moved in together:

> *He was really jealous throughout our relationship. Just little things. But I wouldn't put up with them. We were constantly, fighting cuz I wouldn't put up with his shit.... He totally called me down when we were together, like everything I did was wrong, everything I did was bad.... We only lived together for like a month and that's when he hit me, and that's when I left.... It was really bad, like he raised his fist to my son and that's when I jumped up and I was like, "I don't think so." I told my kids to go outside, and I was on my way behind them going down the stairs, and he kicked me down the stairs. Then he came down and punched me in the face, and I got a black eye. It was really bad.*

Kylie decided to finally leave her partner the first time he physically abused her because she refused to be in another abusive relationship:

> *He only hit me once, but that was enough for me. And that's when I left. I left with my kids that day. I left everything! I left absolutely everything we had ... cuz there's just no way I'd go through that again.... And then I moved to Winnipeg ... to get away from him.*

A few months after Kylie left her partner, she unexpectedly encountered him, and he was physically abusive towards her. At that point, Kylie knew that she was not safe and needed to seek refuge in an abused women's shelter:

> *After moving to Winnipeg, I came back [to Alberta] three months later for a funeral. That's when I saw him again. I had already changed my phone number so there was no way he could contact me, but I just happened to see him at the store, and he grabbed me by the hand pretty hard. I didn't notice until like the next day that my hand was all bruised up. And the girl he was with spit in my hair and my face. Then he started trying to stalk me and stuff, so that's when I came here to the shelter.*

Experiencing abuse has caused Kylie to feel guilty, humiliated, and ashamed about herself as a woman. Kylie blames herself for failing to provide what she refers to as a "normal life" for both herself and her children. However, remaining steadfast, hopeful, and dedicated as a mother for her children's sake has helped Kylie to overcome her negative feelings of self-worth. Experiencing abuse has made Kylie feel stronger about herself as a woman and as a mother and has given her the confidence and knowledge to teach her children to also be strong individuals. Experiencing abuse has also given Kylie the determination to teach her sons not to be like their father, and to instead have respect for women:

> *I just felt really bad for my kids, why I was staying there, and why it was the way it was. I just wish that they had a normal life and not such a messed up dad.... And then I got messed up myself for staying there.... It was really, really hard not to break down and cry in front of them [children] ... and just trying to act and look like you're normal and that everything's okay. Like going to drop them off at their day home and trying to act like everything's okay, when I just felt like shit.... It was really hard! My mom was there a lot, and I was always at my mom's with them....*

I used to feel really bad about myself after it happened. Like I felt really bad about myself and I became anorexic. I went from a size eleven to a size three and ended up in the hospital for an eating disorder, but I just felt so badly about myself. And then it took a while to just kind of build myself back up. I don't know. I feel like a stronger person now. I feel like I could pretty much handle anything now, and I could be there for them [children] and be stronger and teach them how to be strong.... It [being abused] has made me more paranoid and more strict I would say with the boys because I don't want them to be like their dad. So, I'm kind of hard on my boys because I want them to be strong men, and I want them to have respect for women. So I like make them do a lot of things for their little sister so that they'll have respect for her and for me and stuff like that. I've made the choice right now not to get into a relationship for a long time until I'm healthy enough. I know the signs of abuse and all that stuff, and I'll never go through it again so that my kids don't see me go through it, and so that they don't grow up thinking that it's okay.... When people tell me that my kids are really well behaved and really good, it makes me like really proud, and I think oh I must be doing something right for them to be like so good and well behaved.

Since Kylie left her partner, she has been looking for a new daycare for her children and for new employment for herself.

LOUISA

Louisa is a Caucasian woman in her early sixties who was born in Alberta. At the time of the interview, Louisa was residing in an abused women's emergency shelter in southwest Calgary, Alberta. Louisa is the mother of two children—a thirty-one-year-old son and a twenty-eight-year-old daughter both from her relationship with her current abusive partner. Louisa also has one grandchild.

Louisa grew up in what she describes as a "Mennonite home which was not traditional but liberal." Louisa lived with her parents and her two sisters and one brother, and she moved away from home when she was eighteen to attend university, where she earned a bachelor of education degree.

Louisa met her current partner, who is Caucasian, when she was twenty years old. After dating for two years, Louisa and her husband were married, the same year she received her degree. Louisa was married to her husband for thirty-five years but left him nine months prior to our interview. Her husband has a master's degree in engineering from university, and although he is currently retired he does do consulting work. Louisa has a bachelor of education degree from university but has never worked as a teacher. After they married, and particularly once they had children, Louisa's husband allowed her to "have small part time jobs for minimum wage" here and there, but would not allow her to work full time. When she did work, she had to give her husband the money that she did earn, so there was not much incentive for her to work. Louisa believes that if she had made any amount of money, her husband would have felt insecure. When Louisa's children were in school she volunteered in their classrooms, which gave her a chance to socialize with others and escape the constant isolation she felt. Later in life, when Louisa decided that she might need to work if she left her husband, she realized that even though she had a bachelor of education, she could not teach because most school boards would not hire teachers who had been out of the classroom for more than eight years. This has been a "terrible grief" for Louisa, one in which she still deals with today, as it was always her dream to be a teacher. Since Louisa left her husband, she has been working part time at a local boutique.

Throughout their relationship, Louisa's husband was emotionally, psychologically, financially, verbally, physically, and sexually abusive. He began to be psychologically abusive when they were dating:

> *As I think back on it now, it [abuse] started before we were married. It was manipulation and game playing then. I tried to break off the engagement twice because I had all these red flags that were coming up, and then that led to*

actually more abuse and I was afraid. So I thought, okay if I marry him then it'll change you know, because he told me that it would. And so I married him thinking that. And of course um, I really thought that I had to carry through with the decision that I'd made, and I did not think that I would have support from my family for backing out of it [engagement]. Little did I know that my mother said that she would have supported me from day one, cuz she knew there was something very wrong, cuz she said I changed when I met my husband, and I was no longer the same in any way. I became very guarded, very secretive, and that's been a very large grief to me too because I've had to get to know my family again.

Once they were married, Louisa's husband continued to be psychologically abusive, and also became emotionally, financially, verbally, physically, and sexually abusive:

He would ask my input, and I'd do a lot of research about, you know, how to do things, but I didn't feel confident in my knowledge of that because he would override all of my decisions. Anything! Any input that I would have, he would override it or belittle it, or something like that to make me feel insecure about what I had done.... Some of the physical stuff was the pushing, slapping, choking, um, those kinds of things. And also the confinement and rape, that was a lot of what happened earlier in the marriage.... I have memories of like lying on the bed with his arm over my throat and like his full weight of his arm on my throat, which was pretty debilitating. There's not much you can do! When he would rape me, he would twist my arm to the point where I thought it would break.... But if I submitted to him sexually, then it would mean look at you, you actually do want this and you're saying that you don't, but look at you, you actually do! ... There were times when I knew that I had to submit to him sexually in the end or I would be very, very physically hurt, and he had the power to hurt me because I have very fragile bones.... I have had broken ribs and, you know things like that, because when he became aggressive, my bones would break easily and that is very, very painful, and I did not want that to happen if I could help it. So I would give in when I realized that I needed to.

The only times when Louisa's husband was not abusive was when she was pregnant with her children:

I was treated like a princess during my pregnancy.... And that was really a break for me.... It was! I have always been his possession, and his children were also his possessions. So I think that's why he would take care of me during that time [pregnancy]. So it was a break for me. I actually was able to get healthier, and once the baby came, I really was determined to take care of myself, my baby, and my marriage. So it just became like a goal for me to make this work, because even though there were times when I thought I can't do this, I have to take the baby and go, I really knew in my heart it wasn't an option for me at that time.... I would often say to my husband, and it was actually something that was deep in my psyche I think from the brainwashing, I would often say, "If it wasn't for you, I would be living on the street." I think that's what kept me from actually leaving, because I did not believe I would make it if I ever left him, and especially with two children.... I remember that was also said to me very, very often. He would tell me I would be on the street if I ever left him.

Although Louisa's husband was abusive during all thirty-five years of their marriage, the specific forms of abuse that he employed varied and alternated at different times:

The abuse happened in a way that there wasn't always an explanation for it—that I had triggered it or that I had done something to bring it about. So I really believed it was my fault for many, many years. I didn't know exactly what it was that I had done, but it must have been something you know, and that's why I thought, oh I've got to change myself; I've got to do something different. It's my personality, it's my something. Therefore, all the changes. But it [abuse] never stopped. It just changed. It changed to verbal, then it changed to physical, then it changed to mind games, what they actually call, and what I've been counselled is called crazy making. I didn't know there was such a thing! I thought I was losing my mind. I thought I had misunderstood something that he'd said or done or interpreted something wrong. I didn't realize it was a game that we were playing, and it was a game to him to see how much I would take.... Another reason why I stayed in it [relationship] so long, is because when one type of abuse stopped and changed to something else. I thought, okay now we're getting better, we're actually working this out. But it had only changed to something else.... I didn't realize it was the same thing but in another colour.... And so you can deceive yourself into thinking that it's actually improving.... Towards the end of the thirty-five years that we lived together, he was actually verbalizing that he was testing me to see how much I would take. What an eye opener for me! I was just totally devastated because here I'd been trying with everything that I had available to me, and here it is a game. And I thought how can anybody be that cruel! And I think I was pretty much at the end of my rope emotionally, mentally, physically, like everything just on thin threads.

Louisa decided to finally leave her husband when the abuse became constant and incessant and when her husband verbalized that she was no longer safe. It was then that Louisa realized that she needed to leave immediately if she were to remain alive:

I must say he [husband] is very good at doing his job, and he's been a very good provider over the years. We never wanted for anything materially, so he was good that way. But all of us, including myself and my two children, suffered a great deal emotionally. It doesn't matter how much material stuff you have or how wealthy you are, if you don't have emotional safety then nothing else matters. And it took me a long while to realize that money cannot make up for what I was losing.... I had been in counselling for a number of years already talking with different counsellors, and my counselors were telling me that I needed to leave, and I needed to leave quickly. They were also telling me that it was incredibly dangerous because my husband did not remember what he would do after he had done it. Like even to this day, my husband will say to me that he has never done those things, and it would never occur him to him to do things like that. But it's really odd because sometimes he'll refer back to an incident, and it will be some years later, and then I'll think, okay I guess maybe you did remember that after all. So somewhere in the back reaches of his mind, it's still there. And so my counsellors did um, say to me that those types of abusers are the most dangerous kind because they don't have the presence or conscience of mind that in the moment will stop them from doing something very bad. So when you don't have that sort of hold on your conscience from way back, then there's no limit.... But what finally really opened my eyes, even though there had been a lot of physical, emotional and verbal abuse, was that it had come to a point where, you know the cycle of abuse and there's a bit of a lull in it, well in my life there was no longer a lull in it.... After thirty-five years, the spiral had become so tight that there was no break from it, and there was no time when I felt I could actually still breathe and get some energy back to face whatever was coming next. It came to a point where my husband actually told me that I wasn't safe. He said he felt he was no longer responsible for anything that he did towards me, and I could take it or leave it. And I thought, okay, now this is time. I can't fool around with this anymore.

As such, Louisa began to quickly plan out how she would flee because she knew that once she left she could never go back:

> *I planned it. Because I could see this coming I knew that I needed to do something, and I was getting counselling that was saying you need to plan for this, and I was actually getting help financially so that I could hire a lawyer. So I hired a lawyer without my husband knowing about it, and I got advice from her, and I got documents before I actually left cuz I knew that once I was gone, I could never, ever go back. I could not go back and get stuff. I would just have to be gone. So I was doing that for a while. But then there was an opportunity that I had known about—my husband was going to be away for about ten or eleven days, and it was during that time that I had a window. A God-given opportunity actually, because I was really praying about it, like how am I going to manage this and I knew that I had to go. God was telling me that I had to go because of all the stuff that was so obvious now. And it was an opportunity, it was my window to leave, and I did. I made sure that I had everything that I needed, and I just took the basic things that were dear to me and important papers and things like that, and I went and stayed with a friend. I wasn't able to stay with her long because when my husband got back, he found out where I was staying, and so he was stalking me. So I moved frequently during that time just so that I could stay beyond his reach, but, actually, what I found out later on is that he knew exactly where I was all the time. When I got here [to the shelter] it wasn't long, and I saw his car and realized that he knew where I was here too.... It was such a shock to so many people when I left, cuz the people in the church, the people in the community, people wherever just thought we were the ideal family, and that's how we portrayed it. Like my parents knew that there was something wrong, and my sisters knew that there was something very wrong, but they didn't know what it was. When I left then they were like, okay now we know. I have been highly supported from some,*

> *but not from others. Some have said, "Well look at how wonderful you had it! Look at your wonderful life and you just threw it away!" you know, because nobody knew. See, you reap what you sow, and really I had portrayed such a wonderful image of pretense that everything was just fine because I wanted people to think that. And now I couldn't live in that anymore, so I guess it's really not their fault that they didn't know, and they won't know because I'm not going to go explaining it to everybody.*

Even though Louisa left her husband nine months prior to the interview, he continues to psychologically and verbally abuse her:

> *I was afraid that I would have to leave here [shelter] because my husband knew that I was here, but they [shelter staff] have been very gracious.... I also felt very afraid because there were threatening messages on my phone, but then another message would come and he'd say, "Oh I'm not, I only want to make sure that you're okay, and you know I only care for you. I love you. I would never hurt you." And so it was always these very, very mixed messages. And even still, like I get that, like he would never want to hurt me, yet he wants me to be penniless. So it never ever is consistent or makes any sense.... He's still asking if I will come back and that's amazing to me.*

Experiencing abuse for so many years has damaged Louisa to her very core as a woman and a mother. The recurrent and relentless abuse that she experienced over the years at the hands of her husband caused her to feel so much grief, anguish, and distress that she no longer felt like a human being. Louisa found it difficult to deal with the pain and agony she felt on the inside from the abuse and to still portray that she was well, composed, and collected on the outside for the sake of her children. Despite the controlling and oppressive environment in which Louisa lived, the times she most looked forward to and which brought her the most happiness were the times she was alone with her children, when she could truly be herself as a woman and as a mother. Knowing that her children remember these happy times they had together has been a source of strength and comfort for her:

> *When I was being abused it was like I wasn't even a human being anymore.... I would just sort of go inside myself and try to be unaware of what actually was going on, and that's what I would do when I was being physically and sexually abused. I would just tune out and pretend that it actually wasn't happening in a lot of cases.... But the difficult thing was just trying to be okay and just trying to be sane. If I had just come out of the bedroom from being raped, for example, I had to come out and be okay. If I had just had my arm twisted to the point where I thought it would break and there were bruises, I had to wear something long sleeved and come out and be okay [starts crying] ...So the difficult thing was not saying anything, and being okay—putting on a front.... I just recall how much energy I had to put into just being okay and just being okay so that it would look okay for my kids. Whether I was okay inside or not I had to look okay on the outside, and that took an enormous amount of energy.... What I would do was, I would say, "It's okay! I can handle this. It's okay! I'm doing fine. I'm fine, look at how fine I am! I am absolutely fine!" And that's how I'd get through it.... Totally, totally fragmented I'm sure because I wasn't connected at all with what was going on in my heart and in my insides. But my head was saying, "I'm fine! This is okay! Look at how fine we are!" ...When I look back on how unwell I was during the times, when I should have been a healthy, vibrant mother with lots of energy to go and do this and that with the kids, that's been disappointing that I didn't have that. We would go on a vacation, or some time when we were spending intense family time together, it was so difficult, and it wasn't like this free and easy and we all feel really good about being together kind of thing, it wasn't like that. A lot of family vacations fell apart because we just couldn't hold it together for any length of time you know.... But I was there for my children more when my husband wasn't around, and we*

did have some very, very good times and good memories of that. Sometimes when I talk to my kids now, they talk about those times, and it really touches my heart to know that it was meaningful to them, even though it was a really difficult time.... I don't even know how I got the strength to leave. I don't know. I was just running on pure adrenaline, and when I think back on it now, I have no idea how I did it.... Now I don't feel safe in this world. I've come to some situations that are really big eye openers for me now that I'm out in the world a little bit. At this age, I should know what feels good to me and what doesn't feel good. I should know more social graces than I actually do know. I should know more boundaries than I know. So in some ways I feel like I really have to work on my boundaries. I have to work on what is really safe for me to accept and what isn't, and how I portray what's okay for me and what isn't. There's just a lot of fear of doing things on my own, making my own decisions. It's just incredible! I've had to make so many decisions on my own, like my own banking, my own care insurance, my own payment of the rent, my own medical coverage, you know all these things I'm still working on.... So many decisions that, that I need to do all by myself, and I'm finding I'm very, very frightened of that. But we moved I guess probably ten or eleven times during the course of our marriage, and they were large long distance moves. I look back on it now, and I basically did all of that on my own because he was at work doing the earning and the providing. I looked after all our real estate people, the packing up of the house, the moving people and everything. All the setup of the family wherever we were, like, getting all of their needs looked after— doctors, dentists, schools, tutoring, sports. Everything like that was my doing. So I know I can do it. But do I feel confident in it? No, not at all. So that's where I guess my confidence and my self-esteem are very eroded, and I am determined to build it back up. I know that I can, but it's just that solid, solid foundation that most people would have, I think that I don't have.

Since Louisa left her partner, she has been working on a settlement with her husband for their assets through a mediation process with lawyers.

CARLY

Carly is a Caucasian woman in her early thirties who was born in Alberta. At the time of the interview, Carly was residing in an abused women's second-stage shelter in northwest Calgary, Alberta. Carly is the mother of two children—a seventeen-year-old son as a result of sexual assault, and a twelve-year-old son from her relationship with her current abusive partner.

Growing up, Carly lived with her parents, her older brother, and her two younger twin brothers. However, Carly left home when she was only twelve years old because she felt overwhelmed with the responsibility of helping her mother take care of her younger twin brothers. Carly's mother depended on her a lot, something Carly thinks her mother may not have realized at the time. After Carly left home, she stayed with many of her friends' families.

At the young age of fourteen, Carly was sexually assaulted by her older cousin. Shortly thereafter, Carly found out that she was pregnant. Despite the pain and agony of knowing that the child within her was a result of sexual assault, Carly carried through with her pregnancy. Although it wasn't her "choice to be raped," having an "abortion" was "not a choice" in her "books." Carly believes she made the decision to keep the baby because she was brought up in a Christian family. Carly did not initially tell anyone in her family about how she was sexually assaulted by her cousin and then later became pregnant because she was ashamed, but then she eventually confided in her parents. She raised her son on her own, which was hard for her as she missed out on being a teenager—she "never went to prom," and she never had the opportunity to "finish school." Carly spent many years hiding the truth from her son. However, when her son was eleven, he began asking who his father was. Carly felt that "when it comes time to lie, it's time to tell the truth," and she him the truth. Over the years, members of Carly's extended family were gradually informed about the sexually assault and pregnancy. As a result, Carly's immediate and extended family "disowned" this cousin, and he is no longer invited or allowed to attend family functions. Carly's parents are still married today, and she has a good relationship with both of them, although she does not see them very often because they live in British Columbia.

As a result of leaving home and becoming pregnant at an early age, Carly was unable to complete elementary school. The last grade level that she completed was grade seven, but since then has upgraded to grade eleven at a local college. Carly was working full time at a local retail store until she left her partner and began residing at the shelter. Once in the shelter, she had to quit her job because she had no childcare for her children, and the shelter requires that residents ensure that their children are attended at all times, regardless of their ages.

Carly met her current partner, who is abusive, when she was just nineteen years old. Her partner was working in construction for the summer in Alberta. After dating her partner for just three months, Carly found out that she was pregnant. She was in a dating relationship with her partner on and off for almost twelve years but left her partner approximately three months prior to our interview.

Throughout their relationship, Carly's partner was psychologically, financially, and verbally abusive. The abuse began after their son was born and increased as he got older:

> *Not even a year after our son was born…he became pushy, really pushy.... And, you know I found myself doing things that I didn't want to do.... The whole situation was just terrible all the way around, you know. Like once it was Christmas and my paycheck isn't very much, I mean, I'm making ten dollars an hour you know. But he [partner] was like, "Ah, I'll take care of this, this, and this." And I was putting away Christmas presents and what not. And here my son, you know, he takes a lunch everyday to school, but there's no bread, and there's no milk. And he [partner] knows that my cheque is in my purse and I can't cash it because I have these funky hours from eleven pm to seven am. I go, 'You know, I didn't go to the bank,' and here my*

son is crying and picking money out of his piggy bank so I can get him bread and milk cuz he witnessed what was going on. Well, like how is that, you know? He's [partner] got money, but he's like "No, no, no, no." ...It's a control thing. Everybody should do as he says, you know. He's a very angry person. He believes that counseling doesn't help anybody (starts crying), you are the way you are and that's just it. And you know, he thinks that if he doesn't demand respect and intimidate people, then you know they just walk all over him. Well it doesn't work like that, you know. And that's probably the hardest thing right now, is like he was working on things, but as far as counseling or seeking help he thinks that's all a bunch of bullshit. What scares me is that my son is still soft, and loving, and caring, but he's not allowed to feel what he wants to feel, he's not allowed to have his own emotions cuz his dad controls him, you know. If he cries he gets in shit, you know, and that's not fair.

Carly decided to finally leave her partner the first time he physically abused their son. Carly could personally endure the psychological, financial, and verbal abuse that her partner put her through for years, but she could not endure the thought of her son also being put through abuse at the hands of her partner:

The final day that I left I phoned child welfare and found out where I could go and what I could do. Here I'm a small town girl in a big city, you know, I don't know what to do [sighs]. I, um, left because it was about seven thirty in the morning, and he [partner] was just angry and ignorant, and he's a major marijuana user, like six, seven, eight joints a day, you know. Anyways, um, he couldn't get a bag of weed the night before, and that morning, he had gotten upset with my son, and I don't know why. I was still sleeping cuz like I'd just gotten home from work. And he's freaking out on my son, and he had pushed my son and basically from here, the couch, to there [points to a table about ten feet away], that's how far my son flew

> *before he hit the ground. Just by pushing him, you know. And here's my son, he's got his book bag, and he just got up and started running out the door crying. You know, how's that fair for any child to go to school? Not even the fact of going to school, that's no reason to treat a child like that, you know. There was no reason for it! "Oh he was looking at me funny" he [partner] said. So I said, "What do you mean he was looking at you? You know, the kid doesn't know how to look at you because everybody's got to walk on eggshells around you." And that's when I'm there! What happens when I'm not there, you know.... There's still a lot of things, like he overreacts to things, and he uses some of the verbal language, and you know. I find that's just not necessary, and it's just so unfair to intimidate or have anyone live in an intimidated world.... This is not what any child or any person deserves, you know. And I told myself like, you know, this isn't the way to bring kids up.... I'm guilty of putting my kids through too much, you know, my kids have seen too much, and it's not fair [starts crying]. You know, it's hard for a parent to deal with that. You start to feel like a failure and you reach out for that help, and you sure are sorry that you didn't reach out for that help sometimes.*

During one of the times when Carly was not with her current partner, she met and began dating another partner. Carly was in a dating relationship with this second partner for just under a year. This partner was verbally and physically abusive. The abuse began shortly after they started dating. During one abusive incident, Carly's partner threw a case of empty beer bottles at the back of her head as she was walking down the stairs, and she became unconscious. Carly was then rushed to the hospital with a head injury. It was then that Carly decided to leave this partner and move back home to British Columbia with her children. Shortly after leaving this partner, Carly found out that she was pregnant, but did not inform him. Three months after finding out that she was pregnant, she was in a serious car accident and began hemorrhaging; she was then rushed to the hospital and told by hospital staff that she was miscarrying the baby. However, six months late, Carly went to the hospital because she was having cramps, only to find out that she was in labour and had not miscarried after all. Carly gave birth to a little girl, but her daughter was born with a congenital heart defect and died when she was two months old. Losing her daughter has been a very difficult and heartbreaking experience for Carly. She often still thinks of her daughter and wonders what it would be like to have her daughter living with her today.

Experiencing abuse has caused Carly to feel very disappointed in herself as a woman and as a mother. Carly has not only internalized blame for the abuse she experienced but has also held herself responsible for the abuse her children witnessed. This has led Carly to feel dejected, remorseful, and inferior. However, Carly's children have been her biggest source of strength and have given her the courage to talk with them about abuse and to teach them that abuse is wrong, unjust, and unacceptable:

> *I feel like a piece of shit, like a piece of shit [starts crying]. You know, like what have I done? At first it's like you feel sorry for yourself, and you're ashamed, and you're embarrassed, and you're weak, very, very weak. It [abuse] scared me most definitely. It has made me continue to think I'm weak [starts crying], and a lot of things.... I'm a strong person, I'm a very strong person! But you know, I find that one little thing will make me feel so weak, and I'll think back cuz something will trigger a certain time or a certain instance and I start to not believe in myself. I'll be discouraged, and I'll see it myself because I won't do certain things because I feel I'm not worthy or I don't deserve to be.... I wonder what have I done, you know, is it something I've done? ... Is it something I've missed? ... Is it something I am doing wrong? ... Is it somewhere that I have lacked being a mother? Because of the abuse I'm very hard on myself.... But my kids are my biggest strength. My biggest feeling of being ashamed or embarrassed is at what I was doing to them, or what exactly they had seen, or how they were interpreting how they were you know, cuz I would just die if my kids grew up to hit*

> *women.... It would break my heart! And just to talk to them and to discuss with them that this is not right, this is not acceptable, and it's not even okay for me. It's bad and it's wrong for me to be in that situation and for them to witness or to see that kind of situation.... And to make sure that they're aware of that, you know, it's not okay to treat anyone, male or female, men or women, like that.... And you know, try to explain that it's maybe something within someone that needs to be dealt with you know.... Not everybody's bad, and you know it comes from somewhere. Actions come from somewhere, and some people just have a crappy life. I got dealt one of them. In some ways, I'm extremely fortunate, you know, I got two beautiful babies.... I've had a lot of mishaps, I've had a lot of heartbreak in my life [starts crying].*

Since Carly left her partner, she has been trying to find a home for her and her children so that they can begin rebuilding their lives.

BADRIYA

Badriya is an Arab woman in her mid-thirties. She was born in Iraq, but her family moved to Lebanon when she was still a baby and then immigrated to Canada when she was a child. At the time of the interview, Badriya was residing in an abused women's second-stage shelter in northwest Calgary, Alberta. She is the mother of four girls—a ten-year-old, an eight-year-old, a six-year-old, and a three-year-old from her relationship with her current abusive partner. All four of Badriya's daughters were residing with her at the shelter.

Growing up, Badriya's father was physically abusive towards her mother. As such, when Badriya was still young her mother decided to "run away" with her and her three sisters. Badriya's mother left her three brothers with her father. Shortly after, Badriya and her mother moved to Canada, while her brothers and sisters remained in Lebanon as they were all married at the time. She lived with her mother in Toronto, Ontario. Although Badriya completed high school, she has never been employed.

Badriya met her partner when she was living in Toronto, Ontario. Her partner is also Arab and immigrated to Canada from Iraq when he was an adult. The same month Badriya and her husband were married, they moved to Calgary, Alberta. Badriya was married to her husband for eleven years but left him six months prior to our interview.

Throughout their relationship Badriya's husband was verbally and physically abusive and became abusive two months after they were married:

> *He start to abuse me the first two months we was married. Yeah, he was very abusive. But I can't say nothing cuz it's like culture thing, right.... He always like put me down. He never ever say, "I love you." And one time I ask him, "Like why you don't say I love you?" He say, "Because I don't want you be proud of yourself" ... He always tell me I a piece of garbage.... He always say to my kids I'm stupid, and I don't know nothing.... Many times he actually said if he leave me nobody would look at me or at my face. That's what I feel now.... Like even now I feel I'm nothing still. And even I'm going to group [counselling], and we study self-esteem.... He used to hit me too much, like three times a week at least, and my body was bruised everywhere.... Even if I can't give him glass of water cuz I'm sick he used to hit me.... Shouting, calling me names, and hitting it was part of my life.*

The verbal and physical abuse escalated when Badriya was pregnant with their children. Badriya even had two miscarriages as a result of the physical abuse she experienced at the hands of her husband:

> *Since day one when I start to have kids ... he always treat me bad ... especially because he doesn't want have kids.... Each time I find out I was pregnant I was scared if it's girl or boy because I know how much he wants boy. And I'm scared if I find out it's girl, what he would do. He always get mad when he find out I'm pregnant, especially when I*

do ultrasound ... and find out that I have girl ... he doesn't talk to me for one week.... When I go to hospital he doesn't go with me cuz it's girl too.... With all my pregnancies, he used spit at me, hit me, and choke me when I was pregnant. He did many times. Or like he'd throw water at me to wake up.... I went through too much.... I had two miscarriages actually because he hit me too many times.... I was having very, very hard time.... Like every day I used to have panic attacks after the kids go to sleep from like eight or nine o'clock until five o'clock in the morning, straight, never stop. Oh my gosh. I went through lot! Like one time I called the ambulance and I end up in the hospital. The other time I have to wake up the kids around three o'clock in the morning and take them to the hospital with me with their pajama. The time I called the ambulance, I see dark in front of my face, like somebody choke me, and my heart pumping, and I can't breathe [starts crying].

Despite the abuse that Badriya suffered for many years, she frequently denied that such abuse was happening when it was brought to the police's attention, as she feared that her partner would harm her if she reported him or left him:

My neighbour, they used to call the police when he used to hit to me. But I always say to the police, "No he didn't hit me," even when they see bruises.... The first time he hit me after we was married for two months, the police show up and he run out the window.... So I said, "He's not here." They said, "Your neighbour just phoned and said he hit you." I said, "No he didn't," cuz we was like new married, and I don't want to like right away.... So anyways they say, "We can tell," cuz like I was crying, and my eye was bruised. But I said, "No." They said, "We will get him." So they come after one week at two o'clock at night. and he was in the house. They come and they get him, and he has to stay in jail for one night.... But I still said, "No" ... And one time he hit me after I had the third baby, and she was one week old. When I got home he hit me, and all

> *my body was bruised everywhere. So my neighbour called the police and they come. So like I was crying and I said, "Yes he hit me." So they took picture everywhere of my body, and they write statement and asked me to sign it. So when I sign it, right away I don't know what come in my mind, I rip the paper and I say, "I'm not going to charge him." But they said, "Because we see everything on your body, the bruises, we're going to charge him. And because you said that, and your neighbour said that he always do that, and you told us, and you write the statement but ripped it, we going to charge him." So I didn't cuz I was like scared of him.... Anyway, they take him to jail again for one day, and they give him no contact order, like, he can't come to the area for three months.... So anyway he used to phone me and say, "Don't charge me." When it was the court date, I didn't go because he said don't go. And many times he said, "If you go [to court] I will cut you in pieces, put you in the toilet and flush you up, and nobody knows where you are." He used to threaten me too much. So, I didn't go [to court]. So the next day the police show up at my house ... and they said to me, "We coming to take you to jail ... because you have subpoena from the police, and you didn't show up at the court" ... So they said, "Who you have to take care of the kids?" I don't have any friends, nobody, because he wouldn't let me have any friends, and I have no relative, nobody here. So they end up calling the child welfare. The child welfare, they come and they said, "She has to go to jail because she didn't go to subpoena to the courts." So anyway, I went and they take the kids. But at four o'clock, I get out, and they give back to me the kids.... I was crying, I said [to husband], "You see what happened to me! Why you didn't tell me?" He knows this will happen to me, like he's smart he knows, but I didn't know this would happen.*

Badriya decided to finally leave her husband when child welfare became involved and gave her the ultimatum of either leaving her husband or having her children apprehended and taken into custody:

> *One day, I was with my kids, and we was going out and someone rang the door. It was two women and two police, and I said, "Yes can I help you?" and they said, "We are from child welfare, and we're coming to get you out from the house." I said, "Why?" They said, "Your neighbour, they always phone the police because you always crying, your husband always hits you, and there is kids in the house. So if you don't come with us, we're going to take the kids.... This is the third time your neighbour phones. So we have to talk to judge before we come here, so it's not our decision and not your decision. It's court ordered. We have to get out from the house." I start crying and I said, "No he never hit me" ... because I was scared to leave the house, and I wasn't strong. I mean, still I'm not that strong, I know myself I'm not strong person. I am scared to do stuff, you know.... So they said, "If you don't come we take the kids." So he come [husband], he was in the bedroom, he come and he say, "No I never hit her," and he start to shout. So they said, "Enough!" ... And I left because of my kids.... So they find a place at the shelter ... and we went there for eight weeks. Then we end up here.... At that time, he used to phone me, and I didn't answer my cell phone. I didn't answer because how much I accept from him, like hard life.... I realized when I went up, and I see the world, and he wasn't around for controlling and hitting and calling me names non-stop. I was just waiting for somebody to take me away from him or something.... When child welfare was going to close the file, I said, "No don't close it." They said, "You're the first person who say don't close the file." But I want them to stay with me because I feel little bit stronger than before, and he isn't around. I'm so happy I left. My life was saved from him. I know if I stayed with him maybe two or three weeks more I be dead because it comes to the end, and at that time, it too much, like he was choking me almost to death.*

Like the other women in the study, experiencing abuse has been emotionally, mentally, and physically taxing for Badriya. She no longer felt like the same person and often wondered and questioned why she was the victim of abuse, as she never imagined she would find herself in such a position. Badriya coped with the pain of abuse by focusing on and devoting herself to her children. The love and affection that Badriya's children showed her was the only source of happiness in her grief-stricken world:

> *I'm not like before, a normal person right.... It affect me lots. I was stressed and on depression pills.... I used to cry lots. I used to go outside on the balcony or downstairs to the basement and cry and say, "Why this happen to me?" ... I feel like I'm fifty or sixty years old now. No honest! Like I feel I'm very, very tired ... and I feel like I'm very down in my heart ... So I used to just focus on my kids when they come from school. Everything in the house clean, the cooking ready, so I study with my kids.... I go for walk.... I take them swimming ... or we go watch family movie.... Just focusing on my kids for me it's very, very easy.... When I give them love or kiss, they give me back, right. When I'm sad, they give me hug right. So this is the life.... I'm always happy with my kids.*

Since Badriya left her partner, she has been volunteering at two different homeless shelters. She has also been considering going back to school or finding employment.

CONCLUSION

The individual narrative profiles of the women participants shared in this chapter reveal that, despite their various social locations, experiencing abuse influenced and shaped their experiences as women and as mothers. Although the women expressed that being a mother in an abusive situation was often challenging and difficult, they also expressed that mothering provided a primary source of hope, strength, and courage that carried them through the deepest and darkest moments of abuse, something that was expressed by almost all of the women in the study. By focusing on the voices of the women themselves, this helps to shed light on and render more visible the subjective meanings, understandings, and experiences of mothering in the social context of domestic violence. The next three chapters provide an in-depth discussion of the multiple, varied, and complex ways in which abused women experience mothering in light of dominant mothering ideologies and discourses and in relation to their various social locations.

3.

ABUSED WOMEN'S KNOWLEDGE AND UNDERSTANDINGS OF THE DOMINANT IDEOLOGY AND DISCOURSE OF MOTHERHOOD

MOTHERING IS CARING, love, interest, respect, um, validating, like the mirroring thing. Perfection [laughs]... Society expects, like I mean I really don't give a crap, but they expect total self-sacrifice. Like there's no room for a person to be a mother. There may be room for a mother to be a person a little bit, but you know a person is, well he's a man and he doesn't have to worry about that! It's like the difference when you say to somebody, "Oh yes the vice president has four kids she can't make the meeting"; they say, "Uh, okay, so she can't get a babysitter?" But if you say, "The vice president has four kids he can't make the meeting," they say, "Why, he has another appointment?" You know it's just an assumption, like that because you're the mother it's your career and it's your interests that must be sacrificed.... I've seen this in women's magazines and commercials. I mean have you seen the "Swiffer" commercials where she is so excited to do the dusting [laughs]! Or where she makes everything better by baking her son cookies because it's raining out, and he can't go camping! I'm like, oh gosh! Yeah, yeah, sure [laughs]! ... And I think that society has a very inaccurate perception of who gets abused and what abuse is. So when you say abused mother, the picture that instantly comes to mind is like somebody very poor, had a whole bunch of children maybe by different fathers, is married to an alcoholic, and you know her life sucks, and this is just

> *another thing she has to deal with. But it's not true! It's just not true! ... It's anybody can be anybody ... and it's really hard to accept that.... So, I don't think that society knows what an abused mother looks like, and I don't think that they focus very much on the mother. They focus more on the effects on the children, which is fair enough, but there's a woman there who needs help too.... What I've noticed is it's very hard sometimes to articulate all the things that you're feeling, plus you've been told that you're stupid, or crazy, or whatever! So it's easy to sort of see them as incompetent, indecisive, not good, or something like that.... I mean people always ask like, "Why does she stay?" and they don't ask "Well why does he treat her bad?" No, they ask, "Why does she stay? I wouldn't stay there!" ... Well, it's not that easy, but it's easy enough to just sort of look at that end bit. But that's society too right, it's kind of the paternalistic male dominated.* (Quotation from Josephine, a thirty-five-year-old mother of a one child who experienced emotional, psychological, and financial abuse from her previous male partner for four years)

Mothers in the past and in the present have lived under the influence of ideologies of motherhood that promote dominant ideals and standards of mothering against which their lives are judged and regulated. The ideologies of motherhood function as culturally constructed practices, ones that are continuously redesigned in response to changing economic and societal factors. As cultural constructions, ideologies' meanings vary with time and place (O'Reilly, *Rocking the Cradle* 37). These ideologies of motherhood are specific structures of statements, terms, and categories that define how women must mother at given times and places (O'Reilly, *The 21st Century Motherhood*; O'Reilly, *What Do Mothers Need?*; Horwitz). As discussed in the introduction, the current ideology of motherhood is intensive mothering, which emphasizes total self-sacrifice on the part of mothers and promotes a set of expectations that are impossible to achieve (Horwitz). Women who "intensively mother" are regarded as "good" mothers, while women who do not are viewed as "bad" mothers (O'Reilly, *Mother Outlaws* 2).

However, not all women subscribe to the beliefs and expectations of ideologies of motherhood to the degree that they are promoted and perpetuated in current society (Baber and Allen; McMahon). Some mothers, in fact, are aware of, challenge, and even resist these mothering standards through their mothering practices. This resistance is supported by research studies, albeit very limited in number, that explore the process of resistance by mothers and, more specifically, the process of resistance to the social institution of motherhood and dominant mothering discourses (Croghan and Miell; Little). Tula Gordon pioneered research in this area by conducting a study on mothers who resist the social institution of motherhood in their lives and the impact it has on their lived experiences, but only includes women who identify as feminist. Fiona Green conducted a study that examines the experiences of sixteen self-identified feminist mothers and found that they successfully negotiate the tensions between the "institution" and "experience" of motherhood as well as actively challenge and resist patriarchal assumptions about motherhood in their parenting practices ("Feminist Mothers"). These two studies, however, exclude other mothers who do not identify as feminist. Finally, Erika Horwitz conducted a study that explores the experiences of fifteen mothers who do not necessarily identify as feminist but who perceive and state that they actively resist the dominant discourses of mothering. However, this study does not include other mothers who may resist the dominant discourses in their mothering but may not specifically identify themselves as resistant or recognize and name their actions as resisting. Additionally, missing from all these studies is the explicit consideration of mothering experiences as they relate to intersections of gender, race, and social class.

The current gap in the research is problematic because it ignores mothers who indeed resist dominant ideologies of motherhood but do not identify as "feminist" or as "resistant" and mothers who resist in oppressive social milieus, as in circumstances of domestic violence, single motherhood, non-whiteness, and poverty. Consequently, our understanding about the specific ways that mothers in the context of domestic violence comprehend, perceive, and accept or resist expectations of the dominant ideologies of motherhood is very much lacking. One is left to wonder: what is the dominant ideology of motherhood that abused mothers articulate? Do abused mothers articulate the same demands and standards of mothering that are imposed by the dominant ideology of mothering? How does the dominant ideology of motherhood affect abused mothers' lives? Do abused mothers experience the same stress, guilt, depression, and feelings of inadequacy from living under the influence of the dominant ideology of motherhood? Do abused mothers subscribe to or challenge the dominant ideology of motherhood? If so, how and why?

The above quotation from Josephine, one of the women in the study, provides a good example of the role and influence that current standards of mothering play in the lives of abused women. Josephine clearly articulates that the dominant ideology of motherhood is intensive mothering and discusses the related standards that stipulate mothers are solely responsible for the care of their children. In this regard, Josephine states that society expects "perfection" and "total self-sacrifice" from mothers. Josephine also distinctly articulates the associated dominant discourse of the "good mother" versus the "bad mother" and describes how abused mothers are believed to be "bad mothers" for failing to meet the standards of intensive mothering. That is, abused mothers are viewed and portrayed as "incompetent," "indecisive," and "not good" mothers. But, what is interesting is that Josephine does not merely subscribe to the dominant ideology of intensive motherhood that she describes but rather outright challenges it. She questions and criticizes the messages and expectations of this mode of mothering that promote an ideal that is impossible to achieve. She pokes fun at the unrealistic portrayal of self-sacrificial and perfect mothers in commercials that are shown on television. She even outright asserts that she does not "give a crap" what "society expects" of mothers because she knows that the expectations for mothers are based on false and idealistic "assumptions." Finally, she challenges the view and portrayal of abused women as "bad mothers" by stating that "society has a very inaccurate perception of who gets abused, and what abuse is," and, consequently, does not "know what an abused mother looks like." She maintains that abused mothers are not inherently "bad mothers" but rather are falsely portrayed as such due to a "paternalistic male dominated" society. Josephine's narrative is one example that demonstrates that abused mothers not only articulate but also challenge the discourse of intensive mothering.

In the study, I explore the following three main areas: 1) abused women's perceptions of the standards and expectations of mothering that all mothers are held to as well as those that abused mothers in particular face; 2) the ways that abused women view and construct themselves as mothers and what discourses they draw from, resist, and negotiate in constructing their mothering identities; and 3) the ways that intersections of the abusive social context, gender, race, and social class shape abused women's constructions of their mothering identities, which will be discussed in this and the remaining chapters.

This chapter provides greater insight into the first area—abused women's cultural knowledge about motherhood, specifically the ways that they view, understand, and experience the dominant ideology and discourse of motherhood and the impact it has on their everyday lives. First, I present how motherhood-mothering scholars have theorized the nature of motherhood as it is currently perceived and practiced in patriarchal societies as well as the possibility and necessity of maternal empowerment in the lives of mothers. These theories provide a backdrop for understanding the current climate in which women perform their mothering. Second, I discuss the ways the women in the study define the current standards of mothering that they and other mothers are held to. These women's definitions of mothering standards offers important insight into the next two chapters, which discuss how the abused women in this study construct themselves as mothers in relation to these dominant mothering discourses as well as their individual social locations.

FEMINIST THEORIZATIONS OF MOTHERHOOD AND MOTHERING

Motherhood-mothering scholars have long upheld that motherhood, as it is constructed and performed today, is "disempowering if not oppressive" because: 1) the mainstream standards of mothering are idealized and impossible to achieve; 2) mothering is a privatized, all-consuming, and endless act; and 3) the role and work that mothers do is devalued (O'Reilly, *What Do Mothers Need?* 63). Maternal scholars have particularly taken issue with and sought to demystify the disempowering and oppressive nature of these mainstream standards of mothering. Much of the scholarly work is based on and influenced by an important distinction that Adrienne Rich made in *Of Woman Born*. In this work, Rich distinguishes "between two meanings of motherhood, one superimposed on the other: the potential relationship of any woman to her powers of reproduction—and to children; and the institution—which aims at ensuring that that potential—and all women—shall remain under male control" (13). According to Rich, the term "motherhood" refers to the patriarchal institution of motherhood, which is male-defined, controlled and deeply oppressive to women, whereas the term "mothering" refers to women's experiences of mothering, which are female-defined, centred, and potentially empowering to women (Rich; O'Reilly, *Mother Outlaws* 11; O'Reilly, *Rocking the Cradle*; Umansky). Rich argues that the reality of patriarchal motherhood must be distinguished from the possibility or potentiality of empowered mothering. This distinction, Rich makes clear, "is not an attack on the family or on mothering *except as defined and restricted under patriarchy*" (14). Building on Rich, Andrea O'Reilly argues that within patriarchal culture "women who mother in the institution of motherhood are regarded as 'good' mothers, while women who mother outside or against the institution of motherhood are viewed as 'bad" mothers' (O'Reilly, *From Motherhood to Mothering* 2). In this sense, "mothers, in order to resist patriarchal motherhood and achieve empowered mothering must be 'bad mothers' or 'mother outlaws' (O'Reilly, *From Motherhood to Mothering* 2). Rich thus "defines empowered mothers as 'good mothers' and patriarchal mothers as 'bad mothers' (qtd. in O'Reilly, *Mother Outlaws* 2).

The work of Andrea O'Reilly provides the largest and most significant contribution to the further development of Rich's work and to the construction of a feminist theory and practice of empowered mothering. O'Reilly correctly points to an important gap in Rich's work and in the wider feminist motherhood-mothering scholarly work: "there is no discussion of empowered mothering or how its potentiality may be realized" (O'Reilly, "Mother Outlaws" 2). According to O'Reilly, "patriarchal motherhood must be differentiated from the possibility or potentiality of mothering" in order for motherhood to be "recognized and experienced as not naturally, necessarily or inevitably oppressive," and, more importantly, for mothering, when freed from motherhood, to be recognized and "experienced as a site of empowerment, a location of social change" (O'Reilly, *Rocking the Cradle* 11). In *Rocking the Cradle: Thoughts on Motherhood, Feminism and the Possibility of Empowered Mothering*, O'Reilly develops a feminist theory and practice of outlaw mothering known as "Mothering Against Patriarchal Motherhood" to conceptualize empowered mothering and how its potentiality may be realized in mothers' lives. "Mothering Against Patriarchal Motherhood" is a counter-narrative of motherhood and seeks to interrupt the master narrative of motherhood to imagine and implement a view of mothering that is empowering to women (45-48).

As discussed in the introduction, O'Reilly argues that the patriarchal institution of motherhood, as it is expressed in the ideology of intensive motherhood, delineates and promotes mothering in the following eight ways: 1) children can only be properly cared for by their biological mother; 2) mothering must be provided 24/7; 3) mothers must always put their children's needs before their own; 4) mothers must turn to experts for instruction; 5) mothers must be fully satisfied, fulfilled, completed, and composed in motherhood; 6) mothers must lavish excessive amounts of time, energy, and money in the rearing of their children; 7) mothers have full responsibility but no power from which to mother; 8) "motherwork," childrearing specifically, is regarded as a personal, private undertaking with no political import (*Mother Matters*; *What Do Mothers Need?*). Women who conform to the ideology of intensive motherhood are considered "good mothers," whereas women who do not are considered "bad mothers." This social construction of the seemingly normal, seemingly inevitable discursive classification of women as "good mothers" or "bad mothers" sets up norms for women to meet which have little to do with the real lives of women (O'Reilly, *Mother Outlaws*).

Intensive mothering thus does not empower but rather oppresses mothers because each of these eight demands deny mothers' "agency, autonomy, authenticity, and agency to determine" their "own experiences of mothering" (O'Reilly, *Rocking the Cradle* 46). Yet O'Reilly argues that mothers can and do challenge the demands of intensive mothering and the mandate of powerless responsibility (46). In this regard, O'Reilly distinguishes between two types of mothering that women engage in—"patriarchal mothering and empowered mothering" (16, 37-38). Patriarchal mothering signifies an acceptance of patriarchal motherhood, whereas empowered mothering signifies a resistance to patriarchal motherhood and is characterized by agency, authority, autonomy and authenticity (21-23). In specific, empowered mothering consists of mothering practices that resist patriarchal motherhood and, therefore, mark the movement from motherhood to mothering and make possible a "mothering against patriarchal motherhood" (O'Reilly, *Feminist Mothering* 4). An example of such, as O'Reilly explains, would be that "as the patriarchal ideology of motherhood mandates maternal selflessness, a mothering against motherhood practice would insist upon a life outside and beyond motherhood" or "as the patriarchal ideology of motherhood defines mothers as non-sexual subjects in accordance with the age-old whore-Madonna dichotomy, the mother would claim and celebrate a robust and vibrant sexuality" (O'Reilly, *Rocking the Cradle* 12-13). In this sense, "mothering against patriarchal motherhood" is a "transgressive and transformative practice; it seeks to both challenge and change" (12).

O'Reilly also argues that agency, authority, autonomy, and authenticity of empowered mothering are as available to marginalized women as they are to women of privilege and, in fact, are more evident in the mothering practices of mothers who are marginalized such as lesbian women, poor women, and women of colour. This is because marginalized mothers have fewer resources and less status in motherhood and, therefore, are more able to perceive and oppose their oppression (O'Reilly, *Rocking the Cradle*). In this sense, mothers do challenge the demands of intensive mothering and the mandate of powerless responsibility through their mothering (46).

The motherhood-mothering scholarly work is also largely influenced by the work of bell hooks, who points to the importance of recognizing that not all women experience mothering in the same way. Numerous factors influence women's experiences, particularly as they pertain to gender, race, and social class. hooks argues that non-white and poor women's voices have largely been kept out of feminist theorizations about motherhood-mothering. According to hooks, "had black women voiced their views of motherhood, it would not have been named a serious obstacle to our freedom as women. Racism, availability of jobs, lack of skills or education and a number of other issues would have been at the top of that list—but not motherhood" (133). hooks argues that for many non-white women and poor women, motherhood is a source of empowerment because it is "one of the few interpersonal relationships" where women are "affirmed and appreciated," amid a racist and classist society (133). In addition, for many non-white and poor women who often have to balance work outside the home and work inside the home, more time devoted to mothering is welcomed and viewed as liberalizing, as it removes them from the alienating and isolating process of paid work, which takes them away from their homes and children. In this sense, the patriarchal institution of motherhood is not oppressive but rather the ultimate fulfillment of their identity and human needs as women.

The work of Patricia Hill Collins, particularly her theory of "intersectionality and motherhood," provides an important contribution to hooks' call to develop a feminist theorization of motherhood-mothering that puts the voices of black women at the centre. "Intersectionality and motherhood" is a feminist theory on motherhood that places not only race but also class and gender at the centre of theorization of motherhood. Collins argues that "motherhood occurs in specific historical situations framed by interlocking structures of race, class, and gender" (Collins, "Shifting the Center" 45). Intersectionality, therefore, "provides an interpretive framework for thinking through how intersections of race, class, and gender frame and shape mothers' experiences across various social contexts" (Collins, *Black Feminist Thought* 208). In this sense, intersectionality "provides an interpretive framework for thinking through how intersections of, for example, race and class, or race and gender, or gender and class, position mothers within unjust power relations and does so in a way that introduces added complexity to formerly race-, class-, and gender-only approaches" to motherhood (Collins, *Black Feminist Thought* 208). One of Collins important contributions is emphasizing the importance of developing a contextual and specific analysis of mothers with a view to theorizing hierarchies of intersectionality, such that various oppressions are not deemed to be equivalent. Shifting attention to the varying placement of mothers in systems of privilege and non-privilege—whether race, class, or gender—generates divergent understandings of the varied experiences of mothering.

Collins also argues for the need to focus on and examine "motherwork," a term she:

> uses to soften the existing dichotomies in feminist theorizing about motherhood which is centered on white and middle-class women's mothering experiences, and which therefore posts rigid distinctions between private and public, family and work, the individual and the collective, identity as individual autonomy and identity growing from the collective self-determination of one's group (Collins, "Shifting the Center" 47).

Such rigid distinctions reveal themes of mothering that include the following: connections among mothering, aggression, and death; the effects of maternal isolation on mother-child relationships within nuclear family households; maternal sexuality, relationships among family members, all-powerful mothers as conduits for gender oppression, and the possibilities of an idealized motherhood freed from patriarchy" (Collins, "Shifting the Center" 48). However, examining motherwork that is centred on non-white and non-middle-class women's mothering experiences (such as African-American, Native American, Hispanic, and Asian-American women's mothering experiences) merges and connects the divide between private-public, family-work, individual-collective, and identity as individual autonomy-collective self-determination. As a result, different themes of mothering emerge. Themes of "survival, power, and identity" come to light and reveal how women of colour and of lower social classes encounter and shape motherwork (Collins, "Shifting the Center" 49).

In discussing the theme of motherwork and identity, Collins indicates that a dialectical relationship exists between, on the one hand, systems of racial and class oppression designed to strip subordinated groups of subjective identity and a sense of collective peoplehood and, on the other hand, the cultures of resistance extant in various racial and class groups that resist the oppression by maintaining an independent identity. For women of colour and of lower social class, motherwork for identity occurs at this critical juncture (57). Collins discusses two dimensions of the mothering tradition of women of colour and of lower social classes: 1) fostering a meaningful racial identity in children within a society that denigrates people of colour; 2) equipping children with skills to confront the contradiction of the larger effort to assimilate racial children and to challenge systems of racial oppression (57-58).

In this regard, Collins indicates that mothers make varying choices in negotiating the complicated relationship of preparing to fit into yet resist systems of race and class domination. Some mothers submit to racist, class, and sexist ideologies by remaining powerless in the face of oppressive external forces by becoming unwitting conduits of the oppressive dominant ideology or by choosing to fit in for reasons of survival. However, other mothers espouse sophisticated skills that facilitate the appearance of being submissive while, at the same, time being able to challenge inequality (59-60). For women of colour and of lower social class, the struggle to maintain an independent identity takes many forms and is mediated by membership in different racial and social class groups.

The theoretical contributions made by motherhood-mothering scholars help to provide a useful framework for understanding the ways that the women in this study comprehend, experience, and navigate the dominant ideologies and discourses of motherhood in their everyday lives, particularly in light of their various social locations.

ABUSED WOMEN'S PERCEPTIONS OF MOTHERING STANDARDS—ARTICULATING AND CHALLENGING THE DOMINANT IDEOLOGY OF INTENSIVE MOTHERHOOD

The dominant ideology of motherhood is often so deeply entrenched in our everyday culture and society that it becomes internalized by mothers themselves as the one and only way to mother. Many mothers, therefore, attempt to conform to the standards of the dominant ideology of motherhood, ones that are highly idealistic and largely unattainable (Maushart; Mauthner). However, there are mothers who actively challenge and critique the various tenets of these mothering standards (McMahon; Rossiter). In this sense, women may not hold dominant positions of power, but they are able to challenge to various degrees the different ideologies that oppress them (Scott). As indicated by Belenky et al., some women's ways of knowing are passive in that they just take in knowledge without actively involving themselves in questioning or choice. Other women's ways of knowing are focused on their internal intuition, through which they use their "gut feeling" to know and understand the world. Still other women's ways of knowing are through an understanding that knowledge is constructed, as no one truth or reality exists. These women come to know the world through questioning the status quo and the context in which claims to truth are made.

In the study, almost all of the abused women's understandings of "mother" were shaped and influenced by the ideology of intensive motherhood. During the interviews, I asked the women what they thought of when I said the word "mother," and what they thought were the standards and expectations of mothering. What I found was that almost all of the women defined "mother" in relation to the intensive mothering. That is, they had a strong awareness of society's expectations of mothers—that they should "intensely" mother their children. In fact, the women reiterated four of the eight standards of intensive mothering as defined by O'Reilly. These include: 1) children can only be properly cared for by their biological mothers; 2) mothering must be provided 24/7; 3) mothers must always put their children's needs before their own; and 4) mothers must lavish excessive amounts of time, energy, and money in the rearing of their children (O'Reilly, *Mother Matters*). However, the extent of the abused women's awareness of society's expectations of mothers varied. While some abused women articulated all of these standards, others only articulated one or two of them.

Although the majority of the abused women in the study articulated, in one or more ways, the ideology of intensive motherhood in their definitions of "mother," not all of them subscribed to the underlying beliefs and expectations of these mothering standards; rather, many of the women challenged these mothering standards by claiming them to be unrealistic and unattainable. In this sense, some of the abused women were aware that intensive mothering is a mode of mothering that is culturally created. These findings indicate that abused mothers, despite their subordinate position, challenged discourses that oppress them. Below I discuss the four standards of intensive mothering that the abused women most commonly discussed when defining "mother," and the specific ways that they challenged these standards.

i) Children Can Only Be Properly Cared For by Their Biological Mothers

The abused women in this study most commonly cited the standard that children can only be properly cared for by their biological mothers. Many of the women expressed that mothers are expected to be solely responsible for the care of children. As such, the ultimate responsibility of caring for children lay with biological mothers and not fathers. In this sense, mothers have little or no choice but to take responsibility for their children and perform the work involved in mothering. This view reflects the notion of the nuclear family model that is constituted by a heterosexual couple and their biological children; the man earns the wage, and the woman looks after the children and the home. Two abused women provide a clear example of this. Aileen claimed that mothering is primarily women's responsibility because men and women have different and separate roles and obligations in the family.

> *It [motherhood] is supposed to be happiness, brightness, flowers, sunshine, you know, happy home life ... that's what*

> *it's supposed to be.... For them [women] to look after their family, to keep the house clean, to cook, to be loving, and to take care of the husband too.... The husband should ... bring home the bread, the money.... And if the husband doesn't do that or he disappears, well that's very hard for the mother.... Like in the forties and fifties, women did not go to work, and husbands always get the money home.*

As with Aileen, Emma stated that mothers are primarily responsible for caring for children because if they do not, no one else will.

> *Mother is ... women, caring, patience, and responsibility. Like I have to be responsible ... cause nobody is going to do it for me. I got to do it myself.... And I don't expect anybody to feel sorry for me.*

Most of the abused women articulated that mothers are expected to be responsible for the care of their children as a direct outcome of their biology. This biological discourse of maternity equates the maternal role of exclusively caring for children with their bodily capacity to conceive, gestate, and give birth. This view was revealed through women's definitions of "mother" and "mothering" as "maternal instinct," "maternal nature," "maternal love," and "maternal bond," which I discuss below.

Maternal Instinct

Many of the abused women articulated that mothers are expected to be solely responsible for their children because mothering is a "maternal instinct." That is, mothering is considered to be an innate characteristic. In this sense, mothering is seen as something that women are born with and are born to do. This view reinforces a biologically determined paradigm, in which women are viewed solely as procreative. For example, one woman named Madelyn claimed that women's mother instinct begins at the time of conception. In this sense, Madelyn stated that women instinctively begin to care internally for the children in their wombs by caring externally for their individual bodies during pregnancy. Madelyn also claimed that mothers are different than fathers because mothers are innately more loving, giving, dedicated, and responsible.

> *Mothering is like from the onset. Even when the child is still in your womb, that is already mothering. It's how you take care of yourself that you know that your child will be safe inside you, and that you guarantee that you'll give a healthy birth or delivery.... Basically a mother is, you know, there exists a word mother instinct. Mothers are always different from fathers in that they have more love for their children. It's usually always a mother who will want to stay with the kids and have more love.... They go to the extent, or far more than what they can do for their children than the spouse.... A mother is usually the more responsible and the more stronger personality. They're more of your friend. They're more of the hands on. That is a mother.*

As with Madelyn, Tammy stated that women's maternal instinct predisposes them to care for their children, just as their mothers cared for them when they were children. Tammy likened this to a cycle of "dependency" among women.

> *There's the mother instinct that we're in others, whatever that maternal, but no matter what, you're somebody's dependency. Somebody's depending on you with their life! You [mother] should not be neglectful of that.*

Aliya further declared that women's maternal instinct towards their own children extends to other children as well. As such, mothers have an inborn tendency to care not only for their own children but for all children.

> *Mothering is like, um, taking care of. But at the same time, like you can mother anything! You can mother a turtle. So mothering is more like a maternal instincts period.... I know that there's times where my other girlfriends, like if I'm watching their children for them when they ask me to babysit, and I feel a maternal instinct towards their chil-*

dren as well as my own, you know what I mean? Even in a place like this [shelter], everyone, I find, is looking out for everyone's children.

Maternal Nature

Several of the abused women also articulated that mothers are expected to be solely responsible for their children because mothering is considered to be women's "maternal nature," that is, their "natural" role. This mothering role is, therefore, seen as an extension of women's femininity. In this regard, abused women defined mothering as something that comes "naturally" to women. This view reinforces the idea that the womb predisposes women to the role of exclusively caring for children and was revealed in a comment made by Abigail. She asserted that nurturing is a natural and central part of who women are.

Mother is mother earth, and nurture and nature, those aspects of humanity I guess.... And for us [mothers], I think nature is part of it because it's a big part of who we are, how we like to spend our time, and what makes us feel good.

Some abused women expressed that because nurturing comes naturally to women, it is their natural role. These abused women likened women's care of their children to mammals' care of their offspring. In this sense, mothers are viewed as instinctively caring for their children. Taahira stated that women, like the mothers of animals, naturally love and care for their children.

Mother is love, mother is respect, mother is good... It's very normal and natural... You see it in baby animals, where you see mothers are so caring and they love their babies. They don't want that they should fall down or they should be hungry. It's all about care, love, and affection. Mother is the second name of this.

Similarly, Carly claimed that women, like mother hen, naturally care for, guide, and direct their dependent children.

I think of a hen, yes, a mother hen [laughs].... When a child is born they are totally dependent on you, you know. If it's not you, then who? Mother's a strong word.

Likewise, Belinda said that women, like mother bears, are naturally responsible not only to care for but also to shelter and to protect their children.

Well I mean there's always been that mother bear thing, you know, you know don't mess with a mother bear's cubs.

Other abused women expressed that mothering is women's natural calling in life. These abused women compared women's role as nurturing caregivers to the role of comforting religious/spiritual figures. In this sense, mothers' role as caregivers is viewed as their natural and singular vocation. Two abused women compared mothers to the Virgin Mary, a religious maternal figure who naturally and willingly responded to her call to be a mother. Belinda not only compared women to "mother bears" but also to the Virgin Mary. Belinda stated that when she visualizes a mother, she visualizes a woman who is similar to the Virgin Mary.

The Virgin Mary. I kind of picture mothers kind of like that. You know. If that makes sense.

Like Belinda, Aliya also said that she envisions mothers to be like the Virgin Mary because both are naturally nurturing and caring maternal figures.

I'm a Catholic, it's been drilled in my head, so the Virgin Mary comes into my head [laughs]. Um, you know some of that takes a figure that is comforting, open, warm and, nurturing.

Interestingly, two abused women equated mothers to God, a religious figure who is omnipotent and the head of all of humanity. Louisa claimed that when she thinks of a mother, she thinks of God and how he is portrayed in the Bible.

> *I think from reading the Bible, I think of a mother as God.*

As with Louisa, Eden said that she equates mothers with God because when children are born, they view their mothers in an idyllic manner. Eden also related mothers to God because she believes that they are both naturally loving, dependable, and comforting parental figures. In this sense, Eden asserted that mothering is a natural role and calling for mothers.

> *Mother should be natural to mothers ... Mother is also God... I've been reading the Bible a lot, and it says that God and mothers have a partnership because in the baby's eyes they're so innocent. It's almost like they see you as God cuz they're just so dependent on you, and they just love you so much. Like I've never really had a mother or father, they were a pretty shitty mom and dad, and the only one I ever talked to was God. And he's the only person, whatever he is, the only thing that got me through the rough times of my life cuz I could never go to my mom and dad because they were very abusive.*

Maternal Love

A number of the abused women voiced that mothers are expected to be solely responsible for their children because mothers possess a "maternal love" for their children. That is, mothers foster and shape a profound and devoted loving relationship with their children. In this sense, maternal love is considered to be unique to women. This view reinforces the idea that women are more warm, tender, and relational than men and thus should exclusively be assigned the responsibility to care for children. Both Kylie and Leena described mothering primarily on the basis of maternal love.

> Kylie: *Mother is strong, trust, love.... yeah, really loving.*

> Leena: *Mothering is like loving. Yeah. Mothering is loving and being there.*

In addition, two abused women described maternal love in romanticized terms and defined the mother-child relationship as being characterized and exemplified by affection. Lacey stated that mothers are always available to provide affection to their children when they need it.

> *Mother is just someone who's there when you need a hug or a kiss.*

Makayla, however, stated that mothers not only provide affection to their children when needed but also actively, willingly, and constantly bestow affection on their children.

> *Mothering is showing love, holding, cuddling with, and singing.*

Moreover, some of the abused women described maternal love as innate, authentic, selfless, and unconditional. In this sense, caring about and caring for children are seen as two inextricably connected aspects of mothering. Zahra claimed that mothers are expected to inherently express and feel a genuine love for their children.

> *Mothers are supposed to be knowledgeable, they're supposed to be good at disciplining, and they're supposed to be lovable. Like they're supposed to love kids automatically.*

Similarly, Josephine stated that mothers have an altruistic and endless love for their children.

> *Mother is anyone whose heart breaks when your heart breaks you know? Anyone who's happy for you when something good happens ...who wants only the best for you.... Unconditional love, true love.... That's a mother.*

Maternal Bond

A few of the abused women articulated that mothers are expected to be solely responsible for their children because mothers share a "maternal bond" with their children. That is, mothers are considered to be not only physically connected but also emotionally connected to their children. This view reinforces the idea that giving birth in itself exclusively predisposes women to physically and emotionally connecting with and caring for children. For example, Madelyn described mothering not as constricting or restraining but as binding and unifying because of the bond that exists between mother and child.

> *Mothering is like you're bonded. You're connected, you're soul to soul. So mothering is ... not chains ... but a link.... A chain can be broken ... but not a link. You are [mother and child] one ... like a link.*

As with Madelyn, Carly claimed that mothering is characterized by bonding and that this connection between mother and child occurs at birth. However, she also stated that there is an expectation the mother and child disconnect as the child grows older, and that it is mothers who must initiate and direct this withdrawal, distancing, and separation. Carly believes that this process of disconnection is normal and inevitable but hopes that even though her children may no longer rely on her for nurturance, they will still rely on her for guidance.

> *Mothering is bonding, you know, nurturing. When you say mother it's that.... From birth you [mothers] are bonding and nurturing, and they [children] are depending on you.... Gradually, you cut the cord, so to say.... But I hope to God that at thirty or forty my kids still call me for advice, you know what I mean.*

CHALLENGING THE STANDARD THAT CHILDREN CAN ONLY BE PROPERLY CARED FOR BY THEIR BIOLOGICAL MOTHERS

Although many of the abused women cited the standard that children can only be properly cared for by their biological mothers, not all of the women subscribed to the expectations that underlie this standard. In fact, many of the abused women challenged the expectation that mothers are solely responsible for caring for children.

Several abused women challenged the notion of "maternal nature." In this regard, these abused women criticized the expectation that mothers are solely responsible for their children because it is their "natural role." Many of these abused women emphasized that although women carry babies during pregnancy, give birth, and often breastfeed, both women and men are equally able to provide for a child's emotional, psychological, and physical needs. For example, Arika drew attention to the expectation that women are the sole caregivers and, therefore, must stay at home, whereas men are freed from such responsibilities.

> *Moms have to stay home, and the fathers just do what they want when they want with the children. Like they spend time with them when they want to spare an hour.... I hear some people say their dad's babysitting. Well how can their dad be babysitting their own child?*

Maggie pointed out that the expectation that women are the caregivers and men are the providers reinforces a gendered division of labour in the home. Maggie described how mothers are expected to stay home and take care of the children, whereas fathers are expected to go out and earn a wage to financially provide for the family. Maggie claimed that contrary to this societal expectation, she decided to go out and work while her common-law husband stayed at home with their children. Maggie also claimed that her husband stayed home with their children not because he agreed with his wife's desire and decision to work but because he did not want their children to be put in a daycare.

> *It seems like we're [women] always looked at as the ones to stay home and take care of them [children]. Like it seems like we're always the one that has to do everything ... that mothers stay home, and fathers go out and work.... But as I look at it, you know, it works both ways. Like when I was working ... it switched.... He [partner] turned around and was like, "Well, I'll stay home." He didn't want my kids going to daycare, and so he ended up staying home, like taking care of them and taking on my role. But I think*

that how people look at it is that we're [women] supposed to just stay home ... that's what I experienced, that's what I was told to be and to do—stay home.

Kylie emphasized how the current conditions of mothering are the outcome of social processes that constrain women. Kylie described that even though some people may expect mothers to stay home and raise their children, other people, herself included, feel mothers should pursue a career if they so wish. Kylie stated that although her partner had wanted her to stay at home with their three children, she still decided to work outside the home.

Well, a lot of people think a mother should be a stay-at-home mom, and then there's others that think like me, like I want to get out there, I want to have my career and that's why I'm trying to go back to school in September again. When I was with their dad, he expected me to stay at home, he didn't like that I worked.... Yeah I, I don't know whether it was more his jealousy, or whether he wanted to feel like the man and work. So I don't really know.

Leena highlighted the strength and power of the societal expectation that women should remain in the home to care for children. She asserted that the expectation of the "stay-at-home" mother is a stereotype perpetuated by the media, and if mothers do not conform to this stereotype, they are viewed in a negative and deviant light.

There's this belief that mothers should be at home with the kids and cook and clean and not wear the pants but let the man be the boss.... It's just kind of like stereotypes.... If you don't do that, then people are thinking you're like some evil person.... I see this from society itself, like TV *and the media.*

Louisa drew attention to the recent changing and evolving nature of mothering standards. She described how the responsibility of caring for children is being shared more between men and women but also how this final responsibility still largely lies with women and not men. Louisa claimed that this expectation is often perpetuated by other mothers as well as by the media.

> *I would say that maybe now when I look at the, the current generation of mothers and fathers, I think that it's changing because I see how much more of the fathers are having a role than what I knew or than the role my husband played in fathering. So when I look now, I see the nurturing part as both coming from the mom and the dad, way much more than I experienced. And so the standards for mothering are changing I think, because the role is being so much more shared.... In some way, I want to say that because there's so much emphasis put on society caring for children too, I'm wondering if standards of mothering are changing.... A lot of mothers do stay home with their children and nurture their children, but a lot of them don't. They go, and somebody else takes care of their children.... So that all makes me kind of question like what are the standards for mothering right now? Are they changing? Are they being higher or are they being lower? Or are they just changing? I don't know ... society expects mothers to produce wonderful children ... whatever that takes, their children are to be wonderful. When the children aren't wonderful, it's a direct reflection back on the mother in a lot of my observations.... A lot of it is judgment from other mothers, like saying if the kids have not turned out well or they're self-centred or egotistical and then that's entitlement, the entitlement thing, and it is a direct result of how they've been raised in the home.... And I'm thinking mmm, you know, like, I don't know for sure because I think the media has a lot to do with that as well. And we fight hard against the media. Any parent has to fight hard against the media.... So it's a huge job for parents to raise kids, and I don't think it's a total reflection of the parents, but I'm talking about like society and it's still the sort of judgment that's made.... So I hope that it's changing because I'm hoping the fathers are going to be brought into the picture more too.*

One abused woman also challenged the concept of the "maternal bond." Lacey criticized the expectation that mothers are solely responsible for their children because of an enduring connection that only exists between mothers and children. Lacey claimed that mothering should not consist of mothers continually caring for their dependent children but rather should consist of mothers teaching their children to care for themselves and be independent.

> *Mothering is knowing when to let go, like letting them experience things on their own.... But I had to learn that ... because with my family, my mother and my sisters, they all think that you should be there for your kids all the time, and I said, "No you have to let them grow up and, you can't just keep on."*

Clearly, several abused women challenged the message within the intensive mothering discourse that purports children can only be properly cared for by their biological mothers. These women questioned the idea that the sole responsibility of caring for children is the outcome of biological, and not social, processes. Therefore, these abused women recognized that such an expectation constrains women because it frees men from the responsibility of helping care for children.

ii) Mothering Must Be Provided 24/7

The abused women also commonly cited the standard that mothers must care for their children on a constant basis: twenty-four hours a day and seven days a week. Many of the women expressed that children are seen as necessitating extensive care, and, therefore, mothers are expected to give their children constant attention and attendance. As such, the requirement of constantly caring for children rests exclusively on the shoulders of mothers. In this sense, mothering is synonymous with continuous caring. This benevolent discourse of maternity equates the constant maternal work of caring for children with women's motherly obligation to dependent children. This view was revealed through the women's descriptions of "mother" and "mothering" as always "taking care" of children and always "being there" for children.

Two abused women clearly communicated the expectation that mothers care for their children on a 24/7 basis. Mandy claimed that mothering is an endless job and that mothers are always "on call" to respond to the needs of their children. She also claimed that mothering involves not only constantly doing everything for children but also constantly caring about everything pertaining to them.

> *Um, caring of the little ones, there for the child, you know, everything. Just the caring. Being a caring mother that cares about everything that has to do with the child.... It's a 24/7 job.... It's never ending ... just always be ready. You're on call 24/7.*

As with Mandy, Makayla stated that mothering is never ending. It involves not only always being with children but also always taking care of them.

> *Mothering is being with kids twenty-four hours. Like being a mother is washing them [children] up, cooking for them, making sure they don't cry for no good reason.... Yeah I see it on TV, and you're thinking, oh yeah hey it does work, good for them. I've been involved too with child welfare since I've been with my first husband ... they took the kids away ... and so I think that's where I got it from.*

Taking Care of Children

Many of the abused women articulated that mothers are expected to constantly care for children by "taking care" of their well-being, including continuously caring for children's physical and emotional needs. In this sense, maternal work is considered to be holistic work. This view reinforces the idea that mothers are exclusively responsible for always responding to children's needs, desires, and wants. Two women described mothering in terms of the extent and range of care mothers must provide to children. Gabrielle stated that mothering is not just caring for children but deeply caring for them.

Mothering is to care for your child and to care a lot for your child!

Similarly, Louisa claimed that mothering is caring for children in a way that is wide ranging and all encompassing.

A mother is caring for.... Mothering is showing like in a really general way, the path for a child to take in life.... It is all very all encompassing, every aspect of life. Just showing how to do life basically, in a good way.... I'm not describing myself there with those words [laughs]. It's just what I've seen and heard.

Some abused women described this intensive and widespread care by discussing the myriad of ways that mothers must care for children's physical and emotional well-being. Tammy claimed that mothers must constantly ensure their children's physical well-being by safely sheltering, feeding, and cleaning them. Equally mothers must constantly ensure their children's emotional well-being by supporting, securing, and pleasing them.

Mothering, you know, you're taking care of your child, you're being there for support, you're securing them in that safe place, you're making them happy, you're making sure they are fed and kept and clean and happy and organized.

Likewise, Mandy stated that mothers must constantly ensure not only their children's physical and emotional well-being but also their spiritual well-being. Mandy asserted that part of taking care of children's well-being is protecting them from harm.

Mother is caring ... loving ... sheltering. It is caring emotionally, physically, spiritually for children.... Doing the best that she [mother] can to not let harm come to the child.

As with Mandy, April also claimed that protecting children from harm is an important part of consistently ensuring their well-being.

> *A mother is a person that takes care of the baby by providing a stable, financial, loving, kind home for them.... A mother should clean, cook, do the dishes, have a job, pick the kids up from school, take them to daycare, and do all the things.... We're expected to do it all!... A mother loves them [children] and does everything and anything in the world to protect them no matter how much it hurts.*

Being There for Children

Several of the abused women articulated that mothers are expected to constantly care for children by always "being there" for them; mothers must be ever present in order to adequately care for children. In this sense, mothers' presence is considered to be the only means by which children can properly be cared for. Such individualistic mothering practices exclude the involvement of others outside the nuclear family. This view reinforces the idea that mothers are indispensable caregivers in children's lives and, therefore, must exclusively be physically and emotionally available to children at all times. For example, Darri declared that mothers must "take care" of their children but, ultimately, must always "be there" for their children.

> *Mother is a woman that has children and that takes care of them and their upbringing.... A mother should be a person that you can go to and rely on, be safe with. So being there for your children.*

Likewise, Coreen asserted that mothers must "take care" of their children in a myriad of different ways but also must "be there" for their children all the time.

> *Mother is loving ... warm ... hugging.... It's like, feeding, clothing, um, giving money to, helping out, talking, and being there all the time.*

According to Maggie, "always being there" for your children consists of teaching and disciplining them in a caring and loving manner.

> *Someone that will always be there.... I think of it as I guess teaching them what's right or wrong, disciplining them, and also, you know caring for them and loving them.... What you do influences your child.*

Similarly, for Makayla a mother who is "there" for her children is someone who is attentive and involved in her children's lives.

> *Someone who's, um, there. Like someone who's, involved.... Um, probably a listener. Um, um, what do you call that, attentive person, someone who gives them some attention, sits there and talks to them and stuff like that.*

CHALLENGING THE STANDARD THAT MOTHERING MUST BE PROVIDED 24/7

Almost all of the abused women who cited the standard that mothering must be provided 24/7, subscribed to the expectations that underlie this standard. As such, only two abused women challenged the expectation that mothers must give their children constant attention and attendance. One of the abused women questioned the notion of always "taking care" of children's needs, wants, and desires. In this regard, this abused woman criticized the expectation that mothers must constantly "take care" of children in an intensive and all-encompassing way. Kate emphasized that mothers are expected to always appear as though their children are well "taken care of," despite the circumstances in which the mothers and the children find themselves. Kate stated that such an expectation is unrealistic and unachievable.

> *I think, you know, the expectation for every mother is to always take care and be there for kids, even though the reality is nobody can actually do that. We all think, "Oh well look at that woman and her kids, she's obviously not a good mom because her kids are in dirty clothes." You know, we won't consider, oh maybe they were at the park and they were playing in the mud. No, she's just a terrible mother! You see this ... everywhere, you know, from the*

way people talk ... or you see it on TV and all the Leave it to Beaver or Happy Days shows where all the kids were always clean and perfect, and, you know, I think there's some of us, most of us, that do carry that expectation in our heads even though it's not real. Nobody really lives that way!

The other abused woman questioned the idea of always "being there" for children. In this regard, this abused woman criticized the expectation that mothers must constantly care for their children on their own and without the involvement of others. Madelyn pointed to the problematic nature of this expectation, which places the burden of constantly caring for children solely on mothers. Madelyn emphasized how the assumption that children's behaviour is a direct outcome of women's mothering obscures the importance of the diverse social relations and environments in which children are located. Madelyn claimed that when things go wrong in a child's life, it is the mother who comes under scrutiny for what she failed to do in raising the child; it is not the father or society who comes under scrutiny for what they failed to do to help support the mother in raising the child. In this sense, it is only mothers who experience the pressure to constantly care for their children and who are held responsible when something goes wrong with their children.

I'm not really so concerned about society. Like, because you know society they don't really have so much involvement. So, like, they don't care, so it's as if I don't really also care!... But they [society] expects mothers, because the mother is the light of the home to do their part in raising their children and in discipline. Although they [society] don't do more themselves too much. They just expect, but they don't do much. Not much help or programs.... But when a crime happens, in the papers it will always say that this kids became like this because they grew up in an environment like that, or such and such, and then they will blame it on the mother. But that's not a hundred percent correct!

Clearly, the majority of the abused women took for granted the message within the intensive mothering discourse that purports mothering must be provided 24/7. Only two abused women questioned this belief that mothers must constantly care for their children. This demonstrates the power of the intensive mothering discourse and its related standards, which serve the patriarchal institution of motherhood by assigning women the constant responsibility and work of caring for children.

iii) Mothers Must Always Put Their Children's Needs Before Their Own

The abused women cited, to a lesser extent, the standard that mothers must always put their children's needs before their own needs. Many of the women expressed that mothers are expected to care for their children before themselves. In this sense, mothering supersedes all aspects of a woman's self. This sacrificial discourse of maternity equates the maternal act of prioritizing the needs of children over one's own needs with women's maternal commitment to their children. This view was revealed through the women's descriptions of "mother" and "mothering" as making sure children "have everything they need," and as being a "role model" for children. One abused woman, Zahra, clearly communicated the expectation that mothers should care for their children before themselves.

> *As a mother you are supposed to ... do good things for your children, take care of them, be there for them, and no matter what you put them first. They [children] come first in everything you do.*

Children Have Everything They Need

Some abused women articulated that mothers are expected to care for their children before themselves by ensuring that their children have "everything they need." In this regard, mothering is wholly child-centred and places mothers in service to children. That is, mothering implies self-denial and servitude. This view reinforces the idea that mothers are singularly responsible for catering to the needs of children and, therefore, must selflessly adopt the needs of their children by seeing these needs as their own. For example, Belinda asserted that mothers must watch over children to ensure that they have "everything they need."

> *I think of a guardian. Someone loving, nurturing, protecting. Like, overall you make sure that little person has everything they need.*

Likewise, Tammy claimed that mothers must do all within their capacity to ensure that their children have everything they need. It is not a choice but a requirement and an obligation.

> *You do whatever it takes to get that child's needs met and you make sure that it's done. You make sure that you give them all the love and support and mostly care for them. You do what you have to do! You're a mom, do it [laughs]! Well, it's not that you need to, you will, you should [laughs]!*

Mothers Are Good Role Models for Their Children

Some of the abused women expressed that mothers are expected to care for their children before themselves by being "good role models" for their children. In this sense, mothers have a duty to behave and act in a manner that is positive for children. This view reinforces individualistic philosophies that place mothers as being unique forces and the most important influences in children's development. As such, mothers have no alternative but to take on the burden of being the primary role models in children's lives, even if it means putting aside their own experiences, feelings, and needs. The assumption is that the women's mothering behaviour has the potential to greatly affect children. For example, Zahra claimed that mothers should not only "put their children first" but also be a "role model" in their children's lives.

> *As a mom, you're supposed to be their [children's] role model. I have seen it through my mom ... through other moms, you know just all that.*

Also, Taahira said that mothers should be a "good role model" for their children by only "doing good things" and by balancing their children's immediate needs with their long-term needs.

> *A mother is a role model, a good role model.... Someone who do good things only. Who tells you what is right and wrong so that tomorrow you should know the difference. Who tells you what is bad and what is good, and from whom you learn all the good things ... good teachings, good values.*

Similarly, April asserted that mothers should be a "good role model" for their children by never showing that they are emotionally weak or that they engage in any bad behaviour.

> *A mother should be a good role model.... There is the expectations that we're supposed to be, you know, we're not supposed to break down, and we're not supposed to have emotions, and we're not supposed to drink beer, and we're not supposed to smoke cigarettes.*

CHALLENGING THE STANDARD THAT MOTHERS MUST ALWAYS PUT THEIR CHILDREN'S NEEDS BEFORE THEIR OWN

Many of the abused women cited but also challenged the standard that mothers must always put their children's needs before their own needs. These abused women challenged the expectation that mothers must care for their children before themselves.

Several abused women questioned the idea that mothers must make sure their children have "everything they need." In this regard, these abused women criticized the expectation that mothers should exclusively focus on and fulfill all of their children's needs. For example, Kate pointed to how the assumption that women must prioritize the needs of their children over everything else implies that mothering should be women's only and most important activity. Kate declared that, in this sense, mothers are unfairly expected to anticipate and prevent any difficulties and problems that their children may have or may encounter. As such, Kate stated that mothering, according to such expectations, is a "negative" role and experience because mothers are expected to fulfill all of their children's needs.

> *Mothering to me is a really negative word.... You know like somebody's mothering you, like, "Let's look after all the problems, and let's try and look in advance to see what's going to happen to try and stop it from happening," you know. It's looking after everybody's needs, and trying to think what they're thinking so you can anticipate what they're going to need tomorrow. That's mothering to me, and I find that very negative.*

According to Aliya, the expectation that mothers must prioritize the needs of their children over their own needs obscures the fact that mothers themselves also have needs. As such, Aliya declared that society, as in social institutions, has unrealistic expectations for mothers. Such child-centred expectations do not take into consideration or make room for the needs, feelings, and experiences of mothers. Consequently, mothers "easily get worn down" because they are expected to meet all of their children's needs by ignoring and denying their own needs.

> *I think that society, as in like the system and not necessarily as like mother to mother or friend to friend, sometimes has expectations that are unrealistic. I think that people need to realize that mothers are human beings. Mothers get frustrated, mothers get hurt, and mothers get tired.... If a mother has a child, there's only so much time she has besides cooking, cleaning, groceries, and everything else in her life that she has to take care of her son or her daughter. Depending on how many children she has, I think sometimes they need to look more at time and scheduling, and that sometimes a woman, a human being, needs time for herself as well. You have to go do this, you have to do this, and this, and this, and as a woman, you can easily get worn down. You're taking care of your kids, and then, at the same time, you have all these things that you are expected to do. Where is the time to just sit down and have a break?*

Carly also drew attention to the unrealistic expectation that mothers should meet and fulfill all of their children's needs, and that if they do not, their ability to care for their children is called into question by authorities. Carly claimed that these expectations are perpetuated in mothering books, but that such messages are false and oppressive.

> *I think society is trying to raise our children, you know. If you raise your voice to your child in the grocery store, the next thing you know you got child welfare on your doorstep.... I never had my child taken away ... but I've seen a lot of bad things happen.... I learned those messages from the books* What To Expect When You're Expecting *or* What To Expect in The First Year *[laughs]. But it's bullshit! It's all* BS*!*

One abused woman questioned the belief that mothers must be "role models" for their children. This abused woman criticized the expectation that mothers must always be positive examples because they are the most important influence in their children's lives. According to Gabrielle, the expectation that mothers must be role models for their children is so powerful that mothers must publicly portray that everything is well in their private lives, even if it is not. Gabrielle claimed that mothers should not put aside their own needs in order to solely be good role models for their children but rather should make these needs known to the community in which they live in order to receive support.

> *Well, they expect you to be this role model, you know, like if things happen keep it in the house sort of thing.... But I don't think that that's right because I think a community should be, like, if you live in a community, all people should be aware of what happens to help.*

Clearly, several abused women challenged the message within the intensive mothering discourse that mothers must always put their children's needs before their own needs. These women questioned the idea that prioritizing the needs of children is a maternal commitment that women are required to make. Therefore, these abused women recognized that such an expectation is unrealistic as well as emotionally and physically taxing for women.

iv) Mothers Must Lavish Excessive Amounts of Time, Energy, and Money in the Rearing of Their Children

Only a few of the abused women cited the standard that mothers must lavish excessive amounts of time, energy, and money in the rearing of their children. These women articulated that mothers are expected to extensively devote themselves to their children. In this sense, mothering is all consuming. This rigorous discourse of maternity equates infinite maternal care of children with women's maternal dedication to their children. This view was revealed through the women's descriptions of "mother" and "mothering" as "doing everything" for children and as "spending time" with children.

Doing Everything for Children

Two abused women expressed that mothers are expected to extensively devote themselves to their children by "doing everything" for them. In this sense, mothers must allocate excessive amounts of their energy to caring for their children. This view reinforces the idea that mothers' willingness to participate in all areas of their children's lives is an extension of their maternal love, care, and loyalty to their children. One abused woman named Julie provides a good example of this. She declared that mothers must "do everything" for their children, from taking care of their basic physical, emotional, and developmental needs to involving them in and bringing them to extracurricular activities and to being active and involved in their school life.

> *Mothering is nurturing, loving, caregiving, disciplinarian, teaching, being there for your child, and cooking. How my mom was. She was a stay-at-home mom. I grew up on a farm, and she took us to all of our activities. She took care of all of it ... you've got the housework, the cooking, the cleaning, the PTAs, that kind of thing ... do everything!*

Kate also affirmed that mothers are expected to "do everything" for their children and that women's maternal dedication is reflected in their children's behaviour and countenance.

> *There's this expectation that kids are always in clean clothes. Their hair is always done; they're polite in public ... and you're a good mom if your kid's not having a fit in the grocery store. You're taking your kids to every sport possible, you know they're in piano, soccer, and ice skating. They have playdates, you allow other kids to come over ... you do it all ... you're doing everything! ... Yeah, your kids don't talk back to you, but you don't scream at them, and everybody looks normal, and everybody's hair's in place all the time, or else you must be a bad mother.... These are the standards, it doesn't mean their right or wrong.*

Spending Time

Three abused women articulated that the most important way that mothers are expected to extensively devote themselves to their children is by "spending time" with them. In this regard, mothers must assign excessive amounts of their time to caring for their children, which reinforces the idea that mothers must be not only present for their children but also engaged with them. For example, Shyan asserted that mothers must be involved in their children's lives by "spending time" with them in a variety of different ways, including "doing physical things" with them.

> *Mothering is doing things and spending time with your kids.... Get outside with them. Do physical things with them.*

Taahira claimed that mothers must work incessantly for their children and that mothers must spend not only time but "quality time" with them, as it is the truest reflection of a mother's dedication.

> *A mother should work like a machine. She should be very caring, totally devoted ... and fully dedicated. Mother has to tell everything, and mother should spend quality of time with children ... that's the one!*

Mandy also said that mothers must "spend quality time" with their children.

> *A mother should just be a parent, you know being loving, playing games, and just spending that quality time.*

CHALLENGING THE STANDARD THAT MOTHERS MUST LAVISH EXCESSIVE AMOUNTS OF TIME, ENERGY, AND MONEY IN THE REARING OF THEIR CHILDREN

Almost all of the abused women who cited the standard that mothers must lavish excessive amounts of time, energy, and money in the rearing of their children, subscribed to the expectations that underlie this standard. Only two abused women challenged the expectation that mothers must extensively devote themselves to their children. Both of these abused women questioned the notion that mothers are responsible for "doing everything" for their children. Arika pointed out that the assumption that mothers must "do everything" for their children is unachievable and that, in this sense, mothers are expected to be "super women," and to do things for their children that are beyond their actual abilities. As such, Arika affirmed that "too much" is expected of mothers.

> *I think society expects too much out of mothers. Like we're expected to be super women and stuff like that, and it's not like that. Like when the kids go to the hospital, the moms have to stay there all the time. Moms are expected to do everything! I just think that society just expects way too much out of mothers. Way too much!*

Coreen emphasized that the expectation that mothers "do everything" for their children is an expectation that is not imposed on fathers. In this sense, only mothers are expected to extensively devote themselves to their children and are harshly judged if they do not meet this expectation. As such, Coreen stated that the expectations that are imposed on mothers are "really high."

> *The expectations for moms are also really high. I think*

> *really high! Higher than men to be dads. I think ... they expect you to have everything like organized, your whole life totally together, and you don't need help from your partner. They [fathers] don't get talked to, and they don't get talked about. But like when I, you know, if I chose to wait to do that I'd be a bitch, or I'd be you know a horrible mother.... The father gets away with everything, but the mother, it's just like you're bad, you're not good, and you're doing this and you're doing that wrong.*

Clearly, the majority of the abused women also took for granted the message within the intensive mothering discourse that purports mothers must lavish excessive amounts of time, energy, and money in the rearing of their children. Only two abused women questioned this belief that mothers must excessively devote themselves to their children. The small number of women who were critical about demonstrates the power of the intensive mothering discourse and its related standards that serve the patriarchal institution of motherhood by requiring women to extensively devote themselves to the care of their children.

Overall, the abused women's understandings about mothers and mothering were significantly influenced by the dominant discourse of intensive mothering. As discussed above, the abused women defined "mother" according to the following four standards of intensive mothering: a mother 1) is the only person who can properly care for her biological children, 2) provides care to her children 24/7, 3) always puts her children's needs before her own needs, and 4) lavishes excessive amounts of time, energy, and money in the rearing of her children. Although the abused women reiterated these standards of mothering, some also challenged them by actively questioning and criticizing the expectations that are imposed on mothers. As such, abused women were able to not only articulate the dominant discourse of intensive mothering but also identify and challenge its constricting and oppressive nature.

ABUSED WOMEN'S PERCEPTIONS OF THE "ABUSED MOTHER"

Ideologies of motherhood not only define how women must mother but also promote dominant ideals of motherhood against which mothers' lives are regulated and judged. In recent years, several groups of mothers have been stigmatized, criticized, and vilified by the dominant ideology of motherhood for failing to meet the standards of intensive mothering because they have lived in circumstances of abuse. The dominant ideology of intensive motherhood upholds that children's well-being is primarily the responsibility of women. In situations of domestic violence, abused women are accused of failing to ensure the well-being of their children because they have lived in an abusive context and, therefore, have "failed" to protect their children from witnessing and/or experiencing abuse, even in cases where they have not. Consequently, abused mothers are perceived, labeled, and portrayed as "bad mothers." In fact, abused mothers are often re-victimized by systems purporting to help them and their children, such as police, courts, social assistance services, child protection services, and even abused women's shelters because of the "bad mother" label that is applied to them. In this sense, many abused mothers are subject to constant monitoring and control by these social institutions because they are suspected of potential wrongdoing when it comes to their own victimization or their ability to care for their children. For example, abused mothers are more likely to come to the attention of child protection services and be monitored for potential criminality because their ability to shelter, care for, and protect their children is called into question (McDonald-Harker).

In this study, abused women's perceptions of the common understanding or portrayal of "abused mothers," like their understandings of "mother," were shaped and influenced by the dominant discourse of intensive mothering. However, their understandings of "abused mother" were also shaped and influenced by other dominant discourses, including the victim-blaming and mother-blaming discourses. During the interviews, I asked the women if they thought that "mothers who are abused are viewed differently than mothers who are not abused," and if they thought that there are "different standards and expectations of mothering for women who have been abused." What I found was that many of the women described "abused mothers" according to the intensive mothering discourse and its associated "good mother" and "bad mother" discourses. Every single one of the women stated that they experienced being viewed and labeled as a "bad mother" because they had been in a domestic violence relationship— whether or not their children actually witnessed and/or experienced abuse and whether or not they were currently with or had already left their abusive partner. In specific, the women felt that they were portrayed as "bad mothers" for failing to meet two out of the four standards of intensive mothering that they articulated (as discussed above): 1) mothering must be provided 24/7 and 2) mothers must always put their children's needs before their own. Also many of the women stated that they experienced being perceived and characterized in the following stereotypical ways: as careless, selfish, alcoholics, drug addicts, on welfare-social assistance, instigating or deserving the abuse, not caring about their children, allowing their children to witness or experience abuse, and potentially abusing their children themselves—all of which are deemed to be characteristics of a "bad mother."

Although some abused women described "abused mothers" by referring to the dominant discourse of intensive mothering, most of them did so by drawing on and joining the victim-blaming and mother-blaming discourses and then articulating five other deviancy discourses. These women stated that "abused mothers" are portrayed as 1) "weak mothers," 2) "abusive mothers," 3) "looked down on mothers," 4) "to blame mothers," and 5) "in need of help mothers." The women varied in relation to how many of the deviancy discourses they articulated. While some women mentioned only one of these deviancy discourses, other women mentioned several of them.

It is important to note that all of these abused women challenged these negative portrayals of abused mothers. As such, the women's narratives revealed that not only were they able to articulate the dominant discourses that cast abused mothers as "bad mothers" and other deviant mothers but they were also able to identify and challenge its subjugating and unjust nature. These findings indicate that abused mothers, despite their subordinate position, challenge discourses that oppress them.

Below I discuss each of these six discourses that the abused women commonly mentioned when discussing the portrayal of "abused mothers" as well as the specific ways that they challenged these views.

REITERATING AND CHALLENGING THE DOMINANT DISCOURSE OF INTENSIVE MOTHERING—"BAD MOTHER" DISCOURSE

First, some of the abused women described the portrayal of "abused mothers" according to the intensive mothering ideology and its associated "bad mother" discourse. These abused women claimed that abused mothers are largely portrayed as "bad mothers" for failing to meet the following two standards of intensive mothering: 1) mothering must be provided 24/7 and 2) mothers must always put their children's needs before their own. However, these abused women challenged the view that abused women are "bad mothers" by stating that such depictions are false and misleading.

i) Abused Mothers Fail to Mother their Children 24/7

The abused women often claimed that abused mothers are portrayed as "bad mothers" because they are viewed as being unable to care for their children on a constant basis. These abused women stated that they are deemed as being unable to constantly care for their children because they are also coping with the problems, difficulties, and consequences of being abused. However, these abused women challenged these depictions of abused mothers. For example, Makayla asserted that abused mothers are viewed as putting their children in harm's way by being involved in an abusive relationship. As a result, abused mothers are inaccurately portrayed as "bad mothers" who are unable to care for their children. Makayla called into question this unfair comparison and depiction of abused mothers as "bad mothers" and non-abused mothers as "perfect" mothers.

> *Other people look at women who are being abused as "What the hell is going through your head? You've got kids!"... It's like for the abused mother they probably think that oh, well, she's not taking care of her kids, she's not doing the safety of her kids, and a non-abused woman, oh, she's perfect, look at her she's so loving, and you know.... Some*

people probably think a mouthy woman deserves to be hit, and maybe she's not a good mother, and maybe she's like this and that's why she's getting hit, you know.

Similarly, Eden declared that abused mothers are often stereotyped as having a "bad past," or a tendency to use substances such as alcohol or drugs as a coping mechanism. Consequently, abused mothers are falsely portrayed as "bad mothers" who are unable to care for their children. Eden asserted that such a biased perception of abused mothers creates an unfair expectation that abused mothers must "prove" themselves.

I think abused mothers are very, um, what is that word I'm looking for, they're really, misunderstood. Like people think they know who abused mothers are, you know, they think they're bad either way.... So I think when you're abused, a lot of the times they expect you to prove yourself cuz they probably think, oh she's had a bad past or she was probably bad before, she probably drank, did drugs, whatever.... They expect them [abused mothers] to work extra hard. They expect them to prove to everyone that, you know, they're not a bad person and they're not doing drugs or alcohol. But yeah, that exactly, they expect them to prove to everyone that they can have a good life too.... But being abused has taught me that there's all different kinds of forms of ways of mothering and raising a child.

As with Eden, April stated that abused mothers are deemed as mothering under improper conditions because they often reside in abused women's shelters, face financial hardships, or experience emotional difficulties. Therefore, abused mothers are incorrectly portrayed as "bad mothers" who are unable to care for their children. April criticized this misleading assumption that mothers can only properly care for their children by mothering under the same socially prescribed conditions.

I think abused mothers because they're in a shelter or be-

cause they're not financially secure or because they're not emotionally secure and they should be are viewed as bad mothers, un-strong mothers, and not very good mothers.... I just feel like somebody wrote a book and said that this is how you are supposed to be as a mother, and if you don't follow that then you are a bad mother.

ii) Abused Mothers Fail to Put Their Children's Needs Before Their Own Needs

The abused women also claimed that abused mothers are portrayed as "bad mothers" because they are viewed as putting their own needs before their children's needs. They are deemed as prioritizing their own needs over their children's needs because they are not emotionally, psychologically, and physically stable as a result of experiencing abuse. This reflects Krane and Davies recent research, in which they argue that the message given to abused mothers in domestic violence shelters is that a "good mother should always be available, and her children's needs should always come first, no matter what has happened to them" ("Mothering Under Difficult Circumstances" 33). However, the abused women in this study challenged these depictions of abused mothers as "bad mothers." For example, Madelyn claimed that abused mothers are considered to be "submissive," "too kind," and "overpowered." In this sense, abused mothers are viewed as being unable to "stand up" and "protect" themselves and their children. Consequently, abused mothers are erroneously portrayed as "bad mothers" who put their own needs before their children's needs. Madelyn declared that attributing women's victimization to their personal characteristics conceals and denies the fact that abuse can happen to any woman, regardless of who or how she is.

They say that she [abuse mother] is not a good mother. I think that's the first thing that they're going to say.... So she is viewed in a negative way because she is submissive or the kind mother, and then she is, like, overpowered by the spouse. And probably she's so kind that she won't retaliate at all, will accept everything, and accept all the torture.... Sooner or later, she has to fight back, right!

> *Protect herself and protect the children! If she's going to accept everything then what's going to happen? She has to stand up for herself.... But it can happen, you can be abused even if you fight back or even if you're the stronger one or even if you're the timid or submissive one, you can also be abused.*

Similarly, Kate declared that abused mothers are stigmatized as not having the "best problem solving skills" and not "putting their children first" because they are living in an abusive environment. As a result, abused mothers are falsely portrayed as "bad mothers" who think of themselves and their own needs before their children's needs. Kate criticized this biased presumption that abused women are incompetent and neglectful mothers who should be treated as though they have a malady.

> *There's this view that mothers that are abused don't have the best problem solving skills, and they're not putting their kids first you know. Because if you put your kids first and you're in an abusive situation, then you'd get your kids and you'd leave right! So the expectation is that that woman is going to be a loser. I think that society and the way that they treat domestic violence should change completely. They treat abused women like they have Stockholm syndrome or something.... I think that when somebody comes out of an abusive relationship, that she's viewed as just one of those people right! So the expectations is that her kids are going to be unruly. They're going to be dirty, they're going to be rude, they're going to be the bad kids in the class. They'll be the ones doing the drugs, and their moms are so preoccupied with the abuse that they don't really notice their kids anyways. So I think society has almost come to accept that, you know, and they're just those people right, one of those women.... So everybody has to look normal and everybody's hair has to be in place all the time, or else you must be a bad mother.... I've seen this in peoples' reactions to me because I'm not a poor me person. I don't lie about who I am and where I've come*

from, so I do tell. I don't tell it in a way where oh it was a bad thing for me, I'm like this is who I am, and this is where I was, and this is what I've done. And there's some people that are like "Oh well, that's really cool that you're doing something else," you know. And other people are like, "Yeah, so anyways it's time to go." And I mean I've had a few confrontations. There were people at the bus stop by the shelter that I saw every morning, and they said good morning to me until they saw where I came out of. The day they saw where I came out of I went to the bus stop, and they just kind of looked at me and turned away like they didn't want any part of me. And I'm like, "Did I change?" But cuz they didn't know where I was from, as soon as they found that out they're like, "Oh well, you know, we're going to stay away from that person!" So I mean a lot of my perception of that is from just people, you know, and you read it on the news all the time where there's a man and woman fighting and they call the cops after the gun shot right.... So I think people should change their view of abused mothers.

As with Kate, Louisa affirmed that abused mothers' capabilities are called into question. As a result, abused mothers are viewed differently and judged more harshly. Louisa declared that such views contribute to the inaccurate portrayal of abused women as "bad mothers" who prioritize their needs over their children's needs. Louisa called into question this view that abused women lack necessary skills and argued that many abused mothers are capable of dealing with crises and have effective coping strategies because they "hold it together" even under the difficult circumstances of abuse. However, these aptitudes largely go unnoticed.

If you are a person that's been abused people wonder what are you really like. What are you really capable of? Are you really capable of handling a good job? And I don't want a lot of people to know what I've come through because I'm afraid they will view me differently. I don't want to be viewed differently. For that reason I make sure that I look normal and, like, I think anybody should look. I don't want to be different, I don't want to act different, I don't want to speak different, I don't want anything different about me.... If they didn't know me and know my kids, they would make a judgment that I would not be a good mother. That's unfortunate, but I think that how it's gone.... They would probably think I hadn't done very well, and just because I'm abused, I have some other kinds of problems. Not necessarily. But other people may think so..., And how will I deal with, um, say a bad crisis? What would I do in a crisis? Would I be able to handle it? That sort of thing. Actually, I think the opposite is true. I've had lots of crisis in my life, and I've dealt with them really well, so I know how to do that. But the outside observer wouldn't probably think about it that way right off hand. I think a lot of abused mothers have those skills that we don't realize they have. They have wonderful coping strategies and things like that, that we don't often think about. In my own mind, I think the abused mothers that I see out there are very, very strong women, because they have their children. They are holding it together, and I see that a lot of them have jobs.

ARTICULATING AND CHALLENGING OTHER DISCOURSES—REITERATING AND JOINING THE DOMINANT DISCOURSES OF VICTIM BLAMING AND MOTHER BLAMING

Second, while some of the abused women described "abused mothers" by referring to the intensive mothering discourse, most of them described "abused mothers" by joining the victim-blaming and mother-blaming discourses and then articulating five other deviancy discourses. These abused women claimed that "abused mothers" are mostly portrayed as 1) "weak mothers," 2) "abusive mothers," 3) "looked down on mothers," 4) "to blame mothers," and 5) "in need of help mothers." However, these abused women also challenged the portrayal of abused women according to these deviancy discourses by stating that such depictions are biased and misconstrued.

The abused women often made references to the victim-blaming perspective, which places responsibility for domestic violence on the victim. They expressed that abused women are blamed for the abuse because of numerous myths, such as they were insufficiently obedient, subordinate, and attentive to their male partners' needs and desires; they provoked their male partners; and they sought out violent male partners. In this sense, women are blamed for the abuse because it is assumed that it results from their own failures in some capacity. However, the abused women challenged such views by pointing out how preconceived notions about women's responsibility, provocation, and culpability hold them accountable not only for the abuse but also for remaining in the abusive relationship. In this sense, the focus is on why women stay in abusive relationships rather than on why men are allowed to abuse women. The women's narratives reveal the pervasive conceptualization and understanding of power as being equally distributed in all interpersonal relationships, which obscures the reality that women in abusive relationships rarely have power (Radford and Hester, "Overcoming Mother Blaming").

The abused women's references to the victim-blaming perspective were intertwined with their references to the mother-blaming perspective. In this sense, the abused women expressed that they are not only blamed for their victimization, but also for exposing their children to an abusive situation. Abused women are blamed for failing to protect their children from witnessing and/or experiencing abuse because they have lived in an abusive environment. However, the abused women challenged such views by indicating that abused mothers make considerable efforts to protect their children and go to great lengths to counteract the effects of abuse on their mothering. The women's narratives reveal the prevalence of a "deficit" perspective of mothering that "shifts the focus away from men's violence to emphasize women's 'deficiencies' and 'failures' as mothers"; their strengths and efforts are ignored (Lapierre, "Mothering in the Context of Domestic Violence 460).

i) "Weak Mother" Discourse

A large number of women claimed that abused mothers are portrayed as "weak mothers" because they are viewed as not being strong enough to leave their abusive partner and protect their children. These abused women stated that, consequently, there is the assumption that abused mothers must be constantly interrogated and closely monitored to ensure that they are properly caring for their children. However, these abused women challenged this depiction of abused mothers. For example, Zahra affirmed that abused mothers are incorrectly portrayed as "weak mothers" because they became involved and remained in an abusive relationship. Zahra criticized this unfair assessment of abused mothers. She said that they often do not have "the choice" to immediately leave their abusive partner and that if they did have the opportunity to make such a choice, they most definitely would.

> *Abused mothers are seen as weak, as you know not responsible. Definitely weak.... Because why would anybody be in a situation where they get hit and verbally and physically abused. It's like, "What's wrong with them? Why are they in that situation? Why can't they leave?'... You know, if we had a choice to choose then we would choose ... well, we don't have that choice! ... Every society expects every mother to protect their kids. Anybody that's a mom takes care of their kids and protects them, but if you've been abused then it's in question. You know, like, for other moms it's like, "Okay she's a mom, she's good." But for abused moms it's like, "You've been abused, okay is she taking care of the kid? Why is she abused? Is it because she's weak? Is it because she's not smart enough? Is it because she's not educated? She doesn't have the money?" So then if she's all of that, then it's "She's not strong enough or responsible enough to take care of the kids, then she can't protect the kid." So it's out there for them to judge and put things together and take things out of there and play with it.*

Tammy claimed that abused mothers are inaccurately portrayed as "weak mothers" as a consequence of experiencing abuse. In this sense, abused mothers do not have the strength or courage to leave their abusive partner and, therefore, require help. Tammy criticized this biased perception of abused mothers and their abilities, which presumes that leaving an abusive partner is a simple process. Tammy described how leaving her partner was a "big battle" for her and how it took her "eight times" of leaving her partner before she was finally able to successfully leave him and not return. The only reason Tammy stated that she kept returning to her partner was because she was not aware of the resources that are available to abused women. As such, Tammy affirmed that successfully leaving an abusive partner is based on a progressive learning process and not solely on one's personal strength.

> *Mothers who aren't abused got a good family and stuff, and they got a nice enough family. But mothers who are abused, well they're not the person who's got the rich family chalet. I'm not talking about materialistic things, but the kind of family.... And abused mothers are more weaker [laughs'. Yeah, they look at them like they're more weak because of abuse; they need help or something.... But it's a big battle. It's not that easy though. It's taken me eight times of leaving to figure it out.... I finally called the cops, and they brought me here. I didn't know! If I would have known you could have all these tools and resources [at the shelter] three or four years ago, I would not be in this position right now. Cuz I won't be doing this twice.*

Aliya also declared that abused mothers are inaccurately portrayed as "weak mothers" because they have experienced abuse. She further stated that because abused mothers are viewed as "weak," their mothering abilities are called into question and more is expected of them. For example, Aliya described how when she was at the shelter, she felt as though the management staff were "looking down" on her and viewed her as "weak" because she was a victim of abuse. She criticized these unfair views and expectations that are imposed on abused mothers, which she states are "unrealistic" and unattainable.

> *I think women who are abused are looked at as weak. And so I feel like there's more of a spotlight on us. Like*

> *[sighs], for instance when I said politics at the shelter I meant some of the women there, and I'm not talking about my counsellors but my counsellors' supervisors and the women that are running the building and stuff. I would feel as if they were looking down on me like, "You come from a family of abuse, um, that's trashy....You know if you were brought up properly in society with a good home and a good family, you would not be in this situation. And you're weak, and you know you're a statistic now! You're a single mom, living off welfare trying to raise your kid." And, um, I feel almost like they look at it like if we were stronger women and more so in our right mind, we never would have ended up in those situations. At the same time, I feel like it's not so much necessarily expecting, it's can you even mother? Can you do your job? Questioned, I feel that we're questioned much more. But the system isn't the best, and their expectations are unrealistic! How can women last?*

Madelyn elaborated on the expectations that are imposed on abused mothers because they are assumed to be "weak mothers." According to Madelyn, abused mothers are expected to put on a strong face and carry on with their lives for the sake of their children. Madelyn criticized this inaccurate depiction of abused mothers as "weak" and as unable to care for their children by emphasizing that many abused mothers, including herself, protect their children yet are still blamed for not doing so.

> *I think because you are abused, they think you're not capable emotionally, and they expect something of you, like you have to be strong, you still have to be strong because like life goes on. If you're going to be weak what's going to happen to your kids? So you still have to put up a face, even if you sometimes cannot be that strong. So they expect something from you.... And I was blamed for many reasons.... But I was the protective! I was the shield, yes I was the shield, and I was always there ... but they will still blame me!*

Coreen stated that abused mothers are wrongfully portrayed as "weak mothers" because they are believed to be unable to "stand up for themselves." Coreen outright denied this erroneous belief by asserting that abused mothers can and do express their needs, but they falls on deaf ears. Abused mothers are told what they need; they are not asked what they need. As such, there is a disconnection between abused mothers' actual needs and what is perceived to be their needs. Coreen described how when she sought help from the agencies in her community, they offered her help in areas that she did not need, such as help with nutrition and anger management—what she needed was help with clothing her children. As such, there is an assumption that abused mothers lack mothering skills and, therefore, must be taught these skills.

> *In a way, I think they think abused mothers are really weak and can't stand up for themselves, you know, can't say what they need. But they can and they do! But nobody listens! A lot of people don't listen.... Because that's what happened to me with my kids. Like I was asking for this help, yet they were giving me help in a way I didn't need help [laughs], you know like what meals to feed my kids. Like hello, I need clothes here! I don't need you to tell me how to cook for my kids. I know how to cook for them, and I know what they like and what they don't like. And then they're telling me to go to programs for like anger management, and I was like, "Um excuse me? I think he needs to go not me!"*

These abused women's descriptions are consistent with Levendosky, Lynch, and Graham-Berman's ("Mothers' Perceptions") research findings that found abused women are not helpless victims who are solely focused on their abusive partner's needs but rather are active agents who mobilize their resources to respond to the violence on behalf of their children (247).

ii) "Abusive Mother" Discourse

Several abused women also claimed that abused mothers are portrayed as "abusive mothers," meaning mothers who abuse their children. These abused women asserted that because abused mothers have been abused by their male partners, it is believed that they will in turn begin to abuse their children. However, these abused women challenged this depiction of abused mothers. For example, April stated a misconception exists that abused mothers are not only "bad mothers" but also "abusive mothers." April described how when she was in the shelter the counsellors continuously asked her if she was feeling "aggressive" towards her children, as they anticipated that she would surely begin to abuse her children. As such, April criticized this stereotypical belief that abused mothers will, in due course, abuse their children.

> *They think that because we were abused and most people that are abused or have been abused turn into the abuser, you know. And they are just waiting for you to start abusing. They [shelter staff] said, "So how are you feeling today? Are you feeling aggressive towards your kids?" No, I'm not!*

Leena also indicated that abused mothers are portrayed as "abusive mothers." She asserted that this is a false supposition because abused mothers are in fact less likely to abuse their children, as they would never want to subject their children to the same pain and suffering they endured. Leena also asserted that non-abused mothers are just as likely to abuse their children, pointing to the biased and faulty reasoning that is used to suggest that abused mothers are at a higher risk of abusing their children.

> *With abused women, they automatically think that because they're abused they're going be abusive. But then most of the times they change, like they've been abused but then they're not abusive. But people who come from, like, a strict family where they weren't abused, like, they're just as dysfunctional as the person that was getting abused but worse.*

Zahra stated that abused mothers are incorrectly portrayed not only as "weak mothers" but also as "abusive mothers." Zahra upheld that there is an assumption that abused mothers will begin abusing their children, as well as allow their abusive partner to start abusing their children. As such, abused mothers are blamed for the abuse that their male partner perpetrated against them as well as for the potential abuse that their male partner may perpetrate against their children. Zahra denounced this unfair portrayal by indicating that abused mothers are "under the microscope" and, therefore ,many exaggerated and biased assumptions are made about who they are as mothers and how they carry out their mothering.

> *When you're abused, you're under the microscope, and they have different views, different opinions, and different ideas about you. So they might think if you've been abused you're going to abuse your kid or you know you're going to let that abuser that abused you abuse them, and, stuff like that.... Abused moms are out there, everybody knows their story, everybody knows something. Like as humans we know, we think about it, we analyze it, whereas for moms who are not abused, then nobody knows about that. So they are viewed differently.... I've seen it through family and friends and other people in society, just different people that you meet every day, on daily basis that you hear about.*

These abused women's assertions echo Holden and Ritchie's extensive research that found there is no evidence of diminished parenting among abused mothers in comparison to non-abused mothers. Abused mothers are no more aggressive, no more punitive, no less affectionate, no less proactive, and no less capable of providing structure to their children than are non-abused mothers (Holden and Ritchie).

iii) "Looked Down on Mother" Discourse

Many abused women also claimed that abused mothers are portrayed as "looked down on mothers." These abused women maintained that abused mothers are viewed as inferior because they have been abused. Nevertheless, these abused women also challenged this portrayal of abused mothers. For example, both Leena and Emma declared that abused mothers are "looked down on." They claimed that abused mothers are viewed as second-rate individuals who come from bad circumstances and who are unable to make the necessary changes to improve their current life situations. Leena and Emma equally criticized this unfair perception of abused mothers. Leena, who indicated that abused mothers are portrayed as "abusive mothers," also pointed to the erroneous perception that they are "different," "pitiful," and "not good people." Yet Leena affirmed that such views of abused mothers are only "stereotypes."

> *I think it's kind of like stereotyping them [abused mothers]. They [society] think, "Oh she grew up in a good family, they're well off, and she's a good person. But her, look at her! Like she's been abused and did this and that, and you know she's probably not even a good person!" kind of thing, right. Or else look down on them like, "Oh she's so pitiful" or you know, "Feel bad for her" or "She's different," kind of thing.*

Emma drew attention to the naïve presumption that to overcome their abuse all abused women have to do is leave and not return to their abusive partner and seek counselling. However, Emma stated that doing so is "easier said than done" because abused mothers have often lived under controlling conditions for a long time.

> *I don't know, I always feel like society looks down on people like abused women.... Like it's easy to say. "Don't go back to that person, go to counselling, do this do that." Like it's easier said than done because you're so used to being in that kind of environment.*

Carly also claimed that abused mothers are "looked down on" and viewed as "lower class citizens" who willingly allow themselves and their children to be abused. Carly called into question this unfair perception of abused mothers by declaring that it should be the male abusers and not the female victims who are scrutinized and condemned. As such, she emphasized that the focus should be on the abusive behaviour of male partners and not on the potential deficiencies of female victims.

Abused mothers, I believe, are looked down upon.... You know what, I think that child welfare looks at a mother that's been abused as letting themselves and their children be abused. I think they see them like they're a lower-class citizen, you know, they look down at abused mothers and that's bullshit! They should not be looking down at them, but they should stop the abuse, and do something to stop the abuse! ...One thing that I'll say that really hurt me being in the shelter is the books there. I don't think there was one book made pass nineteen eighty-two. Now what kind of updated material is that? That's bullshit! That's more than twenty-five years gone by you know! There's just too much bullshit out there about abused mothers, you know!

iv) "To Blame Mother" Discourse

Other abused mothers asserted that they are portrayed as "to blame mothers." These abused women affirmed that abused mothers are held responsible on all accounts for their own abuse; these abused women, however, challenged this portrayal of abused mothers. For example, Gabrielle said that abused mothers are blamed for getting involved in an abusive relationship in the first place. As such, abused mothers are also accused of and blamed for being unable to care for their children. Yet Gabrielle declared that this blameworthy depiction of abused mothers is but a label.

Well, some people just say, "Well how could you let yourself get in that situation?" So I think society views them [abused mothers] differently. Like they just label you and just say that you can't look after your kids and then, therefore, it's your fault, they blame you.

Mandy said that abused mothers are blamed not only for becoming involved in an abusive relationship but also for provoking the abuser in one way or another. Even in cases when abused mothers return to their abusive partner in an attempt to reconcile their relationship, they are also blamed and criticized for doing so. Mandy criticized this unfair view and assessment of abused mothers by stating that judging rather than understanding abused women's personal situations demeans and diminishes them.

> *Some people will be, like, "well it's their own fault you know," the negative people would be like, "well that's their own fault," so they're blamed because they're the ones who went into the relationship. So the negativeness. Some of the guys who are probably women abusers themselves would be like, "Oh, she probably asked for it,' or "She did something. She probably fucked around on him," or whatever you know.... And say social services for instance, like I've heard stories and I've talked to a few women, and some of them keep going back to the same guy, and then like some of the social workers or even police will have comments like. "Oh well, why? Why go back?" and stuff. But some of the women have this thought. "Oh well no one else is going to love me and my kids. Who's going to do that? This is their father!" So if he says he wants to try it again and stuff, they're going to give him the benefit of the doubt. But it's the negative feedback that they get, the comments and stuff, you know it just brings a mother down more.... Being put down for going back to somebody because you love that person, and that person does love you to an extent but.*

Similarly, Arika asserted that abused mothers are blamed for anything and everything that goes wrong in their and their children's lives. In this sense, the blame is always laid on abused mothers because they were the ones involved in an abusive relationship. Arika called into question this unfair judgment of abused mothers because they mother under different circumstances than non-abused mothers.

> *I feel like mothers who are abused are singled out ... they're blamed.... So if something goes wrong in the child's life or if something goes wrong in our life, it's because of abuse, it's always because of abuse. And the mothers that aren't abused don't have to go through what abused women go through.... They're just two totally different lives.*

v) "In Need of Help Mother" Discourse

Finally, a couple of abused women claimed that abused mothers are portrayed as "in need of help mothers." According to two abused women, abused mothers are viewed as requiring guidance and assistance because they have numerous weaknesses, inadequacies, and limitations. Both of these abused women challenged this false portrayal of abused mothers as "in need of help." For example, Maggie claimed that abused mothers are considered to have a number of emotional and psychological difficulties and, therefore, should go to counselling. Maggie described how she experienced this first hand. When she was residing in a shelter, the staff told her that she should "go to counselling because she 'needed help.'" However, Maggie refuted this assumption and stated that she and her children were indeed happy in many "ways" and at many "times," despite the abusive context in which they lived. As such, Maggie denounced this inaccurate presumption that abused women because they experienced abuse are inherently discontent and despondent.

> *With abused mothers, I think that they always look at them like they need help and counselling, and, like, they should go for counselling and just stuff like that. And it seems like they're just watching out for you, for women that go through abuse. So abused mothers are looked at as people in pain because we're single that's why, and because we were abused.... So I think they just look at it like just to go for counselling, you know.... Because I was told that a lot.... When I first went to a shelter back when we were staying on the reserve, cuz my husband went through some charges, they told me that I should go for counselling, that I still need help. And it just seems like that's how I was getting looked at, you know, like we're not happy. But we were in a way and in times. We were! But I guess it was just when you looked at it, I was always being abused, he was always drinking.*

Tammy declared that abused mothers are portrayed not only as "weak mothers" but also as mothers who are "in need of help."

According to Tammy, abused mothers are perceived as needing help not only for their own benefit but also for the benefit of their children. As such, abused mothers are expected to get help in order to prevent the perpetuation of the cycle of violence in their lives as well as in the lives of their children. Tammy criticized this false supposition that all abused mothers have many problems and, therefore, need help by indicating that everyone, and not just abused mothers, face dilemmas and difficulties in their lives.

> *They think that maybe because you have been in an abusive situation and maybe because it's for the benefit of the children in that household that you get some help because you need help. Plus for the benefit of the child you need help to get stronger, to not repeat a pattern so that it becomes a family cycle. I think there's a little more expectations of that, I would think anyways. But, I think there's lots of different variations besides abuse that are hidden, because everyone's got their dirty skeletons in their closets if you go look.*

These abused women's accounts provide further evidence to support previous research on abused women's mothering that argues that mothers in domestic violence situations often cope very well with the violence and, therefore, do not develop learned helplessness (Buchbinder; Letourneau, Fedick, and Willms; Levendosky et al.). In this sense, many abused mothers compensate for the abuse in their mothering interactions with their children.

Overall, abused women's understandings of the portrayal of abused mothers were influenced by the dominant intensive mothering, victim-blaming, and mother-blaming discourses. The abused women described that "abused mothers" are portrayed as "bad mothers," "weak mothers," "abusive mothers," "looked down on mothers," "to blame mothers," and "in need of help mothers." Although the abused women described the portrayal of abused mothers according to these discourses, they also challenged them by actively questioning and criticizing these negative portrayals of abused mothers. As such, not only were abused women able to articulate the dominant discourses that cast abused mothers as "bad mothers" and other deviant mothers, but they were also able to identify and challenge these discourses' subjugating and unjust nature.

CONCLUSION

Mothers today live under the influence of an ideology of intensive motherhood, prescribes a type of mothering that is wholly child-centred, self-sacrificial, and denies mothers' own selfhood. Nowhere is this more evident than in the narratives of the women who were part of this study. These narratives revealed that most of the women's understandings about mothers and mothering were shaped and influenced by the dominant discourse of intensive mothering (O'Reilly, *Mother Outlaws*). In this sense, the abused women reiterated four of the six standards of intensive mothering, including a mother 1) is the only person who can properly care for her biological children, 2) provides care to her children 24/7, 3) always puts her children's needs before her own needs, and 4) lavishes excessive amounts of time, energy, and money in the rearing of her children. What is significant and notable is the fact that not all of the abused women subscribed to the beliefs and expectations that underlie these standards. In fact, many of the abused women challenged these standards by actively questioning and criticizing the beliefs and expectations that are imposed on mothers. As such, the abused women in this study not only articulated the dominant discourse of intensive mothering but also identified and challenged its constricting and oppressive nature.

The power of the ideology of intensive motherhood is seen in its ability not only to define how women must mother but also to judge and regulate mothers' lives. Abused women are one of the groups of mothers who have been harshly judged, regulated, and labeled as "bad mothers" by the ideology of intensive motherhood for failing to meet it standards. The abused women's narratives in the study revealed that their understandings about how they (as abused mothers) are portrayed were also shaped and influenced by the dominant discourse of intensive mothering, in addition to both the dominant victim-blaming and mother-blaming discourses. The abused women commonly described that they are portrayed as "bad mothers," "weak mothers," "abusive mothers," "looked down on mothers," "to blame mothers," and "in need of help mothers." However, as in their discussions of the social construction of mothers, many of the abused women also challenged this view and portrayal of abused women. They not only articulated the dominant discourses that casts abused mothers as "bad mothers" and other deviant mothers but also identified and challenged their subjugating and unjust nature. As such, despite their subordinate position, abused women were able to challenge to various degrees the dominant discourse of intensive mothering that oppresses them. The next chapter provides a discussion of the ways in which the women in the study construct themselves as mothers and an examination of the discourses that they draw from, resist, and negotiate in constructing their mothering identities.

4.
ABUSED WOMEN'S SUBJECTIVE CONSTRUCTIONS OF THEIR MOTHERING IDENTITIES

The Influence of the Dominant Ideology of Intensive Motherhood and the Discourse of the "Good Mother" Versus "Bad Mother"

I THINK I'M A GOOD MOM. I think I'm a very good mom actually. I think it's one of my strong points as a person and as a woman that I'm a very good mom. I think about how things will influence her [daughter] and then I don't let those situations happen, whereas her dad just doesn't think of the repercussions. At the beginning of this journey, I thought very little of myself as a mother. I still felt like I was doing a good job as a mom, but he would belittle that and cut that on a regular basis and that would affect me. From the time that she's [daughter] been around, I have been the sole parent, the sole person, the sole adult doing the parenting. He [partner] was off working in BC, and then it became at the pub, and so he wasn't ever there. So I would be the sole parent doing the parenting, and I felt like I always made good choices and I felt like I was parenting well, but he would cut that down. Maybe because it was the one thing that I did know that I was doing well. So, he would cut that down. That made me sometimes not have the confidence that I needed to parent effectively.... But there's a difference between a good mother and, um, not necessarily not an effective mother and a bad mother. I guess when I think of a bad mother, there's not many bad mothers that I can think of. I just think, you know, we all have our journey, we're at different places in our life, we have different experiences, we have different learning blocks, we make different choices in life, and there are different things we've come to terms with and different realizations. Especially going through this process [abuse]. When I think about what I used to think of as a bad mother, I don't think of as a bad mother anymore. I just think now of a person in a different place in the journey [laughs], at a different level, and they haven't quite gotten it yet or whatever the case may be. There's some people it comes faster for and some people it comes slower for, and I don't think that's a bad mom because they keep on, they're still trying, they're still plugging away at it, and they're doing the best they can everyday.... Um, so I don't think of that as a bad mom anymore. I used to, maybe because of societal assumptions, but now I realize how sometimes we get pushed to a certain level that we respond badly and that doesn't make us a bad mom it just makes us responding badly. But as long as we're working towards responding well most of the time, I think that makes a good mom. Like what I've gone through, having to stay in shelters, I would have never imagined it in a million years! Never would I have imagined it! Actually, I would have thought of that as a bad mom before. But now, I think of it as a good mom because you're trying to make changes to what happened in your life, and you're doing whatever you can to make that happen. It might have been ideal if I could have waited till I was at a certain level, you know financially and that sort of thing, before leaving. But realistically, that wasn't going to happen. Not with the financial abuse that we had, and everything being stretched, and my credit down the tubes just to have milk, or whatever. It wasn't going to happen. No.... So when I think of mothering I think you have to be very selfless, but you also have to be not selfish, but you have to meet your own needs. That's a big part of what I'm learning now. So a big part of being a good mom is exploring what you need to do and what's true to your soul and doing what you need to do to keep yourself healthy and to keep yourself happy. That helps you to be a good mom. As

> *opposed to before, I just felt like I had to completely focus all of my life on the house, the home, and parenting and trying to make it positive. I used to think that as a mother, I had to be all the hats.... I just felt like I had to do all everything because there's an absentee. But realistically... I don't have to provide all of it. I don't have to be her mother, and her therapist, and her community. She has a good, great one around her, so I just have to open my arms to that.... So I thought I was a good mother before, now I feel like I'm a very good mother.* (Quotation from Abigail, a thirty-seven-old mother of one child and who experienced verbal, emotional, psychological, financial, and physical abuse from her previous male partner for eight and a half years)

Mothers are not only surrounded but also influenced by the dominant ideologies of motherhood. Dominant ideologies of motherhood, which materialize in dominant mothering discourses, are powerful and shape how women view and think about themselves as mothers. In this sense, dominant mothering discourses influence what mothers know and do not know, what they see and do not see, what they say and do not say (Weingarten 12-13), and also how they see and do not see themselves in complex ways. As such, the way mothers come to experience and understand their social identity is discursively constructed (Davies and Harré). By establishing what is accepted as normal, good, and desirable, dominant mothering discourses construct criteria that lead mothers to regulate their own behaviour without the presence of force or coercion. Compliance to the ideals of motherhood occurs when mothers internalize the dominant mothering discourses and, therefore, become self-monitoring subjects (Code; Cooper, "Productive, Relational and Everywhere"). This influences and shapes the ways that mothers view themselves as mothers.

However, dominant mothering discourses are not monolithic and all powerful. Not all mothers are passive victims who merely accept and internalize mothering discourses. Rather, some mothers are active agents who outright question and resist the dominant mothering discourses in their own lives. But our knowledge and understanding about the specific ways that mothers do so is very limited, which raises a number of questions: how do abused women subjectively perceive their mothering? How are abused women's subjective perceptions of their mothering experiences similar or different? What role does the discourse of motherhood play in the lives of abused mothers? How are abused mothers' lives shaped by the discourse of motherhood?

The above quotation from Abigail, one of the women in the study, provides a good example of the role and influence that dominant mothering discourses play in shaping how abused women view and think about themselves as mothers. Abigail clearly draws on the dominant discourse of intensive mothering and its associated "good mother and bad mother" discourses in constructing her identity as a mother. Although the dominant discourse of intensive mothering portrays abused mothers as "bad mothers" for having mothered in the context of abuse, Abigail does not describe herself as a "bad mother." Abigail, instead, describes herself as a "good mother" and makes reference to being a "good mom," not only one time but four separate times. In fact, Abigail states that being a mother is one of her "strong points as a person and as a woman." She does admit that there were times when she thought "very little" of herself "as a mother," particularly when her abusive partner would "belittle" her and "cut" her down. Nonetheless, Abigail always felt as if she was doing "a good job as a mom" because although she was "the sole parent doing the parenting," she carried out her "parenting well," she made "good choices" as a mother, and she thought "about how things" would "influence" her daughter and did not "let those situations happen." In this sense, Abigail asserts that despite having mothered in the context of domestic violence, she is no less capable and no less competent than other mothers. Consequently, Abigail clearly and uniformly evokes images of herself as a mother and details practices of her mothering that illustrate her capabilities as a mother.

What is interesting in this narrative is that Abigail describes herself as a "good mother" and defines a "good mother" not according to the standards imposed by the dominant discourse of intensive mothering but rather according to her own personal standards.

As such, Abigail redefines "good mother" to have more inclusive boundaries. According to Abigail, a "good mother" is someone that "keeps on." is "still trying," is "still plugging away," is "doing the best they can every day," is "working towards responding well most of the time," and is "trying to make changes to what happened" in their "life" by "doing whatever" they can to "make that happen." In this sense, Abigail denies the standard that a "good mother" is someone who puts their children's needs before their own needs and, instead, upholds that a "good mother" is someone who also "meets their own needs," who is exploring what is "true to their soul," and who is doing what they need to do to keep themselves "healthy and happy."

Abigail even recognizes that the understanding of what is a "good mother" and a "bad mother" is based on "societal assumptions." In fact, Abigail's views of mothers changed as a result of her experiences of abuse. She claims, "When I think about what I used to think of as a bad mother, I don't think of as a bad mother anymore." As such, Abigail now claims "there's not many bad mothers that I can think of" and instead of categorizing mothers according to the "bad mother" versus "good mother" discourse, Abigail views and describes mothers as having their own separate "journeys," as being "at different places" in their lives, as having "different experiences" and "different learning blocks," as making "different choices" in their lives, and as "coming to terms" with "different realizations." Indeed, Abigail's narrative is one example that demonstrates that abused mothers resist the dominant discourse of intensive mothering that casts them as "bad mothers" by drawing on the "good mother" discourse and then redefining "good mother" to have more inclusive boundaries.

The previous chapter examined the ways that mothers in situations of domestic violence view, define, and experience the standards and expectations of the dominant discourse of motherhood. This chapter builds on that chapter by examining the specific ways that mothers in situations of domestic violence view and construct themselves as mothers. In this chapter, I present and discuss the specific discourses that the women in the study draw from, resist, and negotiate in constructing their mothering identities.

CONSTRUCTING THEIR MOTHERING IDENTITIES: ACCEPTING AND RESISTING THE DOMINANT DISCOURSE OF INTENSIVE MOTHERING

Dominant ideologies of motherhood dominate, regulate, and constrain women and their mothering because they define how women *should* mother. Intensive mothering, as the dominant mode and discourse of motherhood, is predicated on the eradication, or at the very least sublimation, of a mother's own selfhood and in particular her agency, autonomy, authenticity, and authority (O'Reilly, *Rocking the Cradle*). Despite such demanding criteria, intensive mothering is the mode of motherhood by which all mothers are regulated, evaluated, and judged. Women who practice intensive mothering are considered "good mothers," whereas women do not are considered "bad mothers." Intensive mothering—and the high demands it imposes on mothers to be ever present and available regardless of the circumstances under which their mothering takes place—creates a tension that makes it more difficult for mothers to negotiate their way through motherhood without feeling stressed, discouraged, deficient, and, in sum, blamed (Baber and Allen; Eyer; Hays; Stoppard). To avoid such mother blame, mothers often strive to correct, alter, or adapt their mothering so that it more closely conforms to the standards of intensive mothering. Given that these are idealized standards, they are impossible to achieve. Consequently, mothers inevitably, at one time or another, feel the weight of mother blame, which, in turn, causes mothers to experience shame, guilt, and self-recrimination (O'Reilly, *Rocking the Cradle*). Dominant ideologies and discourses of motherhood, such as intensive mothering, are oppressive to women.

As discussed in previous chapter, O'Reilly distinguishes between two types of mothering that women engage in—"patriarchal mothering and empowered mothering" (O'Reilly, *Rocking the Cradle* 16, 37-38). "Patriarchal mothering" signifies an acceptance of patriarchal motherhood, whereas "empowered mothering" signifies a resistance to patriarchal motherhood and is characterized by agency, authority, autonomy and authenticity (21-23). According to O'Reilly, agency, authority, autonomy, and authenticity of empowered mothering are as available to marginalized women as they are to women of privilege and, in fact, are more evident in the mothering practices of marginalized mothers because they have less resources and status in motherhood and, therefore, are more likely to oppose their oppression.

I argue that O'Reilly's theory-practice of "mothering against patriarchal motherhood" provides a good framework for understanding the role and influence that the dominant discourse of intensive mothering plays in shaping abused women's subjective mothering identities. This theory-practice demonstrates how mothers can and do accept, negotiate, or resist the discourse of intensive mothering not only in their subjective mothering practices, as O'Reilly theorizes, but also in their subjective constructions of their mothering identities that I argue the women in the study do.

In the study, almost all of the abused women constructed their mothering identities by drawing on, negotiating, or resisting the dominant discourse of intensive mothering. During the interviews, I asked the abused women participants how they viewed themselves as mothers. What I found was both unique and significant. While a small minority of the abused women accepted the dominant discourse of intensive mothering and drew on the "bad mother" discourse, the large majority of the abused women resisted the dominant discourse of intensive mothering in subjectively constructing their mothering identities in three main ways: 1) by negotiating the "bad mother" and "good mother" discourses; 2) by drawing on the "good mother" discourse and then redefining a "good mother" to have more inclusive boundaries; and 3) by rejecting both the "bad mother" and the "good mother" discourses and then replacing these discourses with experientially based alternative mothering discourses.

Interestingly, although the abused women stated they are viewed and portrayed as "bad mothers" for failing to meet the standards of intensive mothering, they did not personally perceive and construct themselves as mothers in this negative light but rather overwhelmingly viewed and constructed themselves in a positive ways that were empowering for them. As such, the abused women's narratives reveal that although their views and definitions of themselves as mothers were influenced by the dominant discourse of intensive mothering, they were not passive victims who merely accepted and internalized the discourse of intensive mothering. Many of the women were active agents who questioned and resisted this discourse. I argue that these findings indicate that abused women, despite their subjugated position, engage in "empowered" mothering by constructing their mothering identities in ways that outright resist the discourse of intensive mothering (O'Reilly, *Rocking the Cradle*). Below I discuss the ways that the abused women constructed their mothering identities by drawing on, negotiating, or resisting the dominant discourse of intensive mothering.

ACCEPTING THE DOMINANT DISCOURSE OF INTENSIVE MOTHERING THAT CONSTRUCTS ABUSED MOTHERS AS "BAD MOTHERS"—PATRIARCHAL MOTHERING

In constructing their mothering identities, a small number of abused women accepted the discourse of intensive mothering. That is, these abused women viewed and described themselves as "bad mothers." As such, these abused women engaged in what O'Reilly refers to as "patriarchal mothering" by accepting the dominant discourse of intensive mothering that constructs and portrays abused mothers as "bad mothers." Overall, these abused women had less than positive views of themselves as mothers. Interestingly, none of these abused, women except one, directly referred to the "bad mother" discourse. Instead, these abused women referred to an altered form of the "bad mother" discourse—they described themselves as "not good mothers."

Four of the twenty-nine women engaged in patriarchal mothering by drawing on the "bad mother-not good mother" discourse when describing how they subjectively viewed themselves as mothers. These abused women viewed and claimed that they were "bad mothers or not good mothers" because they failed to meet the standards of intensive mothering, specifically the following standards: 1) mothering must be provided 24/7; 2) children can only be properly cared for by their biological mothers; and 3) mothers must always put their children's needs before their own. Most of the abused mothers stated that they wanted to be "good mothers." As such, in each case, the abused mothers were pressured and constantly made efforts to live by and maintain the standards of intensive mothering. When the abused women failed to achieve the standards of intensive mothering—which are unrealistic and unachievable for any mother to achieve in the first place—they nonetheless judged themselves harshly. These abused women shared a strong commitment to the ideology of intensive motherhood and experienced the push and pull of a no-win situation. In this sense, some, but not all mothers challenged the demands of intensive mothering and the mandate of powerless responsibility (O'Reilly, *Rocking the Cradle*). These abused women who viewed and defined themselves as "bad mothers" did not challenge but rather accepted the standards imposed on them by the dominant discourse of intensive mothering.

i) "Bad Mother"—Fails to Provide Mothering 24/7

Most of the abused women who claimed that they were a "bad mother or not good mother" indicated that they viewed themselves as such because they failed to live up to the intensive mothering standard that stipulates that mothers should provide care to their children on a constant basis, twenty four hours a day, seven days a week. Three of the abused women felt that it was their maternal obligation to constantly care for their dependent children, but they claimed that they were often unable to give their children this constant attention and attendance because they mothered in an abusive context. As a result, these abused women stated that they were unable to always "take care" of and "be there" for their children. Lacey is a good example of an abused mother who viewed and described herself as "not a good mother" because she was not always there to care for her children. According to Lacey, she was often not physically there for her children because she was trying to respond to her abusive partner's needs. When she was not taking care of her abusive partner's needs, she was still unable to physically be there for her children for a variety of different reasons, including the following: she was "always on edge" as a result of being abused; she was away working outside of the home; and she was taking caring of the household duties. Lacey also asserted that she was often not emotionally there for her children as she did not take the time to tell her children that she "loved them," which caused Lacey to feel guilt and sorrow. However, not once did Lacey question the expectation that constantly caring for her children is a responsibility resting exclusively on her shoulders.

> *I tried to be such a good mother but I was not because of everything that was happening.... There's so many things I wanted for the kids, but then with him too, but I ended up ... giving it to him, instead of to the kids! So I always wanted to give the kids everything they wanted, but it was like I was trying to con them, or not conning them, but trying to make up for it ... because I was concentrating on him, instead of concentrating on the kids.... I was always on edge, always, always, always on edge. I couldn't just like play with the kids cuz I was always so busy dealing with him and then dealing with work and then getting the house done.... When I was raising the kids, I guess I wasn't a very happy person. I feel like I was someone who gave up. So I guess I can't say that.... I was always there for the kids.... I guess I just felt as long as they had a home where there was no alcohol and they had their meals. But I guess there was something missing too. Something that I never got that I didn't know how to say and that was that I loved them. It took me a long time to be able to tell someone that I loved them, cuz I never heard it before. And I think my son and daughter felt, well they knew that I was always there, but I guess you need a verbal too.... I don't know how I fell.... I tried, and I tried, and I tried.*

As with Lacey, Aileen described herself as "not a good mother" because she was unable to constantly be there for her children when they were young. Aileen stated that when her children were growing up she was unable to love her children the way she was "supposed to"; she was not able to be with her children as she "wanted to" and, consequently, she was not "close" to her children because she was controlled by her abusive partner and lived in fear. Aileen also claimed that since her children have grown up and moved away from home, she still has been unable to be there for her children because they have cut off communication with her, which has only increased Aileen feelings that she is "not a good mother" and has caused her to feel much pain and regret. As with Lacey, Aileen did not question the expectation that she should be the one exclusively responsible for always responding to her children's needs, desires, and wants.

> *I wanted to be a good mother ... but I was not... [starts crying], and I would have been too. It's really painful because I went through years when I was not able to love my children how it's supposed to be. Opposite of love is hate, but also opposite of love is fear. If you live in fear you cannot love.... Like I could not be with the children as I wanted to. I could not be close to my children. I could not love them because I was controlled somehow, you know. I was full of worry when I was at work— What's happening to the kids? I was worried when I was at home—How will I carry on alone? What if I lost my job? So this constant worrying. It was like my daughter used to say, "Mom you run around like a chicken with her head cut off." Yeah, like, I was panicking you know. I'm getting closer to kill myself. And sometimes, honestly, I thought maybe I should kill my family too. I'm telling you because sometimes people do that, because they wanted something a lot better for the children, but they cannot provide, so they would rather see that they don't suffer, and so it's killing out of love.... And what the psychologist said to us in the Foothills Hospital is, "How a husband acts with the woman, that's how she acts with the children" and this is very, very true. Like I had the death sentence from my husband, and I feel sometimes I give the death sentence to my children. I did not want to, and two years ago, [starts crying], they [children] moved away. and they don't want to talk to me. My daughter said they don't talk to me until I prove myself.*

Taahira also viewed herself as "not a good mother." However, Taahira was the only woman who also explicitly described herself as a "bad mother" because she was both physically and emotionally unavailable to her daughter. Because she was "emotionally broken" from experiencing abuse and because she had to work full time, Taahira was only able to give "twenty percent" of herself and her time to her daughter. Taahira affirmed that she "would have been a more loving and affectionate mother" had she been in a happy and non-abusive relationship. Taahira believed that being a "loving and affectionate mother" should come naturally and normally to all mothers and, therefore, felt much agony and anguish because she was not able to live up to this standard. In this sense, Taahira equated the constant maternal work of caring for and loving children with women's motherly obligation to their dependent children. Taahira held herself to the standard that she must constantly ensure her daughter's well-being by supporting, securing, and pleasing her. Consequently, Taahira expressed that she wanted to be a "good mother" and since she left her abusive partner, she has been doing everything in her power to try to be that "good mother."

> *I don't say I'm very good mother.... I don't say I'm very different mother.... I just think inside "That is kind of example of bad mother you giving her [daughter]."... Emotionally I got broken, you know.... I feel very bad because sometimes when you don't even deserve something, still you have to have it, then you feel demoralized, disappointed. Plus you, you have to fight for the things, and you sometimes you know you lose your strength.... I was only able to be there for her [daughter] twenty percent ... plus I worked so many shifts. If I had, um, happy marriage life and if mostly was good, then I would have been a more loving and affectionate mother....It's not a matter that society expects or I have to do, it is just a natural and normal relationship.... I don't want to be extraordinary mother, I just want to be good mother and strict mother, because I'm alone. I want to teach her discipline, a routine, what life is, what I never saw. In India, I lived like a princess because I was a daughter of a king, I lived like a princess. But, even though my dad had a status, he taught us really good things. My dad taught us hardships. We can live in a hut or we can live in a palace. I don't say we*

are very good, but we are civilized, educated, and disciplined people. So same thing, I just want to be a mother who teach her religious things, good values, how to be a good human, and a disciplined and organized person. So I don't say I'm a very good mother, but I'm still proud of my teachings, what I got from my parents, like all the hardships or just above, and discipline and all that. And I wanted to uh teach her same thing. Until now I couldn't, but now when, she's in my hands, I'm trying my level best to, uh, you know, pass it on her.

ii) "Bad Mother"—Fails to Care For Her Biological Children

Two of the abused women also claimed that they were a "bad mother or not good mother" because they failed to live up to the intensive mothering standard, which stipulates that children can only be properly cared for by their biological mother. These abused women believed that only the mother and no one else should care for their biological children, but they claimed that the abusive social context in which they carried out their mothering required otherwise. As a result, these two abused women asserted that they were not the sole care providers for their children. For example, Lacey described herself as "not a good mother" not only for failing to constantly care for her children when they were younger but also for not remaining at home and close to her children once they were older. At one point, Lacey left home and went to another city to get away from "everybody and everything for a while," particularly her abusive partner. Even though her children were adults, Lacey claimed that they felt as if she had "deserted them." Consequently, Lacey felt "like a failure" for not being there to care for her adult children. But she did not question the standard that she should be solely responsible for providing for her children's emotional and psychological needs.

I ran away from everybody and everything for a while, like when I went to Chilliwack I just left everybody. And I know the kids, even though they're adults, they felt like I deserted them. So like I said, I feel like I'm not a good mother, and I feel like a failure. I should have been stronger

> *and thought more about them [children] than the partner.... But, I'm just so tired of being hurt.*

Likewise, Aileen described herself as "not a good mother" not only for failing to constantly care for her children but also for working outside of the home and sending her children to a daycare. Aileen expressed a lot of remorse and disappointment for not being able to remain at home to care for her children. Consequently, as with Lacey, Aileen felt "like a failure" because she was not able to "enjoy" her children and provide them with a "better life." According to Aileen, she "could have been a very good mother" had she not experienced financial abuse by her partner because then she would have been able to remain at home with her children. Aileen clearly held herself to the standard that her children could only be properly cared for by her and only her, given that she was the biological mother.

> *I supported the family for years, on my own. I always had to leave the children so I can make a living, and I still can remember one occasion when my son says, "Please don't leave me." Well what can I do, you know. I'm just sorry what the kids went through. When I was working they [children] were in a daycare centre. I did not want them to go there. I thought I will always be home. But I did what ever I could. Even when I see young mothers now [starts to cry], I start to cry because I could not enjoy the children for a long time. I wanted to, but ... So, I, it bothers me that my children could have a lot better life. I feel bad, I feel real bad. And this is my wish, that for the rest of my life, try to correct whatever was not right.... I could have been a very good mother if I would not go through this [abuse].... In a way I say I'm a failure.*

iii) "Bad Mother"—Fails to Put Her Children's Needs Before Her Own Needs

Finally, a number of the abused women claimed that they were a "bad mother or not good mother" because they failed to live up to the intensive mothering standard that demands that mothers put their children's needs before their own needs. Three of the abused women believed that mothers must prioritize the needs of their children over their own needs. However, these abused women declared that living with an abusive partner often made putting their children's needs first a challenge; consequently, they found it difficult to live up to this mothering standard and experienced lots of culpability in this regard. Both Lacey and Emma described how they viewed themselves as a "bad mother or not good mother" because they periodically used substances as a way to cope with the abuse. Lacey felt that she was a "bad mother or not good mother" not only for failing to meet the two previously discussed standards of mothering but also for failing to put her children's needs before her own needs because she self-medicated with drugs as a way to cope with living in an abusive environment. As such, Lacey was committed to the standard and belief that she should sacrifice at all times and in all ways her own well- being for the well-being of her children.

> *Actually I found a very good thing to cope with the abuse. I smoked weed to keep me calm rather than drink alcohol.... So of course my son and daughter later started smoking weed, and I couldn't very well say well you couldn't do that because I was doing it too.... I used to hate my mother, and now I find that I did the exact same thing as her, not turned to alcohol but to drugs.... It just calmed me down and I could cope with anything.... So there were times when I was not a good mother.*

Emma is the only woman who unequivocally and only referred to herself as a "bad mother." Emma described herself not only as a "bad mother" but as a "terrible mother." As with Lacey, Emma viewed herself as a "bad mother" for failing to be singularly responsible for catering to the needs of her children. Emma described how she would drink alcohol to "forget" the pain she was experiencing from the abuse and to "calm" her "nerves down" and how she was "not the PTA mom" who devoted all of her time to her children. Consequently, Emma had a low view of herself as a mother because she strongly believed in, and held herself to, the standard that she should prioritize the needs of her children over her own needs.

> *I don't know, sometimes I feel like a terrible mom. Like I'm not the* PTA *mom. I was a bad mom when I drank to just forget, just to calm my nerves down, and to numb myself.... I just feel bad my kids would just look. I felt they were looking down on me. Then they'd be like, "Mom ... you should just quit drinking, we don't like it when you drink." Like that. That's when I feel like a terrible mom.*

A small number of abused women's experiences were influenced by the cultural myths contained in the dominant discourse of intensive mothering as they attempted to live up to the ideal standards of intensively mothering their children. When these women fell short, due to their personal circumstances, they viewed and defined themselves in a negative light—as "bad mothers." As such, these abused women engaged in what O'Reilly refers to as "patriarchal mothering." None of them questioned or resisted definitions of themselves as "bad mothers" as perpetuated by the dominant discourse of intensive mothering. Instead, they believed that they were indeed "bad mothers" and defined themselves as such. In this sense, some but not all mothers challenge the demands of intensive mothering and the mandate of powerless responsibility (O'Reilly, *Rocking the Cradle*). Clearly these abused women did not challenge but rather accepted the standards imposed on them by the dominant discourse of intensive mothering. Attempting but failing to live by the standards of intensive mothering caused considerable guilt, disappointment, and distress in the lives of these abused women, leading even one woman named Aileen to contemplate taking her life, which demonstrates the power of the discourse of intensive mothering. It is not surprising, therefore, that some abused women accepted this discourse. However, it is important to note that although these abused women accepted the discourse of intensive mothering, this did not silence them from voicing the negatives effects that living up to these standards had on their mothering experiences. As such, they may not explicitly resist the discourse of intensive mothering, but they do recognize that it does exist and that it does have an influence on their mothering experiences.

RESISTING THE DOMINANT DISCOURSE OF INTENSIVE MOTHERING THAT CONSTRUCTS ABUSED MOTHERS AS "BAD MOTHERS"—EMPOWERED MOTHERING

In constructing their mothering identities, a large number of abused women resisted the discourse of intensive mothering. Of the twenty-nine abused women, twenty women resisted by 1) negotiating the "bad mother" and "good mother" discourses; 2) drawing on and then redefining the "good mother" discourse to have more inclusive boundaries; and 3) rejecting the "bad mother" and "good mother" discourses and then replacing them with experientially based alternative mothering discourses. As such, these abused women engaged in what O'Reilly refers to as "empowered mothering" by resisting the dominant discourse of intensive mothering that constructs and portrays abused mothers as "bad mothers." Overall, these abused women had positive views of themselves as mothers and, therefore, resisted negative portrayals of being "bad mothers" because they mothered in the context of abuse.

The extent to which these abused women resisted the dominant discourse of intensive mothering varied. While some abused women resisted by negotiating the "bad mother" and "good mother" discourses, other abused women resisted by drawing on and then redefining the "good mother" discourse or by rejecting the "bad mother" and "good mother" discourses and creating new experientially based alternative mothering discourses. These abused women who viewed and defined themselves by negotiating the "bad mother" and "good mother" discourses, by redefining the "good mother" discourse, and by rejecting both the "bad mother" and the "good mother" discourses did not accept but rather challenged the standards imposed on them by the dominant discourse of intensive mothering. In this sense, these mothers challenged the demands of intensive mothering and the mandate of powerless responsibility (O'Reilly, *Rocking the Cradle* 46).

NEGOTIATING THE "BAD MOTHER" AND THE "GOOD MOTHER" DISCOURSES—"I AM A BAD MOTHER AND A GOOD MOTHER"

Two of the twenty-nine women engaged in "empowered mothering" by negotiating the "bad mother" and "good mother" discourses when describing how they personally viewed themselves as mothers. These abused women resisted the "bad mother" discourse by claiming that although at times they may have been "bad mothers," for the most part they were "good mothers." Both of these abused women claimed that, at times, they were "bad mothers" because they mothered in an abusive context and this prevented them from always mothering successfully. However, these abused women claimed that overall they were "good mothers" because despite mothering in an abusive environment, they were very capable and competent mothers. These abused women clearly and uniformly evoked images of themselves and detailed practices that illustrated their attempts to take care of their children and their positive abilities and accomplishments as mothers, despite their circumstances. In this sense, these abused women avoided the cultural claim that they were solely "bad mothers." As such, in both cases, these abused mothers were not always pressured by the standards of intensive mothering, nor did they make efforts to constantly live by and maintain them. When these abused women failed to achieve the standards of intensive mothering, they did not personally judge themselves but rather attributed their deficiencies to the abusive context in which they mothered. Nonetheless, these abused women's views and descriptions of themselves as "bad mothers" and "good mothers" were still based on whether or not they conformed to the intensive mothering standards. As such, these abused women resisted the dominant discourses of intensive mothering by manoeuvring around, but not explicitly subverting these discourses.

The two abused women who claimed that they were both "bad mothers" and "good mothers" indicated that they viewed themselves as "bad mothers" when they were with their abusive partners because they could not be the mother they wanted to be, but once they left their abusive partners, they viewed themselves as "good mothers" because they were able to care for their children on their own. Both of these abused women claimed that they were "bad mothers" when they failed to conform to the standards of intensive mothering and, likewise, that they were "good mothers" when they successfully conformed to the standards of intensive mothering. For example, Leena claimed that when she was with her abusive partner, she was, at times, a "bad mother" because she was not always able to live up to the intensive mothering standard that stipulates mothers should provide care to their children on a constant basis, twenty four hours a day, seven days a week. Being abused caused Leena to feel like she was living under a "fog" and, consequently, she was not able to adequately care for her children at all times. However, once Leena left her abusive partner, she asserted that she was a "good mother" because she was able to conform to this intensive mothering standard and devote more time to her son. Leena also declared that she was a "good mother" when she began to work because she was able to financially provide for her son, and this was in line with the intensive mothering standard that stipulates mothers must lavish excessive amounts of time, energy, and money in the rearing of their children.

> *Sometimes I think I'm a bad mother because when I was with him, and I was abused, I was not super. Like it was very, very hard sometimes because if you have children you can't always take care of them, and you can't do things with them, you know, cuz it's under a cloud and you can't even see the kid cuz it's like a fog right..., But then I know I'm a good mom, and other people see it, and they tell me like, "You know, you're a good mom." Like I was a good mother with my son because I worked. I never had that, I'd never seen my mom work, I just used to see her high and drunk.... I'm a good mom because he [son] tells me, "Mommy I love you, thank you." You know, thank you for this, thank you for that, and then he'll come kiss me and say, "I love you so much," and then he'll kiss me like all over and I'm like, oh I'm a good mom.... He [son] gets everything he wants cuz I give him that cuz I never had that. Then my other kids got taken away when they were*

young, and I wasn't able to give that to them, so I give him that. Like I feel bad that this is what I should have done for them that I didn't because I was too wound up with this and that, and I was abused.... It [abuse] shaped me because being abused until now, I just think of it as a life learning experience and as part of life, and you either go the bad way or the good way. You either go left or right kind of thing, or you either go up or down. So it could be like a bunch of positives and negatives.... But I think it [abuse] made me learn to be stronger, like you learn off it, either good or bad. That's just the way life is.... Like it's hard being a single mother, but then sometimes being single is good ... because my mothering has been up and down, and I just want to keep it up now.

Maggie also alternated back and forth between viewing and describing herself as a "bad mother" at some times and as a "good mother" at other times. She asserted that at times, she felt like a "bad mother" because she did not always live up to the intensive mothering standard that indicates that children can only be properly cared for by the biological mother. When Maggie first left her abusive partner, he took their children and refused to let her see them, which caused her to feel much guilt because she believed that it was her primary responsibility as the mother to care for her children. Nonetheless, once Maggie's children returned to live with her she felt like a "good mother" because she was able to conform to this intensive mothering standard and be solely responsible for caring for her children. As with Leena, Maggie also felt like a "good mother" when she was able to "spend time" with her children, "always be with" her children, and direct all of her "attention" to her children, following the intensive mothering standard that demands mothering should be performed on a 24/7 basis.

I think I'm a good mom. I mean, I know how to handle my kids. I mean like I know my kids are well disciplined, they're well behaved. I don't need to get mad at them. They're very helpful, and, I'm glad they're like that. They're really helpful, especially with the baby, and my daughter's only five, and she's already doing dishes, and she tries to do mom things. So I mean I think I did a good job in raising my kids. I don't know how to say it but, sometimes I don't think I was a good mother. Like when I was with their dad, I used to, like, get mad at them the way my husband would because that's what he wanted. But that was before. Now I realize that I wasn't gonna do that anymore. But, just times like that where it seemed like I wasn't prepared because of him.... Then when me and their dad had split up, he took them and I never spent time with them when they were with their dad. It's not that I didn't want to, it was hard because I wasn't allowed to go there when they were living with their dad. But now they're with me, and now I think I'm a good mom. I mean I take care of my kids. They're always clean, and I try to do the best I can. I know there are times where I can do better. As in like I should have taken them away from the abuse earlier and stuff like that. But now like I'm always with them all the time. Like from when they were born and even after me and their dad split up, and they were living with him until I got them back. I've always been with them.... It seems, like, I feel better when I'm on my own, by myself, taking care of the kids because my attention is always on them. I always put my attention on them and nobody else. Even when I'm visiting, I don't just leave them out, they're always with me. So I think I do better when I'm on my own cuz I can raise my kids on my own. I'm not scared of raising them on my own, it's just unfortunate that they have to grow up being with just one parent. But then I also felt like I was not a good mom when I was with him.

DRAWING ON AND REDEFINING THE "GOOD MOTHER" DISCOURSE: RECONSTITUTING THE BOUNDARIES AND STANDARDS OF THE INTENSIVE MOTHERING DISCOURSE—"I AM A GOOD MOTHER"

Nineteen of the twenty-nine abused women engaged in "empowered mothering" by drawing on the "good mother" discourse and then redefining what a "good mother" is. These abused women did not merely oppose the discourse of intensive mothering; rather, they went beyond this by redefining this discourse. In this sense, these abused women positioned themselves within the existing discourse of good mothering to challenge the label of the "good mother." They then provided alternative explanations to the label of the "good mother" to argue that they were indeed "good mothers." As such, rather than articulating the "good mother" discourse in the same sense as that perpetuated by the standards of intensive mothering, these abused women reframed the "good mother" discourse based on their own standards of mothering that consisted of more inclusive boundaries. These abused women specifically redefined the "good mother" discourse according to the following seven characteristics. A good mother is someone who 1) spends time with her children whenever her circumstances permit; 2) protects her children; 3) rears her children in love; 4) provides for her children's basic needs; 5) rears her children in ways that make both her children and herself happy; 6) teaches her children; and 7) takes care of both her children's needs and her own needs. The majority of the abused women cited several of these characteristics when defining themselves as "good mothers." Of the twenty-nine women, one woman listed four of these characteristics, eight women listed three of these characteristics, eight women listed two of these characteristics, and two women listed only one of these characteristics.

For these abused women, the standards of "good mothering" were dependent on the context in which mothering takes place. According to these abused women, mothering in the context of domestic violence called for different standards and, therefore, these abused women felt that they were "good mothers" because they did all they could within the confines of an abusive social context. As such, these abused women opposed the societal stigma that they were "bad mothers" because they viewed themselves as mothers in positive terms. In fact, many of these abused women cited mothering as the only thing that they felt they did right and did well in their lives. Many of these abused women also mentioned that mothering brought them reprieve from the abuse and that their children brought them much happiness, fulfillment, and hope. These abused women often stated that being a mother and having their children in their lives was the only thing that got them through the abuse and encouraged them to carry on despite the pain and suffering they experienced as victims of abuse. One abused woman named Arika stated:

> *If it wasn't for my children I don't think I'd be alive cuz sometimes I just wished that I wasn't here. But I wouldn't ever do it [end her life], because I know how it is to lose a mom, and I wouldn't want them [her children] to grow up without a mother.*

In this sense, many women lived for their children. Being a mother was a positive experience in their lives, despite living in the context of abuse and the many challenges it posed for them as mothers. Nonetheless, these abused women made many efforts to "do the best" they could as mothers. As such, these abused women resisted the dominant discourses of intensive mothering by explicitly redefining the "good mother" according to their own definitions. Interestingly, during the interviews many of the abused women reiterated numerous times that they were "good mothers." Below I discuss the various ways in which the abused women redefined the "good mother."

i) A "Good Mother" Spends Time with Her Children Whenever Circumstances Permit

The most pervasive theme in the abused women's descriptions of their good mothering focused on spending time with their children whenever they could within their personal and varied circumstances. Ten of the abused women claimed that they were "good mothers" because they made efforts to "spend time" with their children, despite living in an abusive environment. Many abused women described how when they were with their abusive partners, these partners did not support them in performing the work involved in mothering. Other abused women described how when they were with their abusive partner, these partners intentionally and directly targeted and controlled their mothering. As such, these abused women reported that, at times, they felt a loss of control over their mothering. This loss of control was often due to the fact that their abusive partners monitored and restrained so many aspects of their lives, which resulted in significant consequences for their physical, emotional, and mental health. As such, this made it more difficult for these abused women to carry out their mothering the way they personally wanted to. Nonetheless, these abused women went to great lengths to find and create opportunities to spend time with their children, such as doing things with their children when their partners were not home or taking their children to activities outside of the home. Interestingly, these abused women emphasized that it was not necessary for them to be with their children at all times, nor was it necessary for them to do specific types of activities with their children, such as playing, reading, or doing recreational activities in order to be "good mothers." Rather, these abused women asserted that as long as they spent time with their children whenever they could, doing whatever interested them and their children, they were "good mothers."

Many abused women stated that they felt like a "good mother" when their abusive partners were not at home, and they were able to spend time alone with their children. For example, Arika described how she was a "good mother," particularly when she was able to "do whatever" she and her children wanted to do without her partner being there to control them.

> *I think I'm a good mother. But the only time I really felt like a good mom is when I was allowed to spend an hour alone with my children without him there because we could play and fool around and do whatever we wanted. When they got older we could colour, we could read, and I could read the bible to them when their father wasn't there. So it was very seldom that I felt like I could be the mother that I wanted to be.*

Likewise, Carly described how she felt like a "good mother" when she was able to freely spend time with her children and not worry about her partner being there and becoming angry and abusive. Carly stated that spending time with her children—"having fun," "bonding," and "loving one another"—was not always easy because she was dealing with the emotional difficulties of being abused. Nevertheless, Carly made the time to be there for her children and to do "something together," even if it was just "sitting" and "talking" with one another.

> *I'm a good mother. A lot of the time I feel like that. Like being with my boys and them getting along, and us doing something together whether it be just sitting here talking, you know. We could be doing the funniest thing, like, I miss the snow, you know, out there building a snowman. That time with them, and you know nobody's fighting, nobody's under stress, nobody's looking over their shoulder, nobody's worried about some angry person, and nobody's worried about being abused in any way, shape, or form. You're being yourself, you're having fun, you're bonding, and you're loving one another.... But it hasn't been easy.*

Several abused women declared that they felt like a "good mother" particularly once they left their abusive partners and were able to carry out their mothering how they wanted to and not how their partner wanted them to. These abused women indicated that they had much more time to devote to their children, as they were no longer forced to dedicate all their time to meeting the needs of their abusive partners. For example, Josephine considered herself to be a "good mom" because she always spent time just "having fun" with her son and paying attention to his needs. She indicated that since she left her abusive partner, she has realized that she has "much more psychic space to spend" with her son and much more time to just "be there" for him. Josephine felt like a "good mom" on a "daily basis" because although she worked full time and her son went to daycare, she was able to spend time and connect with him in the car on the way to and from daycare. As such, Josephine believed that it was not necessarily the quantity of time but rather the quality of time that she spent with her son that was important. Interestingly, Josephine called into question and criticized the intensive mothering discourse that stipulates specific standards of mothering that all mothers must abide by.

Josephine asserted that there are numerous ways to mother, and none are "good" or "bad."

> *I think I'm a good mom. I think that having fun is a very important part of mothering, and I'm noticing that not every other mother feels that way. My friend Lisa she says that I'm really attentive to my son, like I really pay attention to what he needs and what is going on with him. She says that I'm a good mom, and I'm like I don't know I'm just treating him like I would like to be treated, you know. I don't have anything brilliant to offer, just this is how I would like someone to treat me if I was completely helpless and dependent on them.... So I feel like a good mom on a pretty daily basis. It's pretty fun when we're in the car together and he's like making a noise and I'm like, "What's up?" and he'll go, "Blah blah blah blah," cause he can't talk properly yet, and I'll be like, "Okay here's your milk [laughs]. It's just like I guess anytime that we make that connection, cause he can't talk yet, so communication is a little more tough. You have to be really there, and I am.... But when I was with him [abusive partner], there were demands that everything is kept nice and easy for him. This made it much harder to look after my son and be with him because I had to make sure that my son was conforming to this pattern also, right? ... I really notice how much more psychic space I now have to spend with my son and to be there. Like a lot of real estate was being taken up by taking care of things to do with him [abusive partner], and now that I don't have to do that I'm very much more free.... There are a lot of things lately about labeling mothers which really bother me. I don't do that... It's okay to screw up! I found out fairly early on that they [children] don't remember if you do, so let's hurry up and make all the mistakes now while they don't remember [laughs]. I mean, who's to say what's good or bad. It's hard to sort of put a value judgment on it. It's just I can't see any other way to do it [her mothering]. I mean, I know there are other ways to do it. I see other people do it, then*

> *say, "no I wouldn't do that," but as for which is good and which is bad, who could know? What's right for one child is not right for another.*

Makayla also viewed herself as a "good mom" because she was always "doing stuff" with her children or at least "trying to," even if it meant putting aside the housework. Makayla stated that when she was with her abusive partner she did not really "consider" herself a "mother," since most of her time and energy was spent on "trying to do what" her husband "wanted" more than her "kids." However, ever since she left her abusive partner, she considers herself to be more of a "mother" because she now has the time and energy to focus on her children. Makayla believed that just "having them around" and "being with them" was what really mattered.

> *I think I'm a pretty good mom. Like I said, I like doing stuff with them ... and I am always trying to. But when I was with him [abusive partner], I was always worrying about trying to please them [the children] and trying to please my husband, too. I was just confused! Then I noticed that I was always trying to do what my husband wanted more than my kids. So I really didn't consider myself a mother when I was with my husband cuz I was always worried about him. But since I left and I've been a mother by myself, I find I'm more attentive, my kids are my focus, and I like having them around and being with them. Sometimes it's like, "Ah, go on!" But, overall, I always like having them around, like, they're mine, you know what I mean?*

ii) A "Good Mother" Protects Her Children

Another central theme in the abused women's discussion of their good mothering related to the protection of their children. Seven of the abused women maintained that they were "good mothers" because they prioritized the safety and well-being of their children. These abused women's primary concern related to the protection of their children against the abuse that was occurring in their homes and that was being perpetrated by their abusive partner.

The abused women discussed the various efforts that they engaged in to protect their children. First, they ensured that their abusive partner was not abusive towards their children, and, second, they ensured that their children did not witness their abusive partner's abuse towards them. Some of the abused women remained in the abusive relationship and continued to adopt strategies to ensure that their children did not witness the abuse because, at the time, it was not safe for them and their children to leave. However, most of the abused women eventually decided to leave their abusive partner when it became too difficult to conceal the abuse from their children and when the risk of their children potentially witnessing or even experiencing abuse became too high. These abused women usually left only when it became safe enough for them to leave with their children, as leaving their homes without their children was not an option for any of the abused women, even if it meant continuing to endure the abuse. Clearly, the safety of their children, and not their own personal safety, was their primary concern. As such, these abused women criticized the stereotype that abused mothers are automatically "bad mothers" because they do not immediately leave their abusive partners. These abused women argued that to the contrary, they are "good mothers" because leaving their abusive partners was not always the safest option at the time and, therefore, would not have been in the best interests of their children's safety and protection.

Some of the abused women affirmed that they were "good mothers" because while in the abusive relationship, they made many attempts to prevent their children not only from witnessing the abuse, but also from even being aware that the abuse was occurring. For example, Arika viewed herself as a "good mom" because she "spent time" with her children as well as protected them when she was in the abusive relationship. Arika described how she would take the abuse "silently" so as to not wake her children at night and risk having them witness the abuse. When the marks of abuse were physically visible and her children would inquire, Arika would make up excuses for her injuries to protect her children from worry and fear.

I'm a good mother because when I was with him [abusive

> *partner] I made sure my kids were safe at all times. I was just very protective over them. I never wanted them to go through what I went through. So I was very protective and tried so hard for what happened to me not to happen to them. Everything, every decision that I made was based on the abuse I went through, and I didn't want my kids to go through that.... When my first child, my daughter, was younger and was sleeping he would do things to me, and I wouldn't make a noise. I would take it silently. Then when my kids started to get older, um, I told them lies to hide the abuse. They would ask, "Mom, what happened you have a bruise? How come you got a black eye? How come your nose is bleeding? How come your mouth is bleeding? How come you have a fat lip?" I couldn't tell them the truth, and they used to feel really bad. I know they used to feel really bad for me, but at that time, I thought, well if they don't know, like if they think I fell off the stairs or I banged into the cupboard or something, then they won't be so worried or scared.*

Most of the abused women asserted that they were "good mothers" because they ultimately decided to leave their abusive partner to protect their children. For many of these abused women, this final decision to end their relationship with their abusive partner coincided with an increased risk to their children's safety. For example, Josephine described herself as a "good mother" not only because, like Arika, she spent time with her son, as discussed earlier but also because she finally decided to leave her abusive partner when her son became caught in the middle of the altercations. Even though Josephine loved her abusive partner, she cared more about the safety of her child and resolved that no matter what she would always do whatever it took to keep her child safe. As such, Josephine left her abusive partner without any second thoughts, and this made her realize that she was a "good mother."

> *Once I was sitting in the bathroom holding on to my kid because earlier he [abusive partner] was ranting and raving, and took our son from me and I'm like, "You give me him."*

That makes me cry [starts crying]. I'm like, "You give me my baby now," you know, "Give him to me," and he got all mad... But I wasn't moving you know? And then I felt so bad for putting our son in that situation. I thought this can't go on, I'm not doing the right thing by this child. I'm a mother who won't take any crap. I'm a mother who'll do whatever it takes to keep my child safe, you know, no matter what it costs me personally.

Similarly, April described herself as a "good mother" because she protected her children from potential sexual abuse at the hands of her abusive partner. When April discovered that her abusive partner hid the fact that he sexually abused his six-year-old sister when he was sixteen years old, she was consumed with the fear that he could also sexually abuse her eldest daughter, who was not his biological child, and then hide that from her as well. As such, April chose to immediately leave her abusive partner even though it hurt her to see her children experience so much pain as a result of being separated from their father and only being able to have short visits with him. However, the pain of seeing her children miss their father was outweighed by the costs of the immense guilt she would have to live with ever she ever later found out that her abusive partner had also sexually abused her daughter.

I know I'm a good mother, and I am a good mother because I chose to leave and protect the kids. But his family makes it, like, it's my fault for leaving, and I should have stayed and worked it out, and he was there when I was a drug addict, and blah, blah, blah. They're comparing my experiences with drugs to him being a pig. And I told them, "I beat my addiction, I faced my addiction, and I've been clean and sober. He didn't get any help, he didn't get any counselling, and you guys didn't help him you just swept it under the rug like it was no big deal. You know, you should have put him in counselling." They put her in counselling [his sister that he sexually abused], but they forgot about him. But I feel like I'm breaking their [children's] hearts. My one daughter said, "What did we do for you to leave,

> *daddy?" I said, "It had nothing to do with you, it's mommy and daddy." She then said, "Well, you said he wouldn't play with us," and I said, "Yeah, but that had nothing to do with why I left him," and she's too young for me to state what he did to his sister, and so it's difficult to try and explain to them. Then the baby just doesn't understand at all, and so she's "Daddy, daddy, daddy, daddy." When the visits are over, she's screaming and crying, and, it's hard, it kills me every time. But I just keep telling myself I'd blame myself more if they came to me and told me, "Daddy's touching me," and I could have prevented that. I was sexually assaulted as a teenager, and I know how it felt at sixteen to go through that. So to watch them go through it, I won't, I won't, I won't put them through that! I want them to have a good life.*

Another abused woman named Julie worried about how her daughter would "get through" the confusion and sadness of no longer living with and seeing her father. Nonetheless, she felt like a "good mother" because she knew that she was ultimately protecting her daughter. Julie even contacted child welfare to report that her partner was abusive, even though she knew that her daughter might potentially never be able to see her father again. However, Julie felt that the long-term safety of her daughter was more important than the short-term difficulties she may experience as a result of being separated from her father.

> *When I was being abused, I had a lot of negative thoughts. Like, I was always like, "am I doing this right?" because I was always under the impression I could never do anything right cause I was always asking him like what should I do because whatever I did was always wrong. When I first left, I was really low on myself and stressed and worried about my daughter and how she was going to get through it. But I feel like a good mom for sure because I left him to protect her [daughter]. Like the first time I left, I called child services for help and they said, "No we can't step in because you've already taken her out of the danger."*

iii) A "Good Mother" Rears Her Children in Love

Another important theme in the abused women's descriptions of their good mothering focused on rearing their children in love, which consisted of their ability to meet their children's emotional needs, to be physically affectionate with their children, and to parent with care and respect. Six of the abused women asserted that they were "good mothers" because they were "always there for" their children; they "cuddled, hugged, and kissed" their children, and they raised their children in a "kind and loving" manner, despite mothering in an abusive context. These abuse women discussed how their abusive partner never showed them love and, therefore, they often felt hurt, alone, and even ashamed. As a result, these abused women were determined and committed to show their children love and found much comfort and fulfillment in the loving relationship that they shared with their children.

The abused women also expressed that although they loved their children deeply, they did not feel loving towards them all the time. These abused women explained that children can be very difficult to care for at times, and they acknowledged that, like any other mother, they did not always react with patience and tenderness. As such, these abused women pointed to the false myth of the "perfect mother" and affirmed that to be a "good mother," they did not need to be a "perfect mother."

Some abused women stated that they were "good mothers" because they tried to be emotionally available to their children when their children needed them. For example, one of the abused women named Tammy viewed herself as a "good mom," not because she was a "perfect mom" but because she was doing her "very best" as a mom and tried to "be there" for her son whenever he needed her. In fact, Tammy stated "I don't think there is a perfect mom" and, therefore, points to the ideal of the "perfect mother" as being non-existent. Tammy described how she parented her son by not "following any directions" or prescriptions of how to mother but rather by "doing" her "own thing." As such, Tammy criticized the universal standards of intensive mothering that are imposed on women and, instead, advocated a personal and individual style of mothering.

> *I always think I'm a good mom because I think I'm doing my best. I'm not going to say I'm a perfect mom because I don't think there is a perfect mom, but I am going to say that I'm doing my very best to keep that child happy. So I'm just doing the best I can, and I'm learning as I go. I think I'm a good mom too because I'm wanting, warm, comforting, loving and understanding. I'm the one that's there for him [son] anytime he needs me. I love him, he's the love of my life.... Everyone parents their kid differently. I'm not going to to take a side as to how you should. Just do it on your own, and you may listen to little bits here and there, but the thing is, I never really decided to follow any directions. I just kind of did my own thing. You just kind of take your own path and stick with it.*

Another abused woman named Dani also described herself not just as a "good mother" but as a "good loving mother" because she was there for her children. If ever her children needed her for anything, Dani stated that she was "there for them." She also expressed the fear that others may misjudge and view her as a "bad" mother because she is a victim of abuse, when, in reality, she is a "good" mother regardless of the abuse she experienced.

> *I find that I'm a good loving mother. I take care of my kids, and I'm there for my kids. I try to make them understand that if they ever need me, like for knowledge, advice, anything, I am there for them. I want them to be able to come up to me and ask me, "Hey mom, this is how I feel today' or "I didn't have a good day, Mom," stuff like that. That's what I want for my kids. I want my kids to realize that they have me, that I'm here, you know? I just don't want people to think bad and wrong about me. I'm too good.*

Other abused women affirmed that they were "good mothers" because they showed their children affection. For these abused women, showing physical affection was important to them and was a large part of what made them feel good as mothers. Makayla, for example, described herself as a "good mom" not only because she spent time with her children as previously discussed but also because she often "cuddled" with her children and told them that she loved them, something that her abusive partner never did, at least not sincerely. Makayla also pointed to the fallacy of the "good mother" who appears to be a "good mother" on the exterior because she is organized and her house is cleaned, but who, in reality, is not a "good mother" on the interior, in her heart, because she does not love and show affection to her children. According to Makayla, a "good mother" is someone who sincerely loves her children.

> *I think I'm a good mom because I'm always cuddling, loving, and holding them. I love saying the word "I love you," and I'm always telling them that. I never hear that from him [abusive partner], except after he hurt me then he would say "Oh I love you, I'm sorry it ever happened." But with my kids, I'm actually saying it without having to be mean to them, you know what I mean? They know that it's real and true. So a good mother is someone who just loves her children. It's the way you look at them, and it's the way you actually show some kind of emotion towards them, and it doesn't matter if the house is clean or not. I've seen the difference, like where there's a spotless woman, but she doesn't really like her kids to be with her, and where there's a really messy woman who actually loves her kids.*

Similarly, Aliya stated that although there is always room for improvement, she viewed herself, overall, as a "good mom" because she loves her son and always hugs and comforts him. Aliya criticized agencies such as child welfare who automatically assumed and insinuated that removing her son from her home was in her and her son's best interest, even though she had already left her abusive partner, because she loves her son, and he would be "sick" without her. As such, Aliya called attention to the discourse of intensive mothering that falsely casts abused mothers as "bad mothers" because they have been the victims of abuse and that fails to pay attention to the fathers who perpetrated the abuse in the first place.

> *I always think there's room for improvement, always, always, but for the most part, I think I'm a good mom. It's something I have to take day by day, but I love my son, and I've been taking care of him from day one. I still let him sleep with me [laughs]. There are lots of times I feel like I'm a good mother. Like today I woke up next to my son and felt like a good mom because he was so happy and he was playing and he came up really close to my face. When I hug him I feel like I'm a good mom. When he comes to me when he's upset, and he knows he can come to me, I feel like a good mom. I feel like a good mom because I know how much he needs me and that if he didn't have me, he would be devastated. That's what bugs me about child welfare. If they think they would be doing me a favour by taking him away when I'm all he's had, and it might have only been two and a half years that he's been alive, but when I'm the only one that's been there for him consistently, then if they take him away from me they're going to make him sick.*

Finally, some abused women maintained that they were "good mothers" because their mothering practices and relationships with their children were based on love and kindness and not on harshness and brutality, as in what they experienced in their relationships with their abusive partners. According to these women, to love and raise their children with respect meant accepting their children for who they are and encouraging their children to be the best they can. This was part of learning and getting to know their children in a non-domineering and non-subjugating manner, which constituted "good mothering" for these women. For example, April affirmed that she was a "good mother" and a "great mother" because she knew that she protected her children, as previously discussed, and that she would love her children "no matter what." As such, she tried to always mother in a "peaceful" and "kind" manner. April acknowledged that although she loved her children, she "struggled" as a mother and was not always the perfect picture of serenity and composure. At times, she did get "angry" and she did "yell" at her children. Nonetheless, April stated that this did not make her any less of a "good mother" because her love for her children was "unconditional."

> *I'm a good mother. I love my babies no matter what they do. I struggle as a mother cuz I've never really been in this type of position where I've been a single mom, and a single mom with so much pain behind it. But I'm a good mother, a great mother. I love my kids, I'm peaceful, and I'm kind. I get angry once in a while, and I've yelled at them a few times, and I've lost it with them a couple of times, but, generally, I'm a good mom. Sweet and kind, and caring and unconditional. Everything that I want to be as a mom, so far anyway.*

iv) A "Good Mother" Provides for Her Children's Basic Needs

Another salient theme in the abused women's dialogues about their good mothering focused on fulfilling their children's basic needs for shelter, food, cleanliness, and clothing. Six of the abused women asserted that they were "good mothers' because they ensured that their children's basic needs were always met. Several of these abused women mentioned that their abusive partners' control over the financial resources meant that they sometimes struggled to provide the basic needs—particularly food—for their children on a regular basis. Nonetheless, these abused women used various methods to obtain these basic needs for their children, including accessing food banks and other referral services for food and clothing. A number of these abused women also revealed that they were so physically and emotionally drained from the abuse that they found it difficult to always carry out their daily household duties. However, they always made sure that their children were clean and clothed, which gave them a sense of gratification and satisfaction knowing that their children were well cared for, even while they were going through the abuse. These abused women indicated that to be a "good mother" did not require expending copious amounts of time and money to provide children with all their wants and desires but rather merely required providing for their children's basic needs.

A lot of the abused women declared that they were "good

mothers" because they went to great lengths to find the resources to feed and clothe their children when they were unable to do so within their own means. For example, Badriya, who had four daughters, was on social assistance and her family of five had to subsist on a monthly income of only one thousand dollars. As such, Badriya employed many strategies to make ends meet, which made her feel like a "good mother." Badriya volunteered at drop-in centres where she was permitted to take five items of clothing home with her after each shift; she went to food banks all over the city to get food for her children; and she even employed cost saving strategies to stretch their budget by, for example, bringing food from home instead of purchasing food when they were out doing errands. Badriya felt an immense sense of pride when she found name brand clothing for her daughters in the donation box at the shelter, as she knew how happy they would be. However, Badriya stated that finding ways to provide her children with basic needs such as food and clothing is a taxing work, and it wears her out. She questioned the impact that it will have on her long term. Badriya also criticized the societal view that a "good mother" lavishes excessive amounts of time, energy, and money on their children and that because she is unable to meet this standard, she is somehow a "bad mother." Badriya asserts that this is not true that she is indeed a "good mother" because she provides for her children. She does not need others to judge her or to tell her what kind of a mother she is.

> *I see myself like I'm very good mom. I'm not smart, I'm not beautiful, I'm not strong, but with mom, I'm very good mom. Like, even I act little bit old style, but I'm a very, very good mom. I feel I'm good mom and my kids they are good to me because I volunteer, you know. I volunteer at the Drop-In Centre and I volunteer at the Mustard See, the two homeless shelters and we allowed to take five items per person. I always so happy when I find, like, Lululemon hoodies with the tag in it. I know! I was so happy my kids they were screaming all day they were so happy. Yeah, and um, like my kids now this one she has about ten piece Lululemon [laughs]. Yeah, I know.*

> *But I'm running, working all day for them [children], and then get bread from here, like you know to cover my bills because thousand dollar all I'm getting a month from working. So like running from here cuz otherwise like I can't buy them clothes or something. Like many people, they know, plus they are popular, like how they dress at school. Even I hear, "Everybody talking about your kids." So that make me so happy.... Then we went someday to the mall, so I take them a snack from here [house]. Then we went to Zellers, and I have donation credit for Zellers for twenty dollar. So we bought pizza pop, and we went to the bathroom and we heat it up, you know they have microwave there. We heat up in the bathroom and we sit and eat, and make my kids so happy, and yeah make me so happy. But in the same time, many times it comes to myself you know, if I stay like this I will get tired and sick and older because my life is always the same. Like I told you, like in two to three weeks, if my phone rings, it is just from counselling or something. Nobody phones me. My mom like every three months, she phone me, she's back home [Lebanon], right? I have no one to phone, no one to talk to.... Like of course, like the society, they expect to be good mom: you have education, you teach them, you give them. But, like, I don't go by society. I go by my own, I go by my kids, I go by myself, you know. I'm, as a mom, like, for my kids I know what to do. So I say, you know, I don't wait for my counselling or somebody to tell me, "do this." Even I'm good mom, you know. Like I give, give, give, give and love my kids, but wait for somebody to tell me that? I don't want that.*

Another abused woman named Eden not only described herself as a "good mom" but also as an "awesome mom." As with Badriya, Eden went to great lengths to provide food for her children, particularly when her husband was unemployed, and they did not have any money to buy food to feed their three children. When they would run out of milk for their baby in the middle of the night, Eden would go out searching for resources to obtain milk, even in the middle of winter. Eden felt like a "good mother" because even though she could not afford to cloth herself, she knew that, as she stated, she was "doing everything" to feed her children.

> *Personally I describe myself as an awesome mom.... I'm not perfect, I know that, but I think I'm a good mom.... We're in a bad situation now, but I value myself as a strong woman because I've been through so much.... The time that I felt like a good mother was like when my husband wasn't working, and there were times we had no food and no milk for our children. It would be minus twenty whatever, and I'd get up, I'd go out in the cold, and even though I had no money, I would try my hardest to find resources for food bank or referrals for milk. I remember this one time this resource centre had milk for kids, and it was freezing cold, and I remember walking in the snow to the bus, and I was really, really cold. I remember because I was asking my husband if he can buy me a winter jacket, but he always had an excuse, "We don't have enough money," blah, blah, blah, blah, blah, blah. I remember thinking, well at least I'm doing everything I can to feed my children, even though it's minus twenty whatever. So that experience made me feel like a good mother. Just doing whatever I can to feed my children.*

A number of abused women stated that they were "good mothers" because they always ensured that their children were cleaned and cared for. These abused women asserted that although they were in abusive relationships, it never interfered with their ability to care for their children physically. These abused women said that even though they may not have always had the energy and the ability to "play with" or "entertain" their children, they never neglected to take care of their physical needs. Taking care of their children's basic needs was often the only thing these abused women had control over and was something that they could visibly accomplish and feel satisfied about in their lives, wherein they otherwise experienced control, manipulation, and suffering as a victim of abuse. For example, Shyan described how she was "organized" when it came to "taking care" of her children. When her children were "clean," "fed," "watered," and "in bed," Shyan felt like a "really good mom," although she was abused because she experienced contentment and fulfillment at being able to care for her children.

> *People tell me, I'm a "good mom," and it's not phoniness, either. It's just how I am when we're home alone. Like I would take care of him [son], cause I'll feel better than if I'm taking care of him and bathing him.... I'm organized. I'll be organized for them [children]. I'll do things for them, like make sure they're fed and watered and cleaned, you know? I just feel really close bathing them and stuff. I just feel like a good mom when they're all clean and in bed and fed and watered, that's when I feel like the really good mom. So even though I was abused, I think I'm still a good mother anyways.*

Similarly, Aliya who earlier asserted that she was a "good mother" because she reared her son in love, also affirmed that she was a "good mother" because she always took "really good care" of her son by "feeding," "bathing," and "keeping his clothes clean." According to Aliya, she still had to work on being a better disciplinarian with her son, but the one thing that she felt proud about was her ability to completely provide for her son's physical needs, even while she was living in an abusive context.

> *I really struggle with—I said it over and over again—I really struggle with the whole discipline thing, but I'm working on it. But I know I take really good care of my son with feeding him, bathing him, keeping his clothes clean, and taking care of him. I find I'm very specific about those things, too.*

v) A "Good Mother" Rears Her Children in Ways That Make Both Her Children and Herself Happy

An additional theme that was prevalent in the abused women's descriptions of their good mothering related to their mothering practices, and how they reared their children in ways that made both their children and themselves happy. Six of the abused women declared that they were "good mothers" because both they and their children were happy, despite having lived in an abusive context. A number of the abused women described how living in an abusive context often made it difficult for them to feel joy and contentment because they were being controlled and oppressed by their abusive partner as well as dealing with the pain and suffering of being abused. However, these abused women made many attempts to find ways to experience moments of relief and joy. When these abused women saw that both they and their children were happy, they felt like "good mothers."

For example, Badriya viewed herself as a "good mother" because she not only provided for her children's basic needs, as discussed previously, but also reared her children in ways that made both her children and herself happy. When Badriya left her abusive partner, she found it difficult to raise her four daughters all on her own as she rarely had the opportunity to be alone with just one child. However, Badriya made efforts, whenever she could, to spend one-on-one time with her children. During these times, Badriya felt that she was able to connect with her individual children and express her love and appreciation for them. Badriya described how even spending a few minutes alone with her eldest daughter as they sat in the car in traffic on their way to pick up take- out food brought her such joy. She was able to see that her daughter was happy, as she was, that they were spending time together, just the two of them. As such, Badriya felt like a "good mother" because both she and her daughter were "happy."

> *Being happy, like uh, you know I told you like since day one, like I know I'm good mom. I heard it from million people. But if you want to ask, like, I am very, very happy. Like I'm always happy with my kids, you know, to see them happy. The moment I'm happy with my kids, like it is always to see my kids healthy, just to make them happy. Like yesterday I was a bit stressed, but I have my six-year-old, and her friend, her name Taylor, so she came to my apartment with her mom, and her mom she said, "You know guys, I want to buy you Chicken on the Way,"*

just right here. The mom she give me fifty dollar and she said, "How about if you go buy Chicken on the Way." So I left my kids with her, and then I went with my twelve-year-old, and we went to buy Chicken on the Way. There is too much traffic, and Navine she said, "Oh my gosh, it's too much traffic." I said, "You know what Navine, I love that I have time with you," and I hug her in the car and kiss her. She said, "Oh, yeah, you're right mom." I'm with my four kids, so I never have time with one of my kids. But she was very happy when I was talking to her. I was very happy with her cuz I have time alone with her.

For Belinda, being a "good mom" meant engaging in activities that brought both her children and herself joy. When Belinda was with her abusive partner, and even after she initially left him, she felt worn down and tired because she was trying to overcome her experiences of abuse. As such, Belinda often did not have the energy to physically go out and engage in all sorts of activities with her children. However, she did spend time cooking, doing crafts, and playing sports with her children whenever she could. Also, Belinda did the activities that meant the most to her children, such as going to her son's school dance. This made her children happy and, in turn, made Belinda happy because they were spending time together doing activities that they enjoyed. As such, Belinda felt like a "good mom" because she was with her children.

I think I'm a good mom.... I feel like a good mom whenever I see my kids smiling, and my kids are happy, and that makes me feel like a good mom. But when I was with him and when I first left him, there was not much I could do because I could feel myself just dying inside. I couldn't be playful then, like say, "let's go swimming, let's do crafts, let's bake cookies, let's do something." I just didn't have it in me because I was so drained. Even my sister I remember her saying to me that her and my best friend said talking to me was like talking to a dead person. Because I just couldn't concentrate anymore, and I was just miserable. At one point, I actually thought to myself the only way out would be suicide. It's not something I would have ever considered, but I actually felt like the only way out would be is if I died. So I prayed all the time, cause I believe in God, and I prayed my whole relationship.... So I think it just physically affected me. I started to not have any energy anymore, and I was always, like, I would do something, and it's like okay I just got to sit down for a minute. I was completely exhausted. I would get up and get the kids a drink of juice or do the dishes and I got to sit down for a minute. It completely wiped me out, little things like that, which were not normal. So when I was with him, I tried doing things, like I bought a jogging stroller and I tried to take them out and go for a walk or we would go out in the backyard, things where I wouldn't have to exert too much energy. But since I've been gone now, we've made cookies, we've made pizza together, and I've taught them how to skate, which is something I always wanted to do. I'm still feeling the physical aspect of it, but I'm starting slowly to get a little better. For example, one night at my son's school they were having some dance or something, and I was tired and it was really cold, it was like minus thirty something, and he's like, "Mom let's go to the dance," and I'm like, "Are you sure you really want to go cause I'm really tired and it's cold out there," and he's like, "Mom!" He really wanted to go, and inside I really did not want to go to this dance because I was so tired, and it was minus whatever weather. But then he was disappointed, so then I was like, "Alright let's go, we'll go." And you know, that made me feel like a good mom cause we went, and we had a good time, and he even won a door prize, and my son loves popcorn, and it was like a big popcorn bowl with popcorn in it and pop. So it was this big deal, and he was really happy he got to go. So being with them makes me happy.

Unlike Badriya and Kylie, Zahra only has one child and he was only four months old at the time of the interview. As such, what made Zahra feel like a "good mom" was just being physically present for her son and caring for him to the "best" of her "ability." Zahra described how her son would smile and laugh a lot and that made her, in turn, smile and laugh. At these times, she knew that both she and her son were indeed happy, despite the abusive environment in which they were living, which made Zahra "feel good" and feel like a "good mother." Interestingly, Zahra criticized how mothers, particularly abused mothers, are often judged as either being "bad" or "good" mothers when they make mistakes. But regardless of the mistakes mothers may or may not make, they will always be judged. As such, Zahra claimed that the "only thing" mothers can do is "ignore" and not "care" about what others say. As long as mothers themselves know "deep inside" that they are "good" according to their own definition of "good," then that is all that matters. Clearly, Zahra advocates a personal definition of a "good mother," not the definition of a "good mother" espoused by the intensive mothering discourse.

> *Most of the time, I really felt like I was like a good mom because I do such a good job, and then you know my son is happy, he's healthy, and, you know, I think he's happy cuz of the mom like me and that makes me feel good. When he smiles that makes me happy, too. I take care of him to the best of my ability, and I make sure whatever is going on with me and whatever that's happening doesn't affect him, like at least not in a bad way. When I do that it makes me feel good.... He always makes me laugh. It doesn't matter what kind of night I had or what kind of yesterday I had, like when I wake up and he sees me, he starts laughing so hard. He's like, "Finally somebody's going to get me out of the crib." I like that, so then I take him out. Every day is like a blessing, like I said, not everyone's lucky enough to have kids. And, like, they're the best gift God can give you, you know, the best gift. So he's the best gift, and we're so happy.... But people are always quick to judge. We all make mistakes. But at the end of the day, if people will judge you as bad or as good it doesn't matter, they always have something to say. So the thing you can do is just ignore it, who cares! If deep inside you, you know you're good,*

> *you're doing a good job, and you know you're doing the best you can, then don't worry about others because it's human nature to say, "Oh, I'm not going to look at what I'm doing wrong, but what is she doing wrong?"*

vi) A "Good Mother" Teaches Her Children

Another theme in the abused women's discussions of their good mothering related to teaching their children. Six of the abused women maintained that they were "good mothers" because even though they were not perfect role models for their children as a result of being victims of abuse, they were committed to learning from their experiences of abuse and, therefore, teaching their children. This involved teaching their children to overcome and become stronger from the abuse that they witnessed as well as to understand that abuse is the unacceptable in relationships. Most of the abused women stated that experiencing abuse made them more aware of inequalities between men and women and more determined to teach their children about mutual respect in relationships and about the signs of abuse.

Some abused women were committed to teaching their children strategies to overcome the domestic violence that they witnessed between their parents and, therefore, to become stronger individuals. For example, Abigail viewed herself as a "good mother" because of the way that she parented her daughter. Abigail described how she learned many effective parenting strategies not only from her experiences of abuse but also from taking parenting classes and workshops. She further described how she made many efforts to teach her daughter to build up her self-esteem, to make good choices, and to stand up for herself, particularly when interacting with her father who was often dishonest. Abigail felt like a "good mother" when she saw that as a result of nurturing and guiding her daughter in a "gentle, kind, loving way," her daughter was learning the tools that she was trying so hard to teach her, such as the ability to stand up for herself when her father was controlling.

> *I thought I was a good mother before, but now I feel like I'm a very good mother because I've taken classes and parenting classes and workshops, and it's been quite*

eye opening, you know the importance of her [daughter] self-esteem and how I can help to nurture that, and maybe what I was doing previously was hanging and clinging too tight to her because she's an only child as opposed to giving her the tools that she needs to develop self-esteem. So I think going through abuse, and being a single parent now, I want to make good choices, and, you know, we all make mistakes and we can't always make those good choices, but, in general, it's important to me, especially as I'm a one unit family, to make sure that I make good choices, and that I'm able to pass good choices onto her and move forward and give her the tools that she needs for success. That's really important to me.... And so it's really got me thinking about the choices that we make, and even just general things like how do I react to this, what do I need to, you know, to talk to her about the abuse, how do I incorporate her standing on her own two feet and standing up for herself. She's doing really good with that now. It was really important to me to give her the tools to stand up to dad, because he's the fun parent and quite often he puts her into situations that she's not comfortable, and she'll come home with a broken arm or something from skiing, and it's not because he would purposely do that it's just through negligence. So it's been really important to me to tell her when daddy's lying and saying that it's not dangerous for her and when she feels that it is that she stand up when something is not a good situation for her. Like if they're skiing, and he wants her to do a black run and it's icy, and she knows it's icy, and she's tired that day, to stand up and just say that to him instead of just going along and being put in a situation that she comes home with a broken arm, cuz she couldn't handle it. So, it, it's been important to me to give her that tool. And she's doing good with it, she's developing it. But I see the confusion along the way sometimes, and I just really have to nurture and guide her in a gentle, kind, loving way to give her the tools to do that.... So I really feel like a good mom when I handle a situation well. Like after taking parenting classes and learning the techniques and I handle a situation well.

Other abused women were committed to teaching their children the message that violent behaviour is unacceptable in relationships, which was seen as having more implications for boys than for girls. Although all of these abused women had both sons and daughters, they were specifically concerned about their sons' potential violent behaviour than their daughters' potential victimization. As such, these abused women focused on teaching their sons about equality between men and women and about respecting and not engaging in abusive behaviour towards women, which made these abused women feel like "good mothers." For example, Josephine, who earlier stated that she was a "good mother" because she "spends time" with her children and "protects her children," also proclaimed that she was a "good mother" because she dedicated much time to teaching her son. She taught her son to "respect" and establish "healthy" relationships with other people, particularly as a "man," because she did not want him to ever become an abuser like his father. Consequently, this made Josephine feel like a "good mother" because she was using effective parenting strategies.

You know cause he's [son] going to be a man, so what kind of man is he going to be, right? When he spends time with his dad, I don't worry about his physical safety, but I worry that his dad will play the victim story and get our son to take care of him rather than the other way around. Right now, he's too young for that! So the thing that I really worry about is that he will think that the way to get what he wants is to use other people and manipulate other people rather than coming forward and straightforwardly asking..., But I think the way that I live in general—like I really get upset when I see prejudice, bigotry, unfairness, intolerance—will help. So I think the only thing I can do is just go ahead and do the things that I believe in and hope that that's a strong enough model.... So, I mean, I'm really conscious of inoculating him against that and trying to sort of verbalize, you know, this is what I want, what do you want? And just, like, it's okay to ask for what you want kind of thing, and you know all these things that kind of lead to clean interactions rather than muddied with guilt and manipulation and all that stuff. So I'm talking to him a lot more and that makes me feel good as a mom. But the only thing I can really do is sort of point out what it means to respect people and what healthy looks like, right? Which is, you know, really the main reason I left him because it was not a healthy place to grow up in, right? I mean, for me, I'm strong for myself, but I couldn't do it anymore and take care of my son effectively. I was exhausted and I never had a break, so something was going to slip, and I didn't want it to be him.

Similarly, Makayla, who previously stated that she was a "good mother" because she too "spends time" with her children and "loves" her children, declared that she was also a "good mother" because she was committed to teaching her children to be respectful. As with Josephine, Makayla worried that her son would turn out to be abusive just like his father because he witnessed domestic violence. As such, Makayla tried to teach her son to "show respect to other people," although he had never witnessed his father show respect to her, his mother. As a result, Makayla felt like a good mother because she was trying her best.

I try to teach them [children] respect. I try to teach them to show respect, like respecting other people cuz they've never exactly seen that. My oldest son to this day says, "People always took advantage of you." Sometimes he can be a pretty mean person because he's seen how I was treated, and so when someone takes too much from him, he'll be like, "No!" So I'm scared he might turn out to be abusive and not very good like his dad. I try to take care and teach him respect, so I'd say I'm a good mother.

As with both Josephine and Makayla, Kylie viewed herself as a "good mother" because she put much emphasis on "teaching" her two sons. Kylie worried because when her sons were younger, they witnessed numerous occasions when her abusive partner brutally assaulted her. Although Kylie stated that her sons "don't remember what happened," they are aware that their father was abusive towards her. As such, Kylie teaches her sons to "respect" and "protect" their little sister as well as to do "chores," particularly domestic chores, in the hopes that they will learn to view men and women as equals.

> *I think I'm a good mom. I know it's been hard, but I am. I want the boys to go through some therapy cuz they don't remember what happened, but they know that their dad did abuse me, and I want them to understand what it is and what they went through and stuff, so it doesn't happen again.... So I just teach them to have respect for their sister, just the little things that they do for her and just like they're really protective of her too, like when we're walking, they go run to her and like grab her hand and they walk her across the street. Just little things like that. I taught them how to do chores so they know how to do chores. They do the dishes every day, they sweep the floor, and they clean up. That's what they have to do. I teach them to do chores cuz I'm like, "Men do chores, too." I talk a lot with them cuz they don't really have any male role models, and their dad doesn't work but just lives off his current girlfriend. So I teach and tell them that's not right and when they grow up, I expect them to have jobs too, and I want them to go to school and they know that. So we talk a lot.*

vii) A "Good Mother" Takes Care of Both Her Children's needs and Her Own Needs

The last theme in the abused women's discussion of their good mothering focused on taking care of both their children's needs and their own personal needs. Five of the abused women asserted that they were "good mothers" because they prioritized meeting both their children's and their own needs. Several of the women indicated that when they were with their abusive partners, they were forced to juggle their partners' demands and needs, their children's necessities and needs, and their own wants and needs. Often their partners forced them to sacrifice their own needs in order to meet everyone else's needs, which led many of the abused women to feel much dissatisfaction and discontentment because they believed that they had a right to meet their own personal needs as well. As such, many abused women attempted to meet not only their children's needs but also their own needs when they were with their abusive partner and, particularly, once they left their abusive partner. Once they left, these abused women felt that they were better able to focus on meeting both their children's needs and their own needs, without sacrificing one for the other. What was important to these abused women was keeping a balance between meeting their children's needs and their own needs. When doing so, these abused women felt like "good mothers."

Some women relied on family, friends, and other resources in helping them care for their children. For them, sharing the responsibility not only freed them to take care of and heal themselves from the abuse but also allowed their children to have time away from them and learn to interact with and develop relationships with other adult figures. For example, Josephine viewed herself as a "good mother" not only because she "spent time" with, "protected," and taught her children as previously discussed, but also because she balanced both her children's needs and her own needs. Josephine described how when she was with her abusive partner, she had to completely give up her own interests and projects, things that she knew she needed "to be sane," because her abusive partner refused to help care for their son. As such, Josephine often felt drained and exhausted. Therefore, she accessed and used a serviced called "The Children's Cottage" a few times to receive help with her son. When Josephine had a chance to take care of herself, while ensuring that her son was also safe and taken care of, she felt as if it helped her "mothering" and she was, therefore, a "good mom." According to Josephine, taking care of herself did not make her an inadequate mother but rather helped her to be a better mother.

> *When I was with him, I think what really bothered me too was the fact that I didn't have any time for my own*

> *projects. I didn't have time for my painting, I didn't have time to meditate, I didn't have time to do any of the things that I know I need to do to be sane. And those things help me with mothering also, and I was a good mom. He [abusive partner] would refuse to like take him [son] for a while, you know, like let me get out of the house. He'd come home late and say, "Oh I'm too tired," or, you know, he wouldn't come back when he said he would come and things like that. So getting that time to myself I really missed that, so that made it really hard. So basically no help. I just wanted some help! ... I was just exhausted! ...So I used the Children's Cottage. You can leave your children there for seventy-two hours, but I never left him there for seventy-two hours, but I've left him there for a couple of nights. It's the most awesome thing on the planet. It's a not for profit, so they're just regular people. You don't take milk, you don't take formula, you don't take diapers or wipes, you just take him there and drop him off. It's a beautiful thing. They're really great and they're always like, "Is there anything else we can do to help you? Is there any other services we can give you?" There's quite a lot of paperwork to fill out to use the Children's Cottage. But that doesn't faze me. The paperwork is where you fill out an inventory of how you felt then, and what you did with your time, and how you feel now. I hear about through a postpartum group. A lot of people in my postpartum group were like, "Oh, my husband would never let me do that," and I'm like, "Your what? Your husband would not let you? Okay, then you just give your child to your husband and then you leave for twenty-four hours!"*

Similarly, Dani, who earlier stated that she was "good mother" because she "loves" her children, also affirmed that she was a "good mother" because she tried to find a balance between meeting her children's needs and her own needs. When Dani decided to leave her abusive partner, she left her children at home with her parents and went to stay at a shelter in a nearby city. Dani described how she was probably viewed as "bad mom" because her children were not with her in the shelter, but she was actually doing what was best for both her children and herself. She needed time alone to heal from the abuse, and her children needed to remain at home with her parents so that they could continue to attend school and maintain their regular schedule. Because she was doing what was best for both her children and herself, Dani felt like a "good mother." Clearly, Dani called into question the standards of intensive mothering that demand mothers prioritize their children's needs over their own needs. Dani pointed to the unfair judgment that this demand places on mothers who are in abusive situations—such as herself—and who need to think about not only their children but also about themselves in order to deal with and heal from abuse.

> *All the time I feel like I'm a really good mom. I'm there for all of them [children]. I was always there for my kids right through, from when they were born to their age now. So I think I'm a very good mother.... But like right now, I am in this shelter and I don't have my kids with me. And right now probably people are viewing me as a bad mother because I'm not with my kids, but they don't understand what I'm going through. I don't have them with me because I don't wanna put my kids through this. I could have them, but they belong back at home with my parents because they are in school.*

Other women gave up permanent care of their children to other individuals in order to ensure their and their children's best interests. For these abused women, passing on the care of their children to other individuals was the best choice for all involved. For example, Brandy claimed that she was a "good mother," even though she relinquished the primary care of her children to child welfare, because she put both her and her children's needs first. Brandy stated that she felt that it was beneficial to give up custody of her children to child welfare because she was too young to adequately care for both herself and her children. As such, Brandy did not see herself as the only possible caregiver in her children's lives and, therefore, she resisted the idea that she was the best and only caregiver for her children. According to Brandy, in circumstances such as hers, "good mothering" is not necessarily having your children with you but rather being "there" for your children, communicating with them, and "giving them everything they need," however you can.

> *Society says that a good mom is someone who has her children with her, but I know that I'm a good mom. I think the hardest thing for a mother like myself is to give up their children for the sake of their children, you know? I don't want to blame me being a young mom, and I don't want to make excuses to explain my reason for letting them go to child welfare, but I just couldn't do it. I didn't know how to be a mom. I knew what a mom was, but I just couldn't do it, especially being single. But even if they can't be at home with me, I know I'm there anyway. Like for my oldest girl, you know, thank goodness for Facebook [laughs]. Even though we can't communicate on the phone, we can do it via the internet and stuff, and I can still do the motherly thing of, you know, asking about the boyfriend thing. I ask a lot of questions about him, cuz he's three years older than her. But I try to give them everything they need and then some, however I can.*

REJECTING AND REPLACING THE "GOOD MOTHER" DISCOURSE: CREATING NEW EXPERIENTIALLY BASED ALTERNATIVE MOTHERING DISCOURSES

Three of the twenty-nine women engaged in "empowered mothering" by specifically rejecting both the "bad mother" and "good mother" discourses and replacing these discourses with experientially based alternative mothering discourses. In addition, twenty-two of the twenty-nine women engaged in "empowered mothering" by either negotiating the "bad mother" and the "good mother" discourses, or by drawing on and then redefining the "good mother" discourse, also referred to themselves according to a number of these experientially-based alternative mothering discourses. As with, the abused women who redefined the intensive mothering discourse, these abused women did not merely oppose the intensive mothering discourse; rather, they went beyond this by outright replacing this discourse. In this sense, these abused women positioned themselves outside the existing discourse of good mothering to contest the labels of the "bad mother" and the "good mother." They provided their own definitions of themselves as mothers to describe how they personally viewed themselves. As such, rather than articulating the same "bad mother" versus "good mother" discourses as perpetuated by the standards of intensive mothering, these abused women created their own mothering discourses based on their personal experiences.

The abused women created the following five experientially based alternative mothering discourses: 1) "strong mother"; 2) "loving mother"; 3) "super woman" or "hero mother"; 4) "warrior mother"; and 5) "not a normal mother." These abused women clearly avoided the portrayal of themselves as either "bad mothers" or "good mothers." Instead, they portrayed themselves as mothers in other positive terms, which were based on their own expectations rather than expectations imposed on them by the intensive mothering discourse. In this regard, these abused women had visions of what a mother is, and how they believed they fit into that vision. These visions were based on realistic expectations that they had for themselves as women who were mothering in the context of domestic violence. As such, these abused women were committed to their roles as mothers and tried hard to care for their children, despite the challenges of mothering in the context of domestic violence. Consequently, these abused women felt an immense sense of pride about the quality and adequacy of their mothering. These abused women, therefore, resisted the dominant discourses of intensive mothering in a unique and novel way—by creating other mothering discourses according to their own definitions. Below, I discuss the various ways in which the abused women created these new mothering discourses.

i) "Strong Mother" Discourse

Several abused women viewed and described themselves as "strong mothers." Eleven abused women asserted that they were "strong mothers" because they survived being a victim of abuse while ensuring the well-being of their children. For these abused women, this was an important accomplishment, one that they were proud of. Rather than allowing themselves to feel diminished by their abuse experiences, these abused women chose to learn and grow from their victimization, which, in turn, contributed to improving their and their children's lives. As such, these abused women described themselves in a positive light, which reflected and emphasized their strengths as mothers. For example, Coreen, who was one of the women who exclusively described herself as a "strong mother," stated that she viewed herself in this light because she "made it through" the abuse, and her children were all "safe" and "okay." Although Coreen stated that she would "never be perfect," she was proud of this fact: "I do the best I can with what I have." Coreen clearly had a realistic expectation of what she could accomplish given her circumstances, which made her feel proud of herself. Despite all odds, she was able to leave her partner, "survive" the abuse, and "get through" by doing the "best" she could with what she had.

> *Being abused has affected me a lot. Not negative! I think and feel strong as a mother cuz I've made it through, you know, and my kids are okay, and they're all safe now.... When they were small, I knew I had to get out for their sake, cuz I didn't want him to kill me in front of the kids. Plus my oldest daughter wasn't his, and she was really suffering from it cuz he was really mean to her too because that wasn't his child. And he would like sit her on the couch and beat me up in front of her and tell her, "This is what you're going to get when you're older, you're going to meet somebody that's going to do this too." And my daughter was just crying, and you know, I knew I had to get out for her. But I'm strong cuz I'm trying to survive, I'm trying to get through.... I'll never be perfect, but I do the best I can with what I have.*

Many abused women who viewed themselves as "good mothers," as previously discussed, also viewed themselves as "stronger mothers" as a result of having successfully mothered in the context of domestic violence. Abigail affirmed that when she left her abusive partner, she "felt very little" of herself. With time, she "built up" her confidence in herself and her future. Abigail described how when she left her abusive partner she lost her support system and had to learn as a sole parent how to care for her daughter on her own and how to reach out to other support systems. This made Abigail feel like a "stronger mother," as she had the courage and the ability to be "everything" she could for her daughter.

> *I started from a place where I felt very little of myself, and then I built that up and became a stronger person, a stronger mother. Yes, I'm a good mother, but I'm a stronger mother now because as a single parent it's been really important to me to be a single parent who supports. Our support group is back in Newfoundland where my family is. So, when we left our community in Banff and in Canmore we were out here on our own. So, as no man is a mountain, it takes a community to grow a child effectively, since we left, we don't have that here. So in a lot of aspects it's us on our own here. So having to reach out to other networks, or whatever the case may be within the community to help, as a sole person I just realized how important it is to be positive and to try to be everything that I can be to her [daughter].*

As with Abigail, Kylie also viewed herself as not only a "good mother" but also a "stronger mother" because she survived an abusive relationship and was able to maintain the care and custody of her children. Kylie described how after she left her abusive partner she felt "really bad" about herself to the point of developing an eating disorder and needing to be hospitalized. However, with a bit of time Kylie was able to "build" herself "back up" and, as a result, she felt like a "stronger mother," one who could conquer anything in the name of her children. In fact, Kylie stated that she was "glad" that she went through what she did because she is now aware of the warning signs of abuse. Kylie was proud that despite the difficult experiences she has had in her life, she has always "maintained her children."

> *I used to feel really bad about myself after it [abuse] happened. Like I felt really bad about myself, like I was anorexic, and I went from a size eleven to a size three and then I ended up in the hospital for an eating disorder because I felt so badly about myself. Then it took a while to just kind of build myself back up. I don't know, now I feel like a stronger person and mother. I feel like I could pretty much handle anything now, and I could be there for them [children] and be stronger and teach them how to be strong.... So I'm really glad that I've had that experience. I'm glad I went through what I've went through cuz it's just made me a stronger, better person. It makes me more aware, of people that are around.... I know that it's been really hard, but I've always maintained my kids. Most of my friends have lost their kids at one point or another, but they've always been with me.*

As with both Abigail and Kylie, April viewed herself as a "good mother" and, particularly, as a "stronger mother" because overcoming an abusive relationship has given her the "strength to do whatever it takes to make sure" her children are always "safe," even if it means not dating until her children are adults.

> *I think it's [abuse] made me a stronger mother. In a way because now I know that I have the strength to do whatever it takes to make sure my children are safe, no matter what the consequences may be for myself. So, I will probably never be in a relationship again unless they're [children] over the age of eighteen, and practically married and safe, you know what I mean.*

ii) "Loving Mother" Discourse

Many abused women viewed and described themselves as "loving mothers." Six abused women asserted that they were "loving mothers" because despite having lived in the most heinous of situations where love was certainly not present, they were still able to deeply feel and show love towards their children. Although experiencing abuse had many negative impacts on who the abused women were as women—such as lowering their self-esteem, decreasing their confidence, and casting doubt on their ability to trust both others and themselves—it had the opposite effect on who they were as mothers. These abused women affirmed that experiencing abuse made them become more loving and better able to express their love towards their children. For these abused women, showing love to their children was important for them, as it was something that they never experienced from their abusive partner and something that they yearned and longed for. As such, these abused women did not carry on the cycle of hatred and abuse but rather built up and fortified a cycle of love and respect. These abused women affirmed their loving devotion and care for their children as one of their strengths as mothers. For example, Madelyn and Gabrielle both exclusively described themselves as "loving mothers." These two abused women asserted that they were "loving mothers" because they made many efforts to show their children the love that they were never shown and to shelter their children from the pain and hurt that they themselves experienced. In fact, both of these abused women stated that their love for their children motivated and encouraged them to persevere and to carry on in their lives.

> Madelyn: *I'm a very loving mother. Because of it [abuse], I became more loving, and the love in my heart just doubled, tripled. Right now, like I said earlier, my children are the ones that motivate me to live, to go on with life after what has happened to us.... It's difficult, you have to be so many different personalities in different circumstance. For example, you have to be a father and you have to be a mother at the same time. You have to be so different people in one. So that was for me difficult, and yet I'm able to accomplish it because when you have love, love overcomes everything.... I give support not only emotionally but physically, and the sincerity in my heart is there. True love is there.*

> Gabrielle: *I'm confident, I'm caring, but I'm a loving mom. I want the best for my kids. After how I was raised and*

> *treated, I believe that no one should suffer like hurt and pain. So loving is the way I am with my son and daughter. I am just caring, supportive, compassionate, and loving. I have a lot of perseverance. I strive to look out for my children.*

Similarly, Shyan who viewed herself as both a "good mother" and a "loving mother" declared that she was a "loving mother" because she not only cared for and protected her children but showed them the love that she "never had and was never shown."

> *I'm a loving mother cuz I take care of them and make sure they don't get hurt, you know what I mean? I just try to protect them the best way I know how or can. I try to get along cuz I never want to be hitting any of them cuz I've been hit lots all my life and that's why I'm like that. So I give them the loving I never had and was never shown.*

Lastly, some abused women viewed and described themselves according to other individual mothering discourses. Three abused women described themselves as mothers in relation to their individual and unique circumstances and experiences. These individual mothering discourses include 1) "super woman" or "hero mother"; 2) "warrior mother"; and 3) "not a normal mother." Each of these mothering discourses had positive meanings for the abused women and revealed their varied lives, struggles, and accomplishments as mothers. For these abused women, remaining true to who they were and what they had experienced as mothers was important to their mothering identities. As such, these abused women described themselves as mothers in ways that reflected the individuality and distinctiveness of their mothering. The one common thread that wove through these abused women's narratives was the marked effect that experiencing abuse had on their mothering identities, and how these abused women's positive perceptions of themselves as mothers successfully endured and, in fact, were strengthened, despite having mothered in such oppressive circumstances. Below, I discuss these four other mothering discourses.

iii) "Super Woman" or "Hero Mother" Discourse

Madelyn, who viewed herself as a "strong mother" and "loving mother," also described herself as a "super woman" and a "super hero" mother. As a result of experiencing years and years of domestic violence, being abandoned by her abusive husband, being disowned and threatened by her husband's family, being left to raise her four children on her own, losing her home and all of her belongings, and being forced to move from to Canada to work and earn money to provide for her family—Madelyn felt beat down. Nonetheless, Madelyn survived and persevered, which she attributed to the "super woman" strength and ability that she learned to develop while attempting to endure and overcome the abuse. Although on the inside Madelyn was experiencing tremendous pain and trauma, she had the driving force and determination to put on a strong front for the sake of her children. Even though she stated that this was difficult at times, it actually enabled her to seek out resources to help her with her mothering and to accomplish all of her goals. In this sense, Madelyn viewed herself in positive terms, what she referred to as a "super woman mother."

> *I'm a super woman mother.... When I lived in all that [abuse], after I would close door and then I'm in my room and that's when I cry out all my frustrations to myself and to God. Then before I go out of the room, I put on this face like nothing happened, like I'm this strong superwoman. It was very hard, very hard! Like you have to make believe that there's really nothing wrong, that you can do it, that you are able to do it. I don't want my kids to see me like that when I'm down, cuz I don't want them to be down cuz they're already affected from the time that their father abandoned us. So I don't want to add more to that one. I want to show them that we can do it, we can do it! ... So I did more researching, I tried to learn other things that will help me to be a better mother. There, that's what happened to me. From life experiences, from other people, from books, and from the guidance of God. Believe it or not, God guides me, and he has a helping hand. Although sometimes he does not give it on the spot, sometimes he*

trains you in life and then when you're ready for that, you go to the second stage and then you when you're in the second stage you will understand why you had to undergo the first stage. So because of all that I was able to meet my goals.

iv) "Warrior Mother" Discourse

Josephine who viewed herself as a "good mother" also described herself as a "warrior mother." She experienced intense feelings of betrayal, mistrust, and even disillusionment as a result of experiencing abuse. Given that the abuse came on slowly and subtlety beginning with financial abuse, progressing to emotional abuse, developing into verbal abuse, and then culminating to physical abuse, Josephine did not immediately recognize the signs that she was in abusive relationship, what she referred to as the "red flag." Josephine spent much time trying to work out her relationship with her abusive partner hoping things would get better, but they never did. As such, Josephine felt much pain and regret for having exposed both her son and herself to the abuse. However, once Josephine recognized that she was in an abusive relationship, she immediately left and vowed never to return and never to become involved in an abusive relationship again. Josephine struggled but succeeded in caring for herself and her son on her own. In this sense, she viewed herself as "warrior mother," a mother who will always protect her child and herself, and as a mother who will fight to survive, despite the difficult circumstances in which she may find herself.

I'm definitely more of a warrior mother. Like nobody's going to get me for sure. It's like it's me and my kid and don't mess with us. So it's [abuse] not going to happen again, cause this time I'm more aware, and I've learned some lessons, you know. I can't promise I won't get in that relationship, but the red flag's going to come up a hell of a lot earlier, and, you know, I'm not going to think that I can fix it. I've proved I can do it, that I've found myself a place to live. I have a job, I've figured out the taxes, I go to court. And yeah, I can do this, and I don't need anybody!

v) "Not a Normal Mother" Discourse

Like Madelyn and Josephine, Louisa experienced many challenges as a result of mothering in the context of domestic violence. In fact, Louisa experienced severe abuse at the hands of her husband the whole thirty-seven years they were married and the entire time she raised her two children. As such, Louisa never knew what it felt like to be a mother in a non-abusive environment. Consequently, Louisa described herself exclusively as "not a normal mother."

However, Louisa believed that this description of herself as "not a normal mother" did not have a negative meaning or connotation. Rather, according to Louisa, "not normal" merely meant different as compared to other mothers, particularly mothers who were in non-abusive situations, but it certainly did not mean inferior or deviant. As such, although Louisa did not mother according to the norm, she still had positive views of herself as a mother. She described how her children were "wonderful people" and how she was proud that they "turned out really well." In this sense, Louisa viewed herself as a "not normal mother" who, despite her non-normative circumstances, was still someone who cared deeply about her children and was successful in effectively raising them.

> *I can't say that I'm a normal mother [laughs] because I don't know what being a mother in a non-abusive situation is like because I have never been a mother without being abused.... I'm not a normal mother, but I know that I feel like I had been there for my kids, cared for them as best I could, appreciated them, and like, you know, just helped them to be the best that they can be.... When I step outside myself and sort of think about how another mother would view the kids that I have raised, she would think that she did an okay job, that they turned out really well, and that they're wonderful people.... I feel that my heart is compassionate to others who are experiencing abuse and especially to children, and when my own children are hurting I'm very sensitive to that. Maybe all mothers are, I don't know.*

MOTHERING AGAINST PATRIARCHAL MOTHERHOOD AND MOTHERING TOWARDS WOMAN-CENTRED MOTHERHOOD

Many of the abused women in the study lived under the influence of the cultural myths contained in the dominant discourse of intensive mothering. However, these myths did not influence or affect the way that many of these abused women constructed their mothering identities. The majority of the abused women were not committed to but rather resisted the tenets of the discourse. This resistance was evident by the fact that these abused women held beliefs that were contrary to the discourse of intensive mothering. They did not attempt to live according to the standards of intensive mothering but rather called into question, criticized, and opposed these standards of intensive mothering and their portrayal as "bad mothers" for having been in abusive relationships. These abused women resisted the dominant discourse of intensive mothering in defining themselves as mothers by negotiating the current "good mother" and "bad mother" discourses, drawing on the existing "good mother" discourse but then redefining it to have more inclusive boundaries and, finally, by rejecting both the "good mother" and "bad mother" discourses and then replacing them with experientially based alternative mothering discourses.

I argue that these findings support O'Reilly's theory of "mothering against patriarchal motherhood" by demonstrating that mothers do challenge the demands of intensive mothering and the mandate of powerless responsibility (*Rocking the Cradle*). What is interesting is that although a small number of abused women engaged in "patriarchal mothering" by constructing their mothering identities in accordance with the discourse of intensive mothering, the majority of abused women engaged in "empowered" mothering by constructing their mothering identities in ways that outright resisted the discourse of intensive mothering as set out by patriarchal motherhood.

Some abused women resisted definitions of themselves as "bad mothers," as perpetuated by the dominant discourse of intensive mothering. They did not believe that they were "bad mothers" but rather believed and proclaimed that they were "good mothers" and, therefore, described themselves as such. These mothers insisted on their own authority as mothers and, in doing so, refused to relinquish their power to define themselves to the patriarchal institution of motherhood (O'Reilly, *Mother Outlaws*). For these empowered mothers, the creation of their subjective mothering identities was a site of power where they were able to effect social change in their home and in wider society (O'Reilly, *Mother Outlaws*). This, in effect, made mothering less oppressive for these women, despite the abusive social context in which they carried out their mothering.

Other abused women constructed their mothering identities in ways that not only resisted but also redefined and replaced the dominant discourses of mothering. They defined themselves as neither "good mothers" nor "bad mothers." Instead, they defined themselves according to other discourses, ones that were experientially based and empowering. These mothers were active agents in the face of powerful mothering discourses. Their constructions of their mothering identities revealed not only the power of the discourse of intensive mothering, but also the exercise of agency in their lives. I also argue that these findings suggest new ways of thinking about maternal empowerment, ones that are born out of the strategies of resistance the women in the study actively adopted in their own lives. In keeping with maternal scholars' call for defining and developing theories of maternal empowerment to contest, challenge, and counter patriarchal motherhood (O'Reilly, *What Do Mothers Need?* 63), I put forth and develop a feminist theory-practice of maternal empowerment, what I refer to as "mothering towards woman-centred motherhood."

A feminist theory-practice of "mothering towards woman-centred motherhood," I argue, consists of redefining and even replacing the discourse of intensive mothering, which is male defined and oppressive (as the abused women did in the study,) so that they are female defined and empowering. An example would be if the current ideology of patriarchal motherhood claims that all mothers must selflessly devote all of their time to their children, which in fact it does, "mothering towards woman-centred motherhood" would consist of abolishing this standard of mothering and would, instead, put forth and advocate a standard of mothering that women themselves believe is important, such as spending time with one's children within one's own circumstances and according to one's own schedule—which is what the abused women in the study did.

A feminist theory-practice of "mothering towards woman-centred motherhood," I argue, seeks to demolish a male-centred and oppressive motherhood (patriarchal motherhood) and replace it with a newly created woman-centred and empowering motherhood (woman-centred motherhood) so that it is the only one that exists. This type of feminist theory-practice would allow for women, such as the abused women in the study, to feel empowered in their mothering—not so much through their mothering experience (mothering practices that oppose patriarchal motherhood) because this mothering experience will always be practiced alongside the continued existence of the institution of patriarchal motherhood—but through the process of eradicating this actual institution of patriarchal motherhood and replacing it with an institution of woman-centred motherhood. This can only be accomplished when both mothering as experience and mothering as institution are woman-centred.

Woman-centred motherhood is best defined by what it is—it is female centred, female defined, and based on female experiences and voices. Woman-centred motherhood is taking on discourses by either 1) redefining current discourses or 2) creating new discourses as the abused women did in the study, in a way that seeks to replace the current patriarchal motherhood that makes mothering limiting and oppressive for women, with a woman-centred motherhood that makes mothering liberating and empowering for women. As such, both the experience of mothering and the institution of motherhood would be empowering.

This is not to say that woman-centred motherhood does not oppose and negate patriarchal motherhood because it does. However, opposition and negation are not the primary focus. That is, woman-centred motherhood does not consist of putting patriarchal motherhood (institution) at the centre and then engaging in mothering (experience) that opposes patriarchal motherhood, which is working from the outside in. Rather, woman-centred motherhood is putting women's mothering (experiences) at the centre and then engaging in creating a woman-centred motherhood (institution) by redefining the discourses of mothering and creating new discourses of mothering, which is working from the inside out.

Is woman-centred motherhood possible? In short yes, it is indeed possible but not without challenge. This is evident by the fact that the abused women in the study engaged in woman-centred motherhood. They did not accept but rather resisted the standards imposed on them by the dominant discourse of intensive mothering by redefining the existing discourses and by creating new discourses. I do not suggest that the mothering standards that these abused women defined and created for themselves were right or wrong, as that is not of importance. What is of importance is that the mothering standards that these abused women defined and created for themselves were right for them personally as individuals and were right given their own personal circumstances. As one of the abused women, Josephine, insightfully and rightly stated:

> *Who's to say what's good or bad? It's hard to sort of put a value judgment on it [mothering]. I mean I know there are other ways to do it [mothering], I see other people do it, then say no I wouldn't do that. But as for which is good and which is bad, who could know? What's right for one child is not right for another.*

I put forth a similar logic and argument—who is to say what is good or bad mothering? It is erroneous to put a value judgment on how women "should" mother. Women carry out their mothering in numerous ways, as clearly demonstrated by the abused women in the study. One way of mothering is not better or worse than the other. Just as Josephine stated, "What's right for one child is not right for another," I uphold that what is right for one mother is not right for another mother. Although each of the abused women in the study carried out their mothering in their own unique ways and within their own unique circumstances, all of these abused women did the very best they could and deeply cared about and loved their children. As such, it is no wonder that these abused women felt like "good mothers" because they were, in fact, rightfully good mothers, according to the most just and equitable personal standards of mothering that they set for themselves. These abused women did not live their lives according to the standards set out by the patriarchal ideology of motherhood, which would leave even the most perfect of mothers, if one could ever realistically exist, feeling incapable and deficient. These abused women, instead, set their own personal standards of mothering that worked for them within their own circumstances and then lived their lives according to these standards. Therefore, despite the many difficulties that these abused women undoubtedly faced, viewing and defining themselves according to their own personal standards and definitions caused them to feel a sense of liberation, autonomy, fulfillment, and empowerment in their mothering. Even among the most marginalized and subjugated of women who mother and even in the most constrictive and oppressive of contexts in which women mother, women find ways to exercise agency, resistance, and power. In this sense, the abused women in the study provide a first step to "mothering towards woman-centred motherhood."

CONCLUSION

Mothers are not only surrounded but also influenced by the dominant ideologies of motherhood, which materialize in dominant mothering discourses. The dominant discourse of intensive mothering is powerful and shapes how women view and think about themselves as mothers, which was evident in the narratives of the abused women who were part of the study. These women's narratives reveal that not all abused mothers were passive victims who merely accepted and internalized the discourse of intensive mothering; rather, most were active agents who questioned and resisted this discourse.

While a small minority of the abused women accepted the dominant discourse of intensive mothering and drew on the "bad mother" discourse, the large majority of the abused women negotiated and resisted the dominant discourse of intensive mothering in subjectively constructing their mothering identities. These women specifically resisted the dominant discourse of intensive mothering in defining themselves as mothers in three main ways: 1) they negotiated the "bad mother" and "good mother" discourses. They claimed that although at times they may have been "bad mothers," as they mothered in an abusive context, they were, overall, "good mothers" because they were capable and competent mothers; 2) they drew on and then redefined the "good mother" discourse to have more inclusive boundaries. They defined a good mother as someone who spends time with her children whenever her circumstances permit, protects her children, rears her children in love, provides for her children's basic needs, rears her children in ways that make both her children and herself happy, teaches her children, and takes care of both her children's needs and her own needs; and 3) they rejected both the "bad mother" and "good mother" discourses and replaced them with experientially based alternative mothering discourses that they created, such as "strong mother," "loving mother," "super woman or hero mother," "warrior mother," and "not a normal mother." Interestingly, although these women stated they are viewed and portrayed as "bad mothers" for failing to meet the standards of intensive mothering because they are abused, they did not personally perceive and construct themselves as mothers in this negative light.

I argue that the findings of this study support O'Reilly's theory of "mothering against patriarchal motherhood" by demonstrating that mothers do challenge the demand of intensive mothering and the mandate of powerless responsibility. Although a small number of abused women engaged in "patriarchal mothering" by constructing their mothering identities in accordance with the discourse of intensive mothering, the majority of abused women engaged in "empowered mothering" by constructing their mothering identities in ways that outright resisted the discourse of intensive mothering. I also argue that the findings of this study—which demonstrate that abused women construct their mothering identities in ways that not only resist, but also redefine and replace the dominant discourses of mothering—suggest putting forth and developing a feminist theory-practice that I refer to as "mothering towards woman-centred motherhood." This consists of redefining and even replacing the discourse of intensive mothering, which is male defined and oppressive, so that they are female defined and empowering.

As demonstrated by the women in the study, abused women find ways to resist the discourse of intensive mothering that delegitimized them as mothers in order to create their own unique and distinct mothering identities, ones that are empowering. Many of the women said that they lived for their children and that being a mother was a positive experience in their lives, despite living in the oppressive context of abuse. As such, these women were also strongly committed to their roles as mothers and tried hard to care for their children despite the challenges of mothering in the context of domestic violence. Thus, these abused women felt an immense sense of pride about the quality and adequacy of their mothering

The voices of the abused women in the study add yet another critique to the discourse of intensive mothering. Just because abused women do not fit the idealized model of the "good mother" for having mothered in an abusive context does not mean that they are not "good mothers" or that they in fact view themselves in this negative manner. Quite the contrary. The abused women in the study overwhelmingly spoke about how they effectively cared for their children and personally viewed themselves as mothers in a positive light, which is certainly significant as it demonstrates the agency and empowerment they enacted in their own lives. The next chapter provides a discussion of the ways in which the women participants' social location—based on gender, race, and social class—influences their personal constructions of their mothering identities.

5.

ABUSED WOMEN'S MOTHERING IDENTITIES

Intersections of Gender, Race, and Social Class

I THINK I'M A PRETTY GOOD MOM. Like I said, I like doing stuff with them.... I'm attentive, my kids are my focus, and I like having them around and being with them.... I think I'm a good mom because I'm always cuddling, loving, and holding them. I love saying the word, "I love you," and I'm always telling them that.... I try to teach them [children] to show respect, like respecting other people.... But with us Natives what I experienced is that when Native women get abused, they are thought of as unfit mothers. It's just a racial thing, because right away you would see, okay, like a white woman, a Caucasian woman, with her kids, and they will be doing lesser and they won't be keeping care of their kids, and I've known a few white women like that, and then you would see us sitting there trying to look after our kids, but whose kids will get taken away? It'll be us. I've seen that happen where there's two women in the same shelter, and I'm sitting there watching this one Native lady with her kids and a white woman with her kids, and this white woman will be, like, meeting men on a street corner and saying, "Oh can you watch him [son] for about twenty minutes." Or, the two women's kids would be sick, but the counsellor would come up to the Native woman and tell her, "Take your daughter or your son to the doctor! Look at him or her!" and they would say something to her. Or when a Native woman is trying to discipline her child, like her daughter had a tantrum, like you know one of those screaming tantrums, she got child welfare called on her and boom, her kids were gone. That's happened, I've seen that. So my point of view is that Native women are looked down upon. Like right away if we're abused, boom, well got to get the kids out of there. But if it's a white person they're trying to work with them, you know what I mean? So I got scared and afraid to go to shelters. I'd always ask them [counsellors], "Are you guys going to phone child welfare on me because I've seen it?" Like once I had lived at a shelter and I had to leave her [daughter] who was sleeping in my room just to make a bottle and go right back. So basically I was like make this bottle, boil the water, and race back to the room, then again go back, make a bottle, and race back, you know. So I went to do that and left her in the room, and they [counsellors] came and said, "Who's in this room?" and I said, "That's me," and then I walked out of there and then all these white women tried to avoid me, the face you know. They started complaining about me saying, "Oh, she leaves her kids all the time, blah, blah, blah," and one Native woman goes, "No, she doesn't! No, she doesn't! Why you guys saying that?" and she's like, "Ah," and she walks away. So then she comes and knocks on my door and she goes, "Watch yourself, cuz I've seen a lot of Native women come in here and lose their, you know, they come in here and a week later their kids are all getting taken away." So yeah, I'm constantly walking and looking around, like I'm constantly worried that I'm doing something wrong. Even now that I'm by myself, I have in the back of my head that I am doing something wrong, like say I was late giving her [daughter] a bath I'd feel bad cuz she didn't take a bath for an hour, like you know what I mean. I'm always constantly having to look over what I'm doing and making sure. So like I said, we're treated different. I have to watch everything that I do cuz I'm Native. It just seems like we are a different category, we're all together, and I know it sounds bad but it's what I see. (Quotation from Makayla, a twenty-seven-year-old

> Aboriginal mother of seven children who experienced psychological and physical abuse from her previous male partner for seven months)

In the Western world, mothers are surrounded and influenced by dominant ideologies of motherhood that are based on ideals of gender, race, and social class. The dominant mothering discourses thus construct and present only one group of mothers who are considered "fit" to be mothers—these include married, white, and middle-class women. These mothers' experience is thus positioned and codified as the only "real, natural, and universal" experience of mothering (O'Reilly, *Rocking the Cradle* 80). Mothers who occupy other social locations are considered "unfit" to be mothers on the basis of gender—unmarried women, single women, and lesbian women; on the basis of race—women of colour and immigrant women; and on the basis of social class—sole-support women, women on social assistance, and poor women. These women's mothering is deemed substandard, deficient, and lacking. It is, therefore, difficult, if not impossible, for these mothers to meet the societal image of the "good mother" (Kline). Indeed, "motherhood is conceptualized as a privilege rather than as a right, a privilege that can be withheld both ideologically and in more material ways" for some mothers but not others (312-314). However, the "operation of motherhood ideology within social relations of oppression, including overlapping ones of gender, race, and social class, are often submerged and rendered invisible" (315). This has real consequences for women as they carry out their mothering within these existing power relations. Gender, race, and social class thus matter because they continue to structure motherhood in ways that value some mothers' lives more than others'.

Women's social location based on their gender, race, and social class is fluid and shifting, and represents not only women's individual characteristics but also aspects of their experience and identity. Women's social location, therefore, reflects real differences in the meanings and experiences of mothering. However, our knowledge and understanding about the specific ways that women's social location frames their experiential knowledge of their mothering is limited, particularly among mothers in situations of domestic violence. Very little is known about the ways in which intersections between gender, race, and class produce varied experiences for abused mothers of different marital status, racial and class backgrounds. As such, this lack of knowledge about women's diverse social contexts raises a number of questions: how are abused women's individual social contexts similar and/or different? How do various elements of abused women's individual social contexts intersect to influence their lives as mothers? How do intersections of gender, race, and social class shape abused mothers' views of themselves as mothers?

The above quotation from Makayla, one of the women in the study, illustrates the role that intersections between these various social locations play in shaping how abused women view and think about themselves as mothers. Makayla points to the ways in which the discourse of intensive mothering constructs the racial category "Aboriginal" as less appropriate for motherhood and, therefore, portrays Aboriginal mothers as "unfit mothers." Makayla states, "With us Natives what I experienced is that when Native women get abused they are thought of us unfit mothers." However, Makayla criticizes the discourse of intensive mothering that casts Aboriginal mothers as "bad mothers" by affirming that Aboriginal mothers are not indeed "bad mothers" but rather are constructed as such because it is a "racial thing." Aboriginal mothers are put into a "different category," are "looked down upon," and are "treated different" simply because they are non-white women. Makayla provides many examples of how Aboriginal women's mothering is subjected to greater surveillance and scrutiny, resulting in Aboriginal mothers being judged more harshly than white mothers. Makayla discusses, for example, how Aboriginal women's children are more likely to be apprehended by "child welfare" because they are automatically judged as incapable. Makayla states "Right away if we're [Aboriginal mothers] abused, boom, got to get the kids out of there. But if it's a white person, they're trying to work with them." As such, Makayla describes how she was often "scared and afraid to go to shelters," as she feared that the shelter counsellors would "phone child welfare" because of the false belief that all Aboriginal mothers are "unfit mothers." Makayla even discusses how other Aboriginal mothers are aware of this unfair treatment and try to "watch out" for each other in order to warn, protect, and defend one another.

Interestingly, although the intensive mothering discourse doubly portrays Aboriginal mothers who are abused as "bad mothers," Makayla does not describe herself as a "bad mother" but rather as a "good mother." In this sense, being in a racially marginalized position permits Makayla to see and to resist this discourse of intensive mothering, which is oppressive. Makayla resists by redefining what a "good mother" is according to her own personal mothering standards, as opposed to those set out by the discourse of intensive mothering. As such, Makayla claims that she is a "good mother" because she "spends time" with her children, "loves" her children, and "teaches" her children.

This chapter specifically examines the role that social location plays in shaping the mothering identities of women in situations of domestic violence. In this chapter, I present and discuss the various ways that women participants' gender, race, and social class intersect to influence whether they draw from, negotiate, or resist the discourse of intensive mothering in constructing their mothering identities. This chapter brings together the previous two chapters by linking women's understanding of the dominant ideology of motherhood and their mothering identities to the social locations that they occupy.

CONSTRUCTING THEIR MOTHERING IDENTITIES: THE ROLE OF INTERSECTIONS OF GENDER, RACE, AND SOCIAL CLASS

Motherhood and mothering occur in specific historical and social situations framed by interlocking structures of race, class, and gender, which, in turn, shape mothers experiences (Collins, "Shifting the Center"). Women who are low income and women of colour are often blamed for the difficulties they face in their lives, without any recognition being given to these historical and societal systemic factors like gendered violence, racial oppression, and economic marginalization. These women's marginalized locations are reduced to "personal problems," "lifestyle problems," or choices and situations in which they have placed themselves. Holding women individually accountable effectively serves to denounce and render invisible the marginalized circumstances in which some women find themselves.

Motherhood-mothering scholars have increasingly become vocal about the importance of recognizing the ways in which women's mothering experiences are shaped by intersections of gender, race, and social class. Efforts have been made to develop a model of mothering that draws attention to diversity and variations and that outlines differences in women's mothering experiences. Such a model focuses attention on the complexity of factors that influence women's experiences of mothering. Patricia Hill Collins theory of "intersectionality and motherhood" conceptualizes "an interpretive framework for thinking through how intersections of, for example, race and class, or race and gender, or gender and class, position mothers within unjust power relations and does so in a way that introduces added complexity to formerly race-, class-, and gender-only approaches" to motherhood (Collins, "Shifting the Center" 205). This framework draws attention to how the varying placements of mothers in systems of privilege or non-privilege, whether based on gender, race, or class, frames and shapes mothers experiences across specific social contexts (Collins, "Shifting the Center" 208).

As discussed in chapter three, Collins argues for the need to focus on and examine "motherwork," which is centred on non-white and non-middle-class women's mothering experiences. Collins discusses specifically how women of colour and of lower social class engage in "motherwork for identity," whereby they attempt to foster a meaningful and independent identity in their children by either submitting to or challenging dominant race, class, and gender ideologies. "Motherwork for identity" has two dimensions: 1) fostering a meaningful racial identity in children within a society that denigrates people of colour; and 2) equipping children with skills to confront the contradiction of the larger effort to assimilate racial children and to challenge systems of racial oppression. Mothers make varying choices in negotiating the complicated relationship of preparing to fit into, yet resist, systems of race and class domination. Some mothers submit to sexist, racist, and classist ideologies by remaining powerless in the face of oppressive external forces, by becoming unwitting conduits of the oppressive dominant ideology, or by choosing to fit in for reasons of survival (Collins, "Shifting the Center" 58-59). However, other mothers espouse sophisticated skills that facilitate the appearance of being submissive while, at the same time, they can challenge inequality. For women of colour and of lower social class, the struggle to maintain an independent identity takes many forms and is mediated by membership in different racial and social class groups.

I argue that Collins's theory of "intersectionality and motherhood" provides a useful framework for understanding the role and influence that intersections of gender, race, and class play in shaping abused women's subjective mothering identities. This theory demonstrates how non-white and non-middle-class mothers engage in motherwork for the identity of their children, as Collins theorizes, but also for their own identity as mothers, which I argue some women in the study do through resisting the discourse of intensive mothering in personally constructing their own mothering identities.

In the study, many of the abused women's gender, race, and social class affected the ways that they personally constructed themselves as mothers. During the interviews, I did not directly ask the abused women participants how their gender, race, and social class affected their personal views of themselves as mothers; rather, I asked how the abused women viewed themselves as mothers and why. What I found was many of the women, when discussing how they personally viewed themselves as mothers, brought up and spoke at length about how being single women, low-income women, and women of colour influenced not only how others viewed them but also how they personally viewed themselves as mothers. Women's status as single mothers is particularly related to gender in situations of domestic violence, as women are more likely to flee from men's violence with their children and to then care for these children on their own. Women who occupied these marginalized positions were more likely to resist the discourse of intensive mothering in personally constructing their mothering identities. They were more likely to construct their mothering identities 1) by negotiating the "bad mother" and "good mother" discourses; 2) by redefining the "good mother" discourse according to their own standards of mothering; and 3) by both redefining the "good mother" discourse according to their own standards of mothering and replacing the "bad mother" and "good mother" discourses with their own alternative mothering discourses. These abused women's narratives reveal that occupying multiple sites of marginalization is what allowed them to more readily see and actively resist the discourse of intensive mothering that subjugates them on numerous fronts. These findings indicate that marginalized mothers engaged in "motherwork for identity" in another way—for their own identities as mothers. Below, I discuss the ways that marginalized abused women resisted the discourse of intensive mothering that casts them as "bad mothers," in and through the process of constructing their mothering identities.

INTERSECTIONS OF GENDER, RACE, AND SOCIAL CLASS AND ABUSED WOMEN'S CONSTRUCTIONS OF THEIR MOTHERING IDENTITIES—RESISTING THE DISCOURSE OF INTENSIVE MOTHERING

Although all of the women in the study were abused, not all of the women occupied equivalent positions of marginalization. Some women occupied only one position of marginalization in the areas of gender, race, and social class; other women occupied multiple positions of marginalization in these areas. As such, the women's experiences of oppression varied. Overall, of the twenty-nine abused women interviewed, twelve women were single women, nineteen women were non-white, and twenty-two women were residing in abused women's shelters due to low or a total lack of income. Of these marginalized women, fifteen specifically mentioned and discussed how being single, non-white, and poor influenced their mothering identities. What is noteworthy is that of the twenty-nine abused women in this study, twenty women resisted the discourse of intensive mothering, as discussed in the previous chapter, and of these twenty women who resisted, fifteen (a large majority) of these women were single, low-income women and women of colour. These fifteen abused women resisted the discourse of intensive mothering in constructing their mothering identities in the three ways discussed in the previous chapter. Specifically, only one abused women resisted by negotiating the "bad mother" and "good mother" discourses; a few abused women resisted by redefining the "good mother" discourse according to their own standards of mothering, but the majority of the abused women resisted by both redefining the "good mother" discourse according to their own standards of mothering and by replacing the "bad mother" and "good mother" discourses with their own alternative mothering discourses. As such, these fifteen marginalized abused women engaged in what Collins refers to as "motherwork for identity," not only for their children's identities, as theorized by Collins, but also for their own identities as mothers. They resisted the discourse of intensive mothering that constructs not only abused mothers but also single mothers, non-white, and poor mothers as "bad mothers." Overall, these abused women fostered meaningful and independent identities for themselves as mothers by challenging the dominant gender, race, and class ideologies and thus resisting negative portrayals that they are "bad mothers" for having mothered in the context of abuse, single motherhood, non-whiteness, and poverty.

INTERSECTIONS OF GENDER, RACE, AND SOCIAL CLASS—RESISTING DUAL "BAD MOTHER" DISCOURSES

Of the fifteen abused women who mentioned and discussed their social location, eleven spoke about only one aspect of their social location. These abused women discussed how their gender, social class, or race had an impact on how they viewed themselves as mothers.

i) Gender and Resisting Dual "Bad Mother" Discourses—"Abused Mother" and "Single Mother"

The influence of gender on abused women's views of themselves as mothers was seen in the women's narratives. Six abused women discussed how being a single mother shaped how others viewed them as mothers and how they personally viewed themselves as mothers. These abused women discussed how cultural stereotypes portray single mothers as deficient, incapable, and doomed to lead lives of despair, poverty, and failure. They pointed to how the assumption that female-headed households are worse off socially and economically fails to take into consideration that female household headship is often a positive strategy for survival in the lives of abused women, as remaining with abusive partners poses a risk for them and their children (Chant, "Women-Headed Households").

The negative cultural stereotypes about single mothers are reinforced by the intensive mothering discourse that portrays "single mothers" as "bad mothers." What remains invisible is the fact that "single mothers" are portrayed by the intensive mothering discourse as "bad mothers" because they represent a challenge to hegemonic patriarchal understandings of conventional familial configurations, and to male paternal authority and female maternal subjection within this family structure. As such, many of the abused women in this study stated that they are viewed as "bad mothers," not only because they are "abused mothers" but also because they are "single mothers." In this sense, they are viewed as doubly deviant. Nonetheless, these abused women resisted this intensive mothering discourse that portrays them as "bad mothers" by claiming that being "single mothers" and "abused mothers" does not indeed mean that they are "bad mothers." These abused women pointed to the numerous ways in which they effectively carried out their mothering, despite being single and abused. Several abused women claimed that they were not only "good mothers" but also "strong mothers." These abused women redefined what a "good mother" is according to their own definitions and created the "strong mother" discourse as an alternative discourse. In fact, many of the abused women viewed themselves as "good mothers" and as "strong mothers" because they refused to allow their abusive partners to continue to exercise paternal authority, which manifested itself in the form of control and abuse. They, therefore, left their abusive partners to protect themselves and their children, even if it meant having to care for their children on their own.

Abigail, for example, described how leaving her abusive partner was a "big decision," one that she "struggled with as a mom," because she was aware of the expectation that mothers are responsible for keeping the family unit together. Abigail felt much "disappointment" when she was informed by a police officer that her credibility as a mother would be questioned in the courts if she attempted to seek full custody of her daughter because she had left her abusive partner and was now a "single mother." Abigail explained how she was told that she would have to prove that she was "as effective as she should be" as a mother and that she was, indeed, capable of providing and caring for her children despite the fact that she was single. Although Abigail was aware that she was doubly viewed as a "bad mother" because she was both a single and an abused mother, she did not perceive herself as such. Instead, Abigail resisted this discourse of intensive mothering by claiming that she was a "good mother" and a "stronger mother" because, despite raising her daughter on her own and despite being a victim of abuse, she supported and cared for her daughter by accessing community networks and services.

> *At first we left just the house to be safe, and then we left the community too because it too became unsafe for us because he was always there lurking.... I think it was a big decision [to leave], like it's something that I really struggled with as a mom. As a woman you are expected to hold the pieces together in the family, to be able to make things work, to be the glue of the family, and to make things okay, pleasant, and a nice place to be. I think that is a societal expectation.... One of the big disappointments is that I learned from this constable that women quite often respond in an emotional level, and he said, "You know in the courts, it's a man's world and you have to play the man's game," and he said, "As a single woman, you can't be a woman there, you have to be a man for the best of your daughter. You know, you need to document everything, you need to present this, you need to present that because responding as a woman, quite often what happens is initially women respond with fear, concern, confusion and that sort of thing, and the courts keep on pushing the children more and more with dad because the mom may be not able to be so effective as she should be." So it's been a year later, and the whole time, the judge is saying innocent until proven guilty, and when there's abuse it's difficult to prove guilty. So the judge keeps on pushing them [police] to get more.... Yes, I'm a good mother, but I'm a stronger mother now*

> *because as a single parent, it's been really important to me to be a single parent who supports myself.... So having to reach out to other networks, or whatever the case may be within the community to help, as a sole person, I just realized how important it is to be positive and to try to be everything that I can be to her [daughter].*

As with Abigail, Carly stated that because she left her abusive partner and was now a "single mom," her ability to properly care for her children was subjected to much doubt and speculation. Carly explained that although she shared joint custody with her abusive partner, child welfare only scrutinized and offered her counsel about what she needed to do to improve her parenting. She felt that it was unfair that her mothering and not her partner's fathering was being "looked upon" and judged when she was the victim and her partner was the perpetrator who had abused her. Nonetheless, although Carly was conscious that she was doubly viewed as a "bad mother" because she was both an abused mother and a single mother, she did not view herself in this negative light. Instead, Carly asserted that she was a "good mother" and a "strong mother" because despite the abuse she experienced and despite having to mother her children on her own, she spends time with her children and loves and cares for them. In this sense, Carly resisted the discourse of intensive mothering that cast her as a "bad mother."

> *On the ninth of January, that was the final day that I left. I phoned child welfare and found out where I could go, what I could do, because here I was a small town girl in a big city, and I didn't know what to do.... So since then they [child welfare] are telling me as a single mom that I need to seek this, this, and this, you know. But my son is still with his father. Why is he not in anger management? Why is he not being looked upon? I mean he's supposed to have in-home care. Well, it's been a month and a half, and there hasn't been not one thing happen. Not one thing happen! So what does that say? But yet, you know, they tell me as a single mom, I've got to do this. But they don't even need*

> *to tell me, I've got to do this, this, and this, because I've been asking to do this, this, and this, and to get the ball rolling. I thought that I got the ball rolling. I'm here, I'm at this second stage shelter! ... You know, as many mishaps and misfortunate things that have happened to me, I'm still here for my babies.... I'm a good mother. A lot of the time I feel like that, like, being with my boys and them getting along and us doing something together whether it be, just sitting here talking, you know.... I'm a strong mother too. I'm very strong at being a mother because my babies are my babies, you know. It doesn't matter how big they get. They're still my babies, you know.*

As with both Abigail and Carly, Coreen's mothering was also subject to much inquiry and criticism because she was a "single mom." Coreen discussed how child welfare was constantly informing her about what she "did wrong" as a "single mom" rather than recognizing what she "did right." Yet child welfare did not inquire about or criticize her abusive partner who was not providing child support as he should have been, who was not helping her raise their children, and who was having other children with other women. In this sense, Coreen pointed to and criticized the wider social expectation that mothers, and not fathers, are ultimately responsible for caring for children. Even though Coreen recognized that she was viewed as a "bad mother" because she was not only an abused mother but also a single mother, she resisted this discourse of intensive mothering and, instead, viewed and described herself in a positive light—as a "strong mother." Coreen may have experienced abuse and may have been forced to raise and care for her children on her own as a consequence of leaving her abusive partner, but she still viewed herself as a "strong mother" because she successfully ensured the safety of her children and survived the abuse.

> *I had five kids, and, oh my gosh, they were forever telling me as a single mom what I did wrong. But they weren't looking at what I did right, and then they weren't looking at his [partner's] part. Like he's not giving me child support,*

> *he's not even there to help me discipline these kids, you know, and then he's going out and making more kids you know.... Being abused has affected me a lot. Like really not negative! I think and feel strong as a mother cuz I've made it through you know, and my kids are okay, and they're all safe now.... When they were small, I knew I had to get out for their sake, cuz I didn't want him to kill me in front of them [children].... But I'm strong cuz I'm trying to survive. I'm trying to get through.... I'll never be perfect, but I do the best I can with what I have.*

ii) Social Class and Resisting Dual "Bad Mother" Discourses—"Abused Mother" and "Poor Mother"

Social class also had an influence on how the abused women viewed themselves as mothers. Four abused women discussed how being of lower social class influenced the ways that they were perceived by others as well as the ways that they personally perceived themselves as mothers. These abused women pointed to the cultural stereotypes that pathologize poor mothers and depict them as lazy, dependent, and deprived. These abused women also underlined how suppositions about poor mothers attribute poverty to mothers' personal irresponsibility rather than to structural conditions, such as domestic violence within the home and abused mothers' need to leave their abusive partners and financially provide for the family on their own.

These negative cultural stereotypes about poor mothers are reinforced by the intensive mothering discourse that portrays "poor mothers" as "bad mothers." The intensive mothering discourse defines "good mothering" as involving large financial expenditures on children and devoting a great deal of financial resources to children. What is not readily discernible is the fact that despite social and material contradictions, the intensive mothering discourse remains the normative political and cultural standard against which individual mothers are evaluated. As the monetary cost of normative ideals continues to increase, poor mothers are left at an increasing disadvantage (Adair; Hays; Clarke). In this light, many of the abused women in this study declared that they are viewed as a "bad mother" not only because they are "abused mothers" but also because they are "poor mothers." As such, they are viewed as deviant on two fronts. However, these abused women resisted this intensive mothering discourse that constructs them as "bad mothers" by, instead, defining themselves as "good mothers." These abused women indicated that even though they were victims of abuse—and as a result of fleeing their abusive partner, they did not have the financial means to provide for themselves and their children on their own—they always ensured that their children had shelter, clothing, and food. Despite the most difficult of circumstances, these abused women always provided for their and their children's basic needs. As such, these abused women also redefined the "good mother" according to their own standards of mothering, ones that reflected the realities of their unique circumstances and their abilities to carry out their mothering, even within the very trying circumstances of abuse.

Tammy, for example, spoke about how being homeless affected how she viewed herself as a mother. Tammy described how she remained with her abusive partner because she did not know where to turn for help. She felt that she would not be able to survive financially if she left her abusive partner. However, once she found out about abused women's shelters, Tammy immediately left her abusive partner. Even though she became homeless as a result of leaving her abusive partner and had no other choice but to reside in an abused women's shelter, Tammy viewed herself as a "good mother" because she was doing her "very best" and was always "there" for her son. For Tammy, securing shelter for her and her son defined her identity as a "good mother." As such, Tammy resisted the discourse of intensive mothering that portrays her as a "bad mother" by claiming that she was, in fact, a "good mother."

> *I'm stuck here [in the shelter] because of money. I was stuck there [with abusive partner] cuz I needed money. I used to tell myself, "You can do it," but then I was like, "No, you can't." I honestly thought I could not. There's no steps written down in a format to get you out of it [abuse], and there is nothing even written announcing where you can go or what you need to do when you leave*

him [abusive partner]. There's not a handbook that says, like, okay if you're getting abused go here, go here, or go here, or go talk to this person, and this is the next thing you do. There's not a hand out for that, just like there's not handout for parenting. Luckily, I found out about shelters, and I had to go to a shelter to get help. You know since I've left, I think how I was putting up with it [abuse] to just get the twenty bucks he gave me every day to live. I feel so stupid. But you just don't know though, right? ... But I think ... I'm a good mom, because I think I'm doing my best. I'm not gonna say I'm a perfect mom because I don't think there is a perfect mom, but I am going to say that I'm doing my very best to keep that child happy. So I'm just doing the best I can, and I'm learning as I go. I think I'm a good mom too because I'm wanting, warm, comforting, loving and understanding. I'm the one that's there for him [son] anytime he needs me.

As with Tammy, Badriya also spoke about how experiencing material deprivation affected her identity as a mother. Badriya and her four children resided in a second-stage shelter; she obtained their clothing from donation centres and procured their food from food banks. Badriya described how she enjoyed going to shopping malls with her children and looking at all of the items but also how she often felt such anguish and despair because she did not have the money to buy her children any of the items. In fact, Badriya described how she did not even have the money to buy her children food at the shopping malls and, therefore, she had to pack lunches from home to take with them. Although Badriya did not have the financial means to provide for her children, she resisted the intensive mothering discourse that cast her as a "bad mother" by affirming that she was indeed both a "good mother" and a "strong mother." Badriya viewed herself as a mother in a positive light because both she and her children were happy, and she spent a lot of time with her children.

I take them [children] to the mall, and we go walking in the mall. But I cry sometimes when I look at them cuz I can't,

I can't buy them nothing, not clothes, not toys not even food. I even make them sandwiches and snacks from home and bring them to mall.... Since day one, like, I know I'm good mom.... Like I'm always happy with my kids, you know, to see them happy.... The moment I'm happy with my kids, like always to see my kids healthy, just to make them happy.... I love that I have time [with children] ... I feel myself like a good mom, rich. I don't know how to explain it. Yeah, good mom, strong mom.

Finally, Leena spoke about the social stigma of receiving government assistance and how this affected her identity as a mother. When Leena left her abusive partner, she remained in a shelter for a short period of time, and then she applied for social assistance so that she could move into an apartment on her own with her baby son. As such, the money Leena received from social assistance covered their rent but not their food. Therefore, Leena was required to obtain her food from food banks; she, however, articulated that she felt inferior because she received social assistance and felt that she was, consequently, labeled in a different way than middle-class mothers. Leena described how the popular scripts about "welfare mothers" neglects the difficult experiences of abused mothers who are struggling not only to survive emotionally from their victimizations but also to survive physically from the consequences of leaving their abusive partners and, therefore, having to find the means to meet their basic financial needs. Nonetheless, even though Leena did not have the financial means to provide for all of her and her child's needs, she resisted the intensive mothering discourse by sometimes describing herself as a "bad mother," mostly when she was with her abusive partner. But, for the most part Leena described herself as a "good mother," particularly once she left her abusive partner because she had survived the abuse, spent lots of time with her son, and at one point had a job. Leena also viewed herself as a strong mother because she vowed to never allow herself to be emotionally manipulated and controlled again by an intimate partner. Leena resisted the discourse that constructs her as a "bad mother" by negotiating the "bad mother" and "good mother" discourses as well as by creating new alternative mothering discourses based on her personal experiences.

> *Because I'm low income and then I go to donation centres and food banks and stuff I always feel like people, like, for example, people from my apartment, are just looking down at me and are looking at me weird. Like today I got food bank, and there was a lot of people in my lobby for some reason when I got food bank, and I was signing my papers and saying, "Oh thank you for bringing my food bank up," and I wasn't ashamed but was just real happy, then I noticed that everyone was looking at me, and I felt like they were looking down at me like I'm a bum and just real poor. Yes, I am on welfare, but I'm not so poor that I don't have no place or whatever. Like it pays my rent and my utilities, but not my food, so I get food bank. But you still get that feeling.... You know, when I was with him I felt like a bad mother because it was hard being in an abusive situation and trying to take care of my kids.... I think before I was a bad mother, but now I'm a good mother and I'm a survivor, and I'm a strong mother. I'm not suckered into all that emotional bull anymore.*

INTERSECTIONS OF GENDER, RACE, AND SOCIAL CLASS—RESISTING MULTIPLE "BAD MOTHER" DISCOURSES

Of the fifteen abused women who mentioned and discussed their social location, four women spoke about multiple aspects of their social location. Interestingly, among the abused women who mentioned and discussed their racial position, all of the women but one also mentioned their class position in conjunction with their racial position.

i) Social Class and Race, and Resisting Multiple "Bad Mother" Discourses—"Abused Mother," "Poor Mother," and "Non-White Mother"

The influence of race on abused women's views of themselves as mothers, and particularly how race intersects with social class to affect abused women's mothering identities, was evident in the women's narratives. Four abused women discussed how being a non-white woman influenced how others viewed them as mothers as well as how they personally viewed themselves as mothers. Of these four abused women, all but one of the abused women described how their position as a non-white woman intersected with their class position and affected their mothering identity. As such, these abused women verbally located themselves not only in the race hierarchy with a lack of racial privilege but also in the class hierarchy with a lack of financial privilege.

The intensive mothering discourse certainly does not hold non-white mothers in the highest esteem, regardless of socioeconomic status. This discourse is fueled by centuries of systemic racism and reflects dominant social mores that equate non-whiteness with poverty (Cooper and McCoy 46). As such, it is not difficult to see why race and social class are inextricably linked in many of the abused women's accounts and discussions of their mothering identities. However, it is clear that the poverty of many non-white families, particularly mothers, is "greatly influenced by a host of systemic issues such as inadequate public education, escalated unemployment rates, lack of affordable housing," and, therefore, is not due to mothers' individual deficiencies (Cooper and McCoy 47). Still, non-white families and the mothers within these families are "pathologized." That is, they are blamed for "many of the challenges they incur even when the structural inequality that has evolved over centuries" is what contributes to their "lingering challenges" (Collins, *Fighting Words*). The "politics of blaming" poor non-white mothers for their "family's poverty" is linked to what Collins refers to as "the new politics of containment," which is a "political phenomenon that depoliticizes women's oppression, dissuades their resistance, and helps contain them at the bottom of the socioeconomic and political hierarchies despite other indicators of racial progress (Collins, *Fighting Words* 11). As such, Collins suggests that the new politics of containment "relies much more heavily on surveillance tactics that fix" non-white women in the "public eye" through "the development and maintenance of stereotypical controlling images" (Collins, *Fighting Words* 11). This continues to perpetuate the myth that poverty is "personally induced rather than a result of structural and political realities" (Cooper and McCoy 48).

Most of the abused women who discussed how race and social class intersect to influence their mothering identities were Aboriginal. These abused women discussed how cultural stereotypes that prevail portray non-white mothers as idle, incompetent, reliant on the state, and, ultimately, poverty stricken. First Nation mothers are "particularly vulnerable to being constructed as 'bad mothers' because, as a consequence of colonialist oppression and different cultural norms, they do not always meet the dominant cultural and middle class expectations that constitute the ideology of motherhood" (Kline 308-309). In this sense, it is the individual Aboriginal mothers who are blamed for the difficulties they face as mothers, and no recognition is given to the roots of those difficulties in history and current structures of colonialism and racial oppression. In this sense, Aboriginal women's experiences of domestic violence are often attributed to "personal lifestyle" problems which implies that they asked for the abuse. The characterization of abuse as personal problems emphasizes the individual deficiencies of Aboriginal mothers and obscures the effects of these social ills that are largely the consequence of these historical and continuing colonialist and racist practices.

These negative cultural stereotypes about Aboriginal and low-income mothers are reinforced by the intensive mothering discourse that portrays "non-white mothers" and "poor mothers" as "bad mothers." What is hidden is the fact that "non-white mothers" and "poor mothers" are portrayed by the intensive mothering discourse as "bad mothers" primarily because they do not conform to the white, middle-class model of mothering. As such, many of the abused women in this study stated that they are viewed as "bad mothers," not only because they are "abused mothers" but also because they are Aboriginal mothers and, consequently, are viewed as deviant mothers on multiple levels. However, these abused women did not submit to this discourse of intensive mothering that constructs them as "bad mothers" but rather resisted by declaring that they were in fact "good mothers," "strong mothers," and "loving mothers," although they were abused and non-white. In this sense, these abused women redefined what a "good mother" is according to their own definitions and created the "strong mother" and the "loving mother" discourses as alternative discourses.

Makayla, for example, spoke about how being an Aboriginal mother affected her identity as a mother. She described how when she resided in abused women's shelters, she often felt "looked down on" because she was Aboriginal and how Aboriginal mothers were more likely to have their children apprehended and taken into custody by child welfare merely because they were Aboriginal and, therefore, considered "unfit mothers." Makayla pointed to the stereotype that Aboriginal mothers are less effective mothers compared to white mothers, by describing one incident in particular where the police automatically assumed and then reported that she was poor and was not able to provide food for her children simply because she was Aboriginal. Although Makayla was an abused and a non-white mother, she negated the stereotype that she was automatically a "poor mother." As such, Makayla resisted the intensive mothering discourse that casts her as a "bad mother" by stating that she was indeed a "good mother." Makayla proclaimed that she was a "good mother" because she spent time with her children, she loved her children, and she taught her children.

> *First thing when I go to shelters, I feel really funny, like, looked down on. I see in the shelter how there's two different ways— there's Native and there's white. I've been in the white people's homes and they're just absolutely disgusting, and I've been in the Native's homes and they're, like, clean and I'm thinking, well how come they've got their kids and I have to fight for mine you know, like it's stupid. There was one incident where the kids were actually taken from my home and that wasn't because of lack or food or the house was messy or the kids were dirty. My kids were in the living room watching TV and we had this, well it was supposed to be a social drink in the other room. I wasn't going to allow them to have it in the living room or anywhere the kids can play and touch the alcohol. But then I called the police because a fight had broken out, and it's a good thing I happened to look at the cops report because the cop had said we had no food, that there were liquor*

> *bottles everywhere, and I think it was because we were Native. Honestly, because I'd seen this report and then I opened up the fridge, and I was just like to the police, "Tell me to my face I got no food. Tell me and to my face there are alcohol or beer bottles here," but my kids still got taken.... I think I'm a pretty good mom. Like I said, I like doing stuff with them.... I'm attentive, my kids are my focus, and I like having them around and being with them.... I think I'm a good mom because I'm always cuddling, loving, and holding them.... I try to teach them [children] to show respect, like respecting other people.... But with us Natives, what I experienced is that when Native women get abused, they are thought of as unfit mothers. It's just a racial thing.*

As with Makayla, Shyan discussed how being an Aboriginal mother affected her identity as a mother. Shyan described how abused mothers, particularly abused mothers who are Aboriginal are "pinpointed" as "poor and low income." According to Shyan, it does not matter how successful she is in her family life or from a financial standpoint, she will always be "categorized" as "poor and low income" and, therefore, viewed as a "bad mother" because she is Aboriginal. Shyan declared that she does not "care" what "other people think," and although she is an abused and non-white mother, she criticized the stereotype that she is a "poor mother" who receives financial support from her Aboriginal band. Consequently, Shyan resisted the intensive mothering discourse that she is a "bad mother" by stating that she was not only a "good mother" but also a "loving mother" because she cares for and protects her children the "best way" she knows how and the best way she can.

> *I think abused women are pinpointed like poor and low income. To me, that's what pops into my mind. I don't know why, maybe because a woman's self-esteem is down? Or the way they look at being a Native woman. They think Native mothers probably drink, their kids are probably apprehended, and they're poor, or they're getting*

> *money from their band. But it's not like that, cuz I don't get money from my band cuz I have a poor band. It's like people expect this anyway, so you're already categorized. That's the way I look at it. I mean, I could be having a beautiful home and everything else, but I'll still be judged like this, and I'm already pinned right there.... I don't care like what other people think, really....You can look at any woman, and you don't know what's going on in their life.... People tell me, "You're a good mom," and it's not phoniness either, it's just how I am when we're home alone. Like I would take care of him [son] ... I'm a loving mother cuz I take care of them [children] and make sure they don't get hurt, you know what I mean? I just try to protect them the best way I know how or can.*

Finally, Eden also discussed how being an Aboriginal mother influenced her identity as a mother. According to Eden, there exist master racist narratives about Aboriginal mothers, particularly those who live on Aboriginal reservations, that cast them in a negative light. Eden detailed how Aboriginal mothers are perceived as alcoholics, drug addicts, and impoverished individuals. Consequently, Aboriginal mothers are constructed as "bad" and are expected to prove that they can have "a good life too." However, Eden stated that she knows mothers who are white and who are not abused, yet they do not have a "perfect life," hence highlighting this contradiction. In this sense, Eden pointed to the hegemonic false belief that all Aboriginal mothers are lower class and "bad mothers," whereas all white mothers are middle class and "good mothers." Although Eden is an "abused," "non-white," and "low-income" mother, she did not view herself as a "bad mother" but rather as a "good mother" and a "strong mother." As such, Eden resisted the discourse of intensive mothering that said she was a "bad mother."

> *I think when you're abused a lot of the times they expect you to work extra hard, to prove to everyone that, you know, you're not bad, that you're not doing drugs or alcohol, and that you can have a good life too.... I know*

this comes from, I hate to say it, but a little bit of racism. Like everyone thinks that Native mothers from the reserve are, you know, all drunks, poor, and whatever. And then when you come to the city everyone expects everyone to have this perfect life, like the white picket fence and the big house. But I think both sides are misunderstood. I know some white mothers that are not abused, and I know they don't have a perfect life.... I am Native ... and I am homeless.... but I view myself as a good mom in a bad situation. Now that I left him, my confidence is already starting to go up. I feel proud of leaving him. I feel even though we're homeless right now and we're fleeing, I feel proud that I'm on my way to a better life with my children. Yeah, right now I feel very hopeful and I'm excited for a new life without him.... I value myself as a strong woman cuz I've been through so much.

"MOTHERWORK FOR IDENTITY" FOR THE IDENTITY OF CHILDREN AND FOR THE IDENTITY OF MOTHERS

All of the women in this study were abused but not all of them occupied equivalent positions of marginalization based on gender, race, and social class. While some abused women were marginalized in just one of these areas, other abused women were marginalized in all three of these areas. As such, the abused women occupied various positions of privilege and/or non-privilege and thus were positioned within unjust power relations. However, all of the women who stated that being single, low income and women of colour influenced their mothering identities also resisted the discourse of intensive mothering in constructing these mothering identities. These marginalized abused women were more likely to resist by negotiating the existing "good mother" and "bad mother" discourses; by redefining the "good mother" discourse according to their own standards of mothering; and, finally, by both redefining the "good mother" discourse according to their own standards of mothering, and by replacing the "bad mother" and "good mother" discourses with their own alternative mothering discourses.

By resisting the discourse of intensive mothering in personally constructing themselves as mothers, I argue that these abuse women engaged in motherwork for identity, not specifically for their children's identity as Collins theorizes, but in another way—for their own identities as mothers. As such, I argue that the findings of this study support and build on Collins theory of "intersectionality and motherhood" by demonstrating that abused women also engage in motherwork for their own identities as mothers, what I refer to as "motherwork for (m)other identity," by negotiating, redefining, and replacing the discourse of intensive mothering in constructing their own mothering identities. These marginalized mothers confronted and challenged the contradictions of the intensive mothering discourse. Collins argues that marginalized mothers engage in motherwork for the identity of their children because the survival of their children depends on gaining the skills of fighting class and racial oppression (Collins, *Fighting Words* 321). The class and racial identities of the children are not validated by the schools, the media, and other social institutions. Likewise, I argue that marginalized mothers engage in "motherwork for (m) other identity" because their survival as mothers also depends on gaining the skills necessary for fighting the oppression that they face as marginalized mothers. Like their children, marginalized women's identity as mothers is not validated by the schools, the media, nor other social institutions. As such, marginalized mothers, as demonstrated by the abused mothers in the study, have to cope with and survive within systems that oppress them as mothers, and they do so by defining and creating their own mothering identities. Indeed, the marginalized mothers in the study did not remain powerless in the face of hegemonic intensive mothering discourses that encourage and fortify their alienation and oppression as mothers. They outright resisted these intensive mothering discourses and, in doing so, found ways to support their own self-definitions as mothers, ones that were empowering and not repressive.

Placing the experiences of single, low-income women, and women of colour in the centre of the study's analysis revealed that marginalized mothers perform "motherwork for identity," which challenges not only "social constructions of work and family as separate spheres" and "male and female gender roles as dichotomized" but also the discourse of intensive mothering that constructs and divides mothers as either "good mothers" or "bad mothers." These marginalized abused mothers may not have had gender, social class, and racial privilege, but they did seek to create personal autonomous identities for themselves as mothers instead of submitting to identifying themselves as members of a stigmatized group of "bad mothers." In this sense, these marginalized abused women struggled for the right to self-definition as mothers in the face of much oppression and adversity. The abused women's narratives in the study revealed that marginalized mothers sought self-definition for themselves as mothers, hence revealing that issues of identity are crucial to all motherwork. In this sense, marginalized abused mothers are also conduits for mothers' empowerment and engage in ways to free motherhood from patriarchy. These findings are useful because they suggest how feminist theorizing about motherhood can shift when marginalized mothers' voices become central in feminist research and theory.

CONCLUSION

Mothers occupy different social locations based on gender, race, and social class. While some mothers occupy positions of privilege, other mothers occupy positions of marginalization. It is within these diverse existing power relations that women carry out their mothering. Indeed, mothers various social locations frame their experiential knowledge of their mothering and reflect real differences in their mothering experiences, which were evident in the narratives of the abused women who were part of the study. What is significant is the fact that abused mothers' positions of marginalization affected the way that they personally constructed their mothering identities. The abused mothers who were single, low income, and women of colour were more likely to resist the discourse of intensive mothering that casts them as bad mothers (on multiple levels) in constructing their mothering identities. These marginalized abused mothers diverged by negotiating, resisting, and redefining the intensive mothering discourse. Even though they were portrayed as "bad mothers" because they were not only abused but also single, low income, and women of colour, these mothers did not remain powerless in the face of hegemonic intensive mothering discourses that reinforce and propagate their subjugated positions. Instead, they stood firm in their belief and description that they were indeed "good mothers" who loved and cared for their children, despite the marginalized circumstances in which they performed their mothering, exposing the flawed construct of "good mothering."

I argue that the findings of this study support and build on Collins's theory of "intersectionality and motherhood" by demonstrating that abused women also engage in motherwork for their own identities as mothers, what I refer to as "motherwork for (m) other identity," by resisting the discourse of intensive mothering in constructing their mothering identities. In the study, the abused women's social location based on gender, race, and social class affected the way that they personally constructed themselves as mothers. Those who were single women, low income, and women of colour were more likely to resist the discourse of intensive mothering in constructing their mothering identities.

Despite the realities of abuse, single motherhood, racism, and poverty, abused women find ways to resist the exclusionary and oppressive discourse of intensive mothering. The marginalized women in the study created, valued, and fortified empowering identities for themselves as mothers in the face of the discourse of intensive mothering, which delegitimizes and subjugates them as mothers because of their marginalized circumstances. Many of the abused women who were single pointed to the numerous ways in which they effectively carried out their mothering, despite being the sole caregivers for their children. These mothers often stated that they left their abusive partners to protect themselves and their children, even if it meant having to care for their children on their own. Moreover, many of the abused women who were mothering in situations of poverty highlighted that they always ensured their children's basic needs were met, including providing them with shelter, clothing, and food. These mothers stated that leaving their abusive partner meant that they no longer had the financial means to provide for themselves and their children on their own, but they still managed to effectively care for their children, even in situations of economic marginalization. Finally, many of the abused women of colour, of which most were Aboriginal, expressed that they loved and cared for their children, despite colonial-based stereotypes that portray them as incompetent mothers, responsible for their own marginalized circumstances and reliance on the state. These women fought against such demeaning portrayals of themselves as mothers.

The voices of the women in the study contribute to new ways of viewing and defining mothering, ones that are inclusionary and that shift attention to the larger societal and cultural forces in which women perform their mothering. Marginalized abused mothers do not fit the idealized model of the "good mother" on multiple fronts, but this does not necessarily mean that they do not engage in good mothering or do not view themselves as "good mothers." Because of their multiple marginalizations these abused women uniformly and strongly evoked detailed practices of their capabilities as mothers and viewed themselves as mothers in affirmative ways. The abused women's narratives in the study reveal, in a very real and powerful way, how the dominant standards of intensive mothering are indeed unjust, subjugating, and deeply oppressive.

CONCLUSION

Finding Empowerment through the Storms of Motherhood and Domestic Violence

DESPITE YEARS OF AWARENESS and research in the area of domestic violence, little is known and little has been written about abused women's mothering experiences from their perspectives, voices, and lived experiences. Many of the women in this study pointed to the dearth of research and knowledge about mothering in domestic violence situations which is based on the authenticity of women's own experiences. These women spoke about the necessity of increasing knowledge in this area. One woman named Tammy spoke about the importance of being aware of the particular challenges that mothers in situations of abuse face, and the importance of then gathering and disseminating such information in ways that helps mothers.

> *I just hope that you can get this research out there and help others cuz there's really nothing out there. At least I could help you with this so that everyone could be educated on what it's like to be a mom who is abused. I'm sure there's millions of women out there right now that are going through what I just went through.*

Another woman named Carly spoke about the struggle that many abused mothers, including herself, face as a result of mothering in the context of domestic violence and about the necessity of gaining more knowledge in this area:

> *I can't take much more, you know. I'm grasping right now*

> *at being an abused mother, and I'm grasping for my children and myself. I don't know where to go, and I don't know what to do, but you're here and the research you're doing is going to help women be able to reach out and grab that knowledge, you know.*

Finally, one woman named Louisa spoke about the need to gain a greater understanding about abused women's mothering and the support that women can offer one another by sharing their stories:

> *The questions that you're asking are deep and thought provoking and often something I had never actually thought about, so I'm glad for that. I hope I've provided some insight into that because we need so much more knowledge about this. If I can be of some help some way, I want to do that. I don't think that I have gone through this for nothing. I'm hoping I haven't, and I don't think God would allow that to happen. There's got to be some good that comes out of my experience, and I want to work towards that good. If I helped in this way, then I'm happy for that.*

These women's narratives demonstrate that there is a great need to give abused mothers a voice, to pay close attention to their everyday lives and realities, and to understand the particular challenges and complexities that they face in order to open up discussions about their unique mothering experiences.

This book was written as a way to contribute to a greater knowledge and understanding of abused women's subjective meanings, understandings, and experiences of mothering in circumstances of domestic violence. It was born out of my strong conviction of the importance of seeking to understand women's experiential knowledge of their mothering from their own voices rather than through the voices of judgment of others. This book is thus about giving a voice to these women who have been marginalized, kept on the periphery, and largely excluded from discussions about their mothering in the context of domestic violence. Only when we give abused mothers a voice, pay close attention to their subjective experiences, and shine a light on their everyday lived realities, are we able to begin to understand their unique mothering experiences, which have been silenced and neglected for far too long.

Indeed, there has been a burgeoning literature in both the area of domestic violence and motherhood-mothering. However, little overlap exists between these literatures, as both of these literatures have examined domestic violence and motherhood-mothering as two separate issues, despite the fact that many abused women are also mothers. Recently, a small body of feminist sociological literature has begun to examine mothering within the social context of domestic violence. This literature examines the impact of domestic violence on mothering practices, the impact of domestic violence on mother-child relationships, and, to a lesser extent, the impact of protective interventions on mothering. However, there are a number of gaps in this literature: this literature does not specifically consider abused women's personal mothering experiences, nor does it critically examine abused women's mothering in light of dominant ideologies of mothering and individual social contexts. Consequently, there is little knowledge about abused mothers' personal meanings, understandings, and experiences about the role that dominant ideologies of mothering play in their lives, and how individual social contexts based on gender, race, and social class shape their experiences. Given the limited manner in which abused women's mothering has thus far been framed, examined, and understood in scholarly work, a full picture of how women mother in and through domestic violence has not yet developed. This book has been an attempt to contribute to a more informed picture of the lives and experiences of women in such situations.

This book provides a window into the ways that the women in the study 1) perceive the standards and expectations of mothering that women are held to; 2) view and construct themselves as mothers and the discourses that they draw from, resist, and negotiate in constructing their mothering identities; and finally 3) occupy different social location based on gender, race, and social class and how these shape their constructions of their mothering identities. The findings provide numerous insights. First, the findings reveal that the abused women in the study were not only able to articulate many of the standards of intensive mothering (they reiterated four of the eight standards of intensive mothering as defined by O'Reilly (*Mother Matters*; *What Do Mothers Need?*), but were also able to identify and challenge their constricting and oppressive nature. The abused women's narratives also demonstrate that they recognized and felt that perceptions about abused mothers in general, are often influenced by the dominant discourses of intensive mothering, victim-blaming, and mother-blaming. The abused women commonly described that they are portrayed as "bad mothers," "weak mothers," "abusive mothers," "looked down on mothers," "to blame mothers," and "in need of help mothers." However, many of the abused women also challenged the portrayal of mothers in abusive situations according to these discourses.

Second, the findings show that many of the abused women resisted the intensive mothering discourses in the ways that they personally constructed their mothering identities. In fact, the large majority of the abused women engaged in "empowered mothering" by resisting the "bad mother" discourse (O'Reilly, *Rocking the Cradle*). These abused women resisted in three ways: 1) they negotiated the "bad mother" and "good mother" discourses; 2) they drew on and then redefined the "good mother" discourse to have inclusive boundaries; and 3) they rejected both the "bad mother" and "good mother" discourses and replaced them with experientially based alternative mothering discourses that they created. Abused women, evidently, are a group of marginalized women who find ways to empower themselves in and through their mothering. The study, therefore, makes important contributions to current understandings of mothering in the context of domestic violence, as it illustrates that abused mothers are not passive victims who merely accept and internalize the discourse of intensive mothering. Instead, they are active agents who question and resist these powerful mothering discourses. These women found ways to resist the discourse of intensive mothering that delegitimized them as mothers in order to create their own unique and distinct mothering identities, ones that were empowering. Many of the women stated that they lived for their children and that being a mother was a positive experience in their lives, despite living in the oppressive context of abuse. As such, these women were also strongly committed to their roles as mothers and tried hard to care for their children, regardless of the challenges of mothering in the context of domestic violence.

Finally, the findings demonstrate that intersections of gender, race, and social class played an important role in the ways that the women viewed and constructed themselves as mothers, as did the discourses that they drew from, resisted, and negotiated in constructing their mothering identities. Abused women who were single women, low-income women, and women of colour were more likely to resist the discourse of intensive mothering in constructing their subjective mothering identities. These marginalized abused women resisted by negotiating, redefining, and replacing the intensive mothering discourse. In this sense, they engaged in "motherwork for identity" for their own identities as mothers (Collins, *Fighting Words*). Making another important contribution to current understandings of mothering in the context of domestic violence, this study illustrates that marginalized abused mothers do not remain powerless in the face of hegemonic intensive mothering discourses that encourage and fortify their alienation and oppression as mothers. They outright resist these intensive mothering discourses and, in doing so, find ways to support their own self-definitions as mothers, ones that are empowering and not repressive. These women created empowering identities for themselves as mothers in the face of the discourse of intensive mothering that delegitimizes and subjugates them as mothers because of their marginalized circumstances.

Abused mothers, like other marginalized mothers, are more likely to challenge the demands of intensive mothering because they have less resources and status in motherhood and, therefore, are more able to perceive and oppose their oppression (O'Reilly, *Rocking the Cradle*). Because they have mothered in the most difficult of contexts (domestic violence), the abused women in the study are better able to perceive that the standards of intensive mothering that mothers are held to and judge against are idealized, unnatural, unrealistic, exclusionary, and, indeed, unachievable. Recognizing that these intensive mothering standards are social constructions allows these mothers not only to resist but also to carve out new inclusive mothering standards and new empowering mothering identities.

This study and the findings discussed in this book have a number of important implications when it comes to motherhood-mothering scholarly work, feminist theory and practice of motherhood-mothering, and domestic violence policies, practices, and services. In terms of the motherhood-mothering scholarly research and work, this study is one of the first qualitative studies that focuses specifically on abused women's personal mothering experiences as they relate to dominant mothering ideologies and intersections of race, class, and gender. This study, therefore, contributes many informative insights into women's subjective experiences and meanings of mothering within the social context of domestic violence. The findings provide a detailed account of the challenges, struggles, strategies, and triumphs of mothering in the context of abuse by putting abused women's experiential knowledge of their mothering at the forefront and making their subjectivity visible. The findings also highlight the influence that historically specific systems of meaning have on abused women by directing attention to the ways that abused women's experiential knowledge of their mothering is framed. They also demonstrate the diversity in abused women's lives by focusing on variations in their experiential knowledge of their mothering. Overall, the findings point to how even in the most constrictive and oppressive of contexts in which women mother, and even among the most subjugated and marginalized of women who mother, women do find ways to exercise agency, resistance, and power. Far from supporting a deficit model of mothering, the women in the study demonstrated that they love and care deeply for their children, that their mothering is something they feel proud of, and that they overall have positive views of themselves as mothers, despite dominant discourses of mothering and marginalized social locations that cast them in a negative light. Such a reality points to the necessity of research locating women's experiences at the centre of analysis in order to truly obtain a comprehensive understanding of the role and impact that social organization, structure, and location have on the lives of women who mother in and through domestic violence.

In regards to feminist theory and practice of motherhood-mothering, this study is one of the few that builds upon and contributes to maternal empowerment in the context of domestic violence, which is currently lacking. As such, it contributes many informative insights towards building theorizations about abused women's mothering experiences. The findings support and expand O'Reilly's theory of "mothering against patriarchal motherhood" and also contribute towards envisioning what I refer to as "mothering towards woman-centred motherhood." This is evidenced by the fact that the women in the study constructed their mothering identities in ways that not only resisted but also redefined and replaced the discourses of intensive mothering. A feminist theory-practice of "mothering towards woman-centred motherhood," I argue, consists of redefining and even replacing the discourse of intensive mothering, which is male defined and oppressive (as the abused women did in the study,) so that they are female defined and empowering. A feminist theory-practice of "mothering towards woman-centred motherhood," I argue, seeks to demolish a male-centred and oppressive motherhood (patriarchal motherhood) and replace it with a newly created woman-centred and empowering motherhood (woman-centred motherhood) so that it is the only one that exists. This type of feminist theory-practice would allow for women, such as the abused women in the study, to feel empowered in their mothering—not so much through their mothering experience (mothering practices that oppose patriarchal motherhood) because this mothering experience will always be practiced alongside the continued existence of the institution of patriarchal motherhood—but through the process of eradicating this actual institution of patriarchal motherhood and replacing it with an institution of woman-centred motherhood. This can only be accomplished when both mothering as experience and mothering as institution are woman-centred. Woman-centred motherhood is female centred, female defined, and based on female experiences and voices. The findings also support and build on Collins theory of "intersectionality and motherhood," which is demonstrated through the ways that the women in the study engaged in motherwork for their own identities as mothers, or what I refer to as "motherwork for (m)other identity." The women in the study performed "motherwork for (m)other identity" by resisting the discourse of intensive mothering in constructing their subjective mothering identities. "Motherwork for (m)other identity," I argue, consists of marginalized mothers engaging in defining and creating their own mothering identities, in ways that resist the oppressions (gender, race, and social class) they face as marginalized mothers. It is a type of "motherwork" that marginalized mothers engage in to find ways to support their own self-definitions as mothers, ones that were empowering and not repressive. These contributions provide a more comprehensive understanding of abused women's unique experiences as mothers, and are examples of the ways that maternal theory and practice can be applied to studies conducted on mothers, motherhood, and mothering.

In respect to domestic violence policies, practices, and services, the findings contribute important insights in terms of support for women who are escaping abuse. In specific, the findings highlight that the dominant discourse of intensive mothering constructs abused mothers as "bad mothers." Therefore, abused mothers are often automatically perceived and viewed as "bad mothers" and the focus is placed on their deficiencies as mothers among those in wider society, such as domestic violence shelters counsellors, child welfare workers, and school staff, among others. Many of the abused women in the study claimed that they were reluctant to access domestic violence services, and when they did access these services, they were fearful that their mothering abilities would be called into question. This has significant implications for domestic violence services because it suggests that services and supports for victims of domestic violence ought to move away from a deficit model of mothering. Instead, the focus should be shifted to an understanding of abused women's own personal experiences of mothering, and the ways that they themselves feel they can best be aided and assisted with their mothering. Such a shift will result in less mother blame and more supportive practices and resources offered to help women overcome and heal from domestic violence.

In this book, I positioned the voices of the abused women in the centre as a way to contribute to a greater knowledge and understanding about their subjective meanings, understandings, and experiences of mothering in circumstances of domestic violence. By doing so, we see that these women, despite their marginalized conditions, have strength, fortitude, and conviction in their mothering. Just because abused women, like the women in the study, are deemed to be "bad mothers" for failing to live up to ideology of intensive motherhood, does not necessarily mean that they are or that they envision themselves as such. The women in the study clearly sought to demystify the disempowering and oppressive nature of intensive mothering discourses that denigrated them by creating positive and empowering mothering identities for themselves. This knowledge is not only necessary but crucial to end to the oppressive and restrictive bifurcation of mothers into categories of either "good" or "bad" mothers and to re-envision a more inclusive understanding of mothering, one that is empowering to all mothers, regardless of differences in their lives and social circumstances. Our conceptions, understandings, and discussions of not only abused mothers but all mothers need to be reframed to account for the various and diverse ways in which women carry out mothering. Going forward, we must attempt to envision ways for creating spaces where we empathize rather than dismiss, support rather judge, and build up rather than tear down mothers. It is only then that we will truly achieve maternal empowerment for all mothers.

WORKS CITED

Abrahams, C. *The Hidden Victims: Children and Domestic Violence.* London: NCH Action for Children, 1994. Print.

Adair, Vivyan C. "Branded with Infamy: Inscriptions of Poverty and Class in the United States." *Signs* 27.2 (2002): 451–471. Web. 8 Dec. 2015.

Astin, M.C., K. J. Lawrence, and D.W. Foy. "Posttraumatic Stress Disorder Among Battered Women: Risk and Resiliency Factors." *Violence and Victims* 8.1 (1993): 17-28. Web. 8 Dec. 2015.

Baber, Kristine M., and Katherine R. Allen. *Women and Families: Feminist Reconstructions.* New York: Guilford Press, 1992. Print.

Baca Zinn, Maxine. "Adaptation and Continuity in Mexican-Origin Families." *Minority Families in the United States: A Multicultural Perspective.* Ed. Ronald L. Taylor. Upper Saddle River, N.J.: Prentice Hall, 1998. 64-81. Print.

Baca Zinn, Maxine. "Family, Feminism, and Race In America." *Gender & Society* 4.1 (1990): 68-82. Web. 8 Dec. 2015.

Belenky, Mary Field, Blythe M. Clinchy, Nancy R. Goldberger, and Jill M. Tarule. *Women's Ways of Knowing: The Development of Self, Voice, and Mind.* New York: Basic, 1986. Print.

Berk, R. A., S.F. Berk, D. R. Loseke, and D. Rauma. "Mutual Combat and Other Family Violence Myths." *The Dark Side of Families: Current Family Violence Research.* Ed. David Finkelhor. Beverly Hills: Sage Publications, 1983. 197-212. Print.

Bograde, M. "Feminist Perspectives on Wife Abuse: An Introduction." *Feminist Perspectives on Wife Abuse.* Eds. Kersti Yllo and M. Bograde. Newbury Park, California: Sage Publications,

1988. 11-26. Print.
Bowker, Lee H. *Beating Wife-Beating*. Toronto: D.C. Heath, 1983. Print.
Browne, Angela. *When Battered Women Kill*. New York: The Free Press, 1989. Print.
Buchbinder, Eli. "Motherhood of Battered Women: The Struggle for Repairing the Past." *Clinical Social Work Journal* 32.3 (2004): 307-26. Web. 8 Dec. 2015.
Cascardi, Michele, and K. Daniel O'Leary. "Depressive Symptomatology, Self-Esteem, and Self-Blame in Battered Women." *Journal of Family Violence* 7.4 (1992): 249-59. Web. 8 Dec. 2015.
Chant, Sylvia. "Women-Headed Households: Poorest of the Poor?: Perspectives from Mexico, Costa Rica and the Philippines." *IDS Bulletin* 28.3 (2009): 26-48. Web. 8 Dec. 2015.
Chant, Sylvia H., and Jo Campling. *Women-Headed Households: Diversity and Dynamics in the Developing World*. New York: St. Martin's, 1997. Print.
Chase, Susan E., and Mary F. Rogers. *Mothers & Children: Feminist Analyses and Personal Narratives*. New Jersey: Rutgers University Press, 2001. Print.
Clarke, Alison J. "Consuming Children and Making Mothers: Birthday Parties, Gifts, and the Pursuit of Sameness." *Horizontes Antropologicos* 3.5 (2007): 263-87. Web. 8 Dec. 2015.
Code, Lorraine. *What Can She Know?: Feminist Theory and the Construction of Knowledge*. Ithaca: Cornell University Press, 1991. Print.
Collins, Patricia Hill. "Shifting the Center: Race, Class, and Feminist Theorizing About Motherhood." *Mothering: Ideology, Experience, and Agency*. Eds. Evelyn Nakano Glenn, Grace Chang, and Linda Rennie Forcey. New York: Routledge, 1994. 45-66. Web. 20 Jan. 2016.
Collins, Patricia Hill. *Black Feminist Thought: Knowledge, Consciousness, and the Politics of Empowerment*. Boston: Unwin Hyman, 1991. Print.
Collins, Patricia Hill. *Fighting Words: Black Women and the Search for Justice*. Minneapolis: University of Minnesota Press. 1991. Print.
Cooper, Camille Wilson, and Shauntay Z. McCoy. "Poverty and

African American Mothers." *Journal of the Association for Research on Mothering* 11.2 (2009): 45-55. Web. 7 Dec. 2015.

Cooper, Davina. "Productive, Relational and Everywhere? Conceptualising Power and Resistance within Foucauldian Feminism." *Sociology* 28.2 (1994): 435-54. Web. 8 Dec. 2015.

Cossman, B. "Family Inside/Out." *Feminism and Families*. Ed. M. Luxton. Halifax, Nova Scotia, Canada: Fernwood, 1997. 124-141. Print.

Crawford, C. "The Continuity of Global Crossings: African-Caribbean Women and Transnational motherhood." *Journal of Motherhood Initiative for Research and Community Involvement* 2.2 (2011): 9-25. Web. 8 Dec. 2015.

Croghan, R., and D. Miell. "Strategies of Resistance: Bad Mothers Dispute the Evidence." *Feminism and Psychology* 8.4 (1998): 445-465. Web. 8 Dec. 2015.

Davies, Bronwyn, and Rom Harré. "Positioning: The Discursive Production of Selves." *Journal for the Theory of Social Behaviour* 20.1 (1990): 43-63. Web. 8 Dec. 2015.

Dobash, R. Emerson, and Russell Dobash. *Violence against Wives: A Case Against the Patriarchy*. New York: Free, 1979. Print.

Dobash, R. Emerson, and Russel Dobash. "Research as Social Action: The Struggle for Battered Women." *Feminist Perspectives on Wife Abuse*. Ed. Kersti Yllo and M. Bograde. Newbury Park, California: Sage Publications, 1988. Print.

Douglas, Susan J, and Meredith W. Michaels. *The Mommy Myth: The Idealization of Motherhood and How It Has Undermined Women*. New York: The Free Press, 2004. Print.

Edelson, J., L. Mbilinyi, and S. Shetty. *Parenting in the Context of Domestic Violence*. San Francisco: Judicial Council of California/ Administrative Office of the Courts. 2003. Print.

Ennis, Linda Rose. *Intensive Mothering: The Cultural Contradictions of Modern Motherhood*. Bradford, Ontario: Demeter Press, 2004. Print.

Eyer, Diane E. *Motherguilt: How Our Culture Blames Mothers for What's Wrong with Society*. New York: Times /Random House, 1996. Print.

Featherstone, Brid. "Taking Othering Seriously: The Implications for Child Protection." *Child and Family Social Work* 4 (1999):

43-53. *Wiley*. Web. 8 Dec. 2015.

Featherstone, Brid, and Liz Trinder. "Familiar Subjects? Domestic Violence and Child Welfare." *Child and Family Social Work* (2003): 147-59. *Wiley*. Web. 8 Dec. 2015.

Ferraro, Kathleen J., and John M. Johnson. "How Women Experience Battering: The Process of Victimization." *Social Problems* 30: 325-39. Web. 8 Dec. 2015.

Firestone, Shulamith. *The Dialectic of Sex: The Case for Feminist Revolution*. New York: Bantam, 1971. Print.

Follingstad, Diane R., Anne F. Brennan, Elizabeth S. Hause, Darlene S. Polek, and Larry L. Rutledge. "Factors Moderating Physical And Psychological Symptoms Of Battered Women." *Journal of Family Violence* 6.1 (2001): 81-95. Web. 8 Dec. 2015.

Friedman, Hilary Levey. *Playing to Win: Raising Children in a Competitive Culture*. Berkeley: University of California Press, 2013. Print.

Garey, Anita Ilta. "Constructing Motherhood on The Night Shift: 'Working Mothers' As "Stay-at-Home Moms." *Qualitative Sociology* 18.4 (1995): 415-37. Print.

Gilman, Susan Thomas. "A History of the Sheltering Movement for Battered Women in Canada" *Canadian Journal of Community Mental Health* 7.2 (1988): 9-21. Web. 8 Dec. 2015.

Glenn, Evelyn Nakano. *Mothering: Ideology, Experience, and Agency*. New York: Routledge, 1994. Print.

Gordon, Tuula. *Feminist Mothers*. Basingstoke, Hampshire: Macmillan, 1990. Print.

Green, F. "Moms under Surveillance: Noticing and Challenging the Idea of the 'Good Mother'" *What do Mothers Need*. Ed. Andrea O'Reilly. Toronto, ON: Demeter Press, 2012. 21-34. Print.

Green, F. "Feminist Mothers: Successfully Negotiating the Tensions between Motherhood as 'Institution' and 'Experience.'" *Mother Outlaws: Theories and Practices of Empowered Mothering*. Ed. Andrea O'Reilly. Toronto, ON: Women's Press, 2004. 31-42. Print.

Hays, Sharon. *The Cultural Contradictions of Motherhood*. New Haven: Yale University Press, 1996. Print.

Hazen, A., C. Connelly, K. Kelleher, R. Barth, and J. Landsverk. "Female Caregivers' Experiences with Intimate Partner Violence and Behavior Problems in Children Investigated as Victims of Maltreatment." *Pediatrics* 117.1 (2006): 99-109. Web. 8 Dec. 2015.

Hebert, C. and J. Foley. "Building Shelter, Taking Down Walls." *Ties that Bind: An Anthology of Social Work and Social Welfare in Newfoundland and Labrador.* Ed. J. Symonds. St John's, NF: Jesperson, 1997. 187-221. Print.

Holden, George W and Kathy L. Ritchie. "Linking Extreme Marital Discord, Child Rearing, And Child Behavior Problems: Evidence From Battered Women." *Child Development* 62 (1991): 311-327. Web. 8 Dec. 2015.

Holden, George W., J. D. Stein, K. L. Ritchie, S. D. Harris, and E. N. Jouriles. "Parenting Behaviors and Beliefs of Battered Women." *Children Exposed to Marital Violence: Theory, Research, and Applied Issues.* Ed. G. W. Holden, R. Geffner, and E. N. Jouriles. Washington, DC: American Psychological Association, 1997). 289-334. Print.

hooks, bell. *Feminist Theory from Margin to Center.* Boston, MA: South End, 1984. Print.

Horwitz, Erika. *Through the Maze of Motherhood: Empowered Mothers Speak.* Bradford, Ontario: Demeter Press, 2011. Print.

Hyden, Margareta. *Woman Battering as Marital Act: The Construction of a Violent Marriage.* New York: Oxford University Press. 1994. Print.

Jaffe, Peter, Michelle Zerwer, and Samantha Poisson. "Access Denied: The Barriers of Violence and Poverty for Abused Women and Their Children Search for Justice and Community Services After Separation." Centre for Children and Families in the Justice System, 2014. Web. 8 Dec. 2015.

Jarvis, Kelly L., Erin E. Gordon, and Raymond W. Novaco. "Psychological Distress Of Children And Mothers In Domestic Violence Emergency Shelters." *Journal of Family Violence* 20.6 (2005): 389-402. Web. 8 Dec. 2015.

Jasinski, J. L. "Theoretical Explanations for Violence against Women." *Sourcebook on violence against women.* Eds. C. M. Renzetti, J. L. Edleson, and R. K. Bergen. Thousand Oaks, CA: Sage Publications, 2001. 5-21. Print.

Johnson, Holly. "Violence against Women in Canada". Nelson,

BC: Canadian Centre for Justice Statistics (1996). Print.

Kline, Marlee. "Complicating the Ideology of Motherhood: Child Welfare Law and First Nation Women." *Queen's Law Journal* 18 (1993): 306-342. Web. 8 Dec. 2015.

Knowles, Jane Price and Ellen Cole. *Woman-Defined Motherhood.* New York: Hawthorn Press, 1990. Print.

Krane, J., and L. Davies. "Sisterhood Is Not Enough: The Invisibility of Mothering in Shelter Practice With Battered Women." *Affilia* 17 (2002): 167-90. Web. 8 Dec. 2015.

Krane, J., and L. Davies. "Mothering under Difficult Circumstances: Challenges to Working With Battered Women." *Affilia* 22.1 (2007): 23-38. Web. 8 Dec. 2015.

Kurz, D. "Social Science Perspectives on Wife Abuse: Current Debates and Future Directions." *Gender & Society* 3.4 (1989): 489-505. Web. 8 Dec. 2015.

Ladd-Taylor, Molly. "Mother-Work: Women, Child Welfare, and the State, 1890–1930." *Journal of Historical Geography* 21.2 (1994): 231-33. Web. 8 Dec. 2015.

Lambertus, Sandra. *Addressing Violence Perpetrated against Aboriginal Women in Alberta. bwss.org.* Battered Women's Support Services, 2015. Web. 8 Dec. 2015.

Lapierre, Simon. "Mothering in the Context of Domestic Violence: The Pervasiveness of a Deficit Model of Mothering." *Child & Family Social Work* 13 (2008): 454-63. Web. 8 Dec. 2015.

Lapierre, Simon. "More Responsibilities, Less Control: Understanding the Challenges and Difficulties Involved in Mothering in the Context of Domestic Violence." *British Journal of Social Work* 40.5 (2009): 434-451. Web. 8 Dec. 2015.

Lapierre, Simon. "Striving to Be 'Good' Mothers: Abused Women's Experiences of Mothering." *Child Abuse Review* 19 (2010): 342-57. Web. 8 Dec. 2015.

Lenton, R.L. "Power Versus Feminist Theories of Wife Abuse." *Canadian Journal of Criminology* 7 (1995): 305-330. Web. 8 Dec. 2015.

Leonard, V. W. "Mothering as a Practice." *Caregiving: Readings in Knowledge, Practice, Ethics, and Politics* Eds. S. Gordon, P. Benner, and N. Noddings. Philadelphia, PA: University of Pennsylvania Press (1996): 124-140. Print.

Letourneau, N. L., C. B. Fedick, and J. D. Willms. "Mothering and Domestic Violence: A Longitudinal Analysis." *Journal of Family Violence* 22.8 (2007): 649-59. Web. 8 Dec. 2015.

Levendosky, Alytia A., and Sandra A. Graham-Bermann. "The Moderating Effects of Parenting Stress on Children's Adjustment in Woman-Abusing Families." *Journal of Interpersonal Violence* 13 (1998): 383-97. Web. 8 Dec. 2015.

Levendosky, Alytia A., and Sandra A. Graham-Bermann. "Behavioral Observations of Parenting In Battered Women." *Journal of Family Psychology* 14 (2000): 80-94. Web. 8 Dec. 2015.

Levendosky, Alytia. A., S. M. Lynch, and S. A. Graham-Bermann. "Mothers' Perceptions Of The Impact of Woman Abuse on Their Parenting." *Violence Against Women* 6 (2000): 247-71. Web. 8 Dec. 2015.

Levendosky, Alytia A., Alissa C. Huth-Bocks, Deborah L. Shapiro, and Michael A. Semel. "The Impact of Domestic Violence on The Maternal-Child Relationship and Preschool-Age Children's Functioning." *Journal of Family Psychology* 17.3 (2003): 275-87. Web. 8 Dec. 2015.

Little, D. L. "Independent Workers, Dependable Mothers: Discourse, Resistance, and AFDC Workfare Programs." *Social Politics: International Studies in Gender, State & Society* 6.2 (1999): 161-202. Web. 8 Dec. 2015.

Luxton, Meg, ed. *Feminism and Families Critical Policies and Changing Practices*. Halifax, Nova Scotia, Canada: Fernwood, 1997. Print.

MacLeod, F. *Transition House: How to Establish a Refuge for Battered Women*. Ottawa, Ontario: National Clearinghouse on Family Violence, Health and Welfare Canada, 1989. Print.

Maushart, Susan. *Mask of Motherhood*. New York: New Press, 1999. Print.

Mauthner, Natasha S. "'Feeling Low and Feeling Really Bad about Feeling Low': Women's Experiences Of Motherhood and Postpartum Depression." *Canadian Psychology/Psychologie Canadienne* 40.2 (1999): 143-61. Web. 8 Dec. 2015.

McCloskey, Laura Ann, Aurelio Jose Figueredo, and Mary P. Koss. "The Effects Of Systemic Family Violence On Children's Mental Health." *Child Development* 66 (1995): 1239. Web. 8 Dec. 2015.

McDonald-Harker, Caroline. "Mothering in the Context of Domestic Violence and Encounters with Child Protection Services: From Victimized to 'Criminalized" Mothers.'" *Criminalized Mothers: Criminalizing Motherhood.* Eds. J. Minaker and B. Hogeveen. Toronto: Demeter Press (2015): 323-354. Print.

McMahon, Martha. *Engendering Motherhood: Identity and Self-Transformation in Women's Lives.* New York: Guilford Press, 1995. Print.

Mirlees-Black, Catriona. *Domestic Violence: Findings from a New British Crime Survey Self-Completion Questionnaire.* London: Home Office, 1999. Print.

Moore, T. E., and D. J. Peppler. "Correlates of Adjustment in Children at Risk." *Children Exposed to Marital Violence: Theory, Research, and Applied Issues.* Eds. G.W. Holden, R. Geffner, E.N. Jouriles. Washington, DC: American Psychological Association 1988. 157-184. Print.

Morrel, T. M., Dubowitz, H., Kerr, M.A., and Black, M. M. "The Effect of Maternal Victimization on Children: A Cross-Information Study." *Journal of Family Violence* 18.1 (2003): 29-41. Web. 8 Dec. 2015.

Mullender, Audrey. *Children's Perspectives on Domestic Violence.* London: Sage Publications, 2002. Print.

Nixon, Kendra. L. "Intimate Partner Woman Abuse in Alberta's Child Protection Policy and the Impact on Abused Mothers and their Children." *Current* 8.1 (2008): 172-193. Print.

O'Reilly, Andrea. *Mother Matters: Motherhood as Discourse and Practice: Essays from the Journal of the Association for Research on Mothering.* Toronto: Association for Research on Mothering, 2004. Print.

O'Reilly, Andrea. *Mother Outlaws: Theories and Practices of Empowered Mothering.* Toronto: Women's Press, 2004. Print.

O'Reilly, Andrea. *From Motherhood to Mothering: The Legacy of Adrienne Rich's Of Woman Born.* Albany: State University of New York, 2004. Print.

O'Reilly, Andrea. *Rocking the Cradle: Thoughts on Feminism, Motherhood, and the Possibility of Empowered Mothering.* Toronto: Demeter, 2006. Print.

O'Reilly, Andrea. *Maternal Theory: Essential Readings.* Toronto:

Demeter, 2007. Print.

O'Reilly, Andrea. *Feminist Mothering*. Albany: State University of New York, 2008. Print.

O'Reilly, Andrea. "Outlaw(ing) Motherhood: A Theory and Politic of Maternal Empowerment for the Twenty-First Century." *Hectate* 36.1.2 (2010): 17-29. Web. 8 Dec. 2015.

O'Reilly, Andrea. *The 21st Century Motherhood Movement: Mothers Speak out on Why We Need to Change the World and How to Do It*. Toronto: Demeter, 2011. Print.

O'Reilly, Andrea. *What do Mothers Need?* Toronto: Demeter Press, 2012. Print.

Palladino, Hallie. "The Cultural Contradictions of Fatherhood: Is There an Ideology of Intensive Fathering?" *Intensive Mothering: The Cultural Contradictions of Modern Motherhood*. Ed. Linda Rose Ennis. Bradford, Ontario: Demeter Press, 2014: 280-298. Print.

Peled, E., and I. B. Gil. "The Mothering Perceptions of Women Abused by Their Partner." *Violence Against Women* 17.4 (2011): 457-79. Web. 8 Dec. 2015.

Pleck, E., J. H. Pleck, M. Grossman, and P. B. Bart. "The Battered Data Syndrome: A Comment on Steinmetz' Article." *Victimology: An International Journal* 2 (1977-1978): 690-684. Web. 8 Dec. 2015.

Radford, L. "Domestic Violence, Understanding Social Problems: Issues in Social Policy." *Understanding Social Problems*. Eds. M. May, R. Page and E. Brunsdon. Oxford: Blackwell Publishers, 2001: 70:83. Print.

Radford, L. and M. Hester. "Overcoming Mother Blaming? Future Directions for Research on Mothering and Domestic Violence" *Domestic Violence in the Lives of Children: The Future of Research, Intervention, and Social Policy.* Eds. S.A. Graham-Bermann and J. L. Edleson Washington, DC: American Psychological Association, 2006: 135-156. Print.

Radford, L. and M. Hester. "Introduction." *Women, Violence and Male Power.* Eds. M. Hester, L. Kelly, and J. Radford. Buckingham. Open University Press, 1996. 1-16. Print.

Ranson, G. "Paid Work, Family Work, and the Discourse of the Full Time Mother." *Journal of the Association for Research on*

Mothering 1.1 (1999): 57-66. Web. 8 Dec. 2015.

Ribbens, J. *Mothers and their Children: A Feminist Sociology of Childrearing*. London: Sage Publications, 1994. Print.

Rich, Adrienne. *Of Woman Born: Motherhood as Experience and Institution*. New York: Norton, 1986. Print.

Rizzo, Kathryn M., Holly H. Schiffrin, and Miriam Liss. "Insight Into the Parenthood Paradox: Mental Health Outcomes of Intensive Mothering." *Journal of Child and Family Studies* 22.5 (2013): 614-20. Web. 8 Dec. 2015.

Rossiter, Amy. *From Private to Public: A Feminist Exploration of Early Mothering*. Toronto: The Women's Press, 1998. Print.

Ruddick, Sara. "Maternal Thinking." *Philosophy, Children, and the Family* 6.3 (1980): 101-26. Web. 8 Dec. 2015.

Ruddick, Sara. *Maternal Thinking: Toward a Politics of Peace*. New York: Ballantine Books, 1989. Print.

Ruddick, Sara. "Thinking Mothers/Conceiving Birth." *Representations of Motherhood*. Eds. D. Bassin, M. Honey, and M. M. Kaplan. New Haven, CT: Yale University Press, 1994. 29-46. Print.

Rullo, Guiseppina, and Tullia Musatti. "Mothering Young Children: Child Care, Stress and Social Life." *European Journal of Psychology of Education* 20.2 (2005): 107-19. Web. 8 Dec. 2015.

Russell, Diana E. H. *Rape in Marriage*. New York: Macmillan, 1982. Print.

Schechter, Susan. *Women and Male Violence: The Visions and Struggles of the Battered Women's Movement*. Boston: South End Press, 1982. Print.

Scott, J. "Deconstructing Equality-Versus-Difference: Or, the Uses of Postructuralist Theory for Feminism," *Conflicts in Feminism*. Ed. A. Hirsh. New York: Routledge, 1990. 134-148. Print.

Seagram, Samantha, and Judith C. Daniluk. "'It Goes with the Territory' The Meaning and Experience of Maternal Guilt for Mothers of Preadolescent Children." *Women & Therapy* 25.1 (2002): 61-88. Web. 8 Dec. 2015.

Stack, C. and L. Burton. "Kinscripts." *Journal of Comparative Family Studies* 20.2 (1993): 157-170. Web. 8 Dec. 2015.

Statistics Canada. "The Violence Against Women Survey (1993)." Government of Canada, 2015. Web. 8. Dec. 2015.

Statistics Canada. "Transition Home Survey 2011-2012." Gov-

ernment of Canada, 2015. Web. 8. Dec. 2015.
Stoppard, Janet M. *Understanding Depression: Feminist Social Constructionist Approaches*. London: Routledge, 2000. Print.
Sullivan, Cris M., Huong Nguyen, Nicole Allen, Deborah Bybee, and Jennifer Juras. "Beyond Searching For Deficits." *Journal of Emotional Abuse* 2 (2000): 51-71. Web. 8 Dec. 2015.
Takševa, Tatjana. "The Commercialization of Motherhood and Mothering in the Context of Globalization: Anglo-American Perspectives." *Journal of Motherhood Initiative for Research and Community Involvement* 3.1 (2012): 134-148. Print.
Takševa, Tatjana. "How Contemporary Consumerism Shapes Intensive Mothering Practices." *Intensive Mothering: The Cultural Contradictions of Modern Motherhood*. Ed. Linda Rose Ennis. Bradford, Ontario: Demeter Press, 2014. 211-232. Print.
The Public Health Agency of Canada. *Aboriginal Women and Family Violence (2002). phac-aspc.gc.ca*. The Government of Canada, 2015. Web. 8 Dec. 2015.
Thurer, Shari. *The Myths of Motherhood: How Culture Reinvents the Good Mother*. New York: Penguin Books, 1995. Print.
United Nations. *Strategies for Confronting Domestic Violence: A Resource Manual (1993)*. United Nations, 2015. Web. 8 Dec 2015.
Umansky, Lauri. *Motherhood Reconceived: Feminism and the Legacies of the Sixties*. New York: NYU Press, 1996. Web. 8 Dec. 2015.
Vandenbeld Giles, Melinda. *Mothering in the Age of Neoliberalism*. Bradford, Ontario: Demeter Press, 2014. Print.
Walker, Gillian. *Family Violence and the Women's Movement: The Conceptual Politics of Struggle*. Toronto: University of Toronto Press, 1990. Print.
Walker, Lenore E. *The Battered Woman*. New York: Harper & Row, 1980. Print.
Wall, G. "Mothers' Experiences with Intensive Parenting and Brain Development Discourse." *Women's Studies International Forum* 33.3 (2010): 253-263. Web. 8 Dec. 2015.
Weingarten, K. "Radical Listening: Challenging Cultural Beliefs for and About Mothers." *Cultural Resistance: Challenging Beliefs, About Men, Women, and Therapy*. Ed. K.Weingarten,

New York: Haworth Press, 1995. 7-22. Print.
Wilson, C. "Domestic Violence in the Child Protection System: Seeing Double." *Journal of Interpersonal Violence* 13 .2 (1998): 289-293. Web. 8 Dec. 2015.
Zeanah, C. H., B. Danis, L. Hirshberg, D. Benoit, D. Miller, and S. S. Heller. "Disorganized Attachment Associated with Partner Violence: A Research Note." *Infant Mental Health Journal Infant Mental Health Journal.* 20 (1999): 77-86. Web. 8 Dec. 2015.

Caroline McDonald-Harker is a Sociologist and a Professor in the Department of Sociology and Anthropology at Mount Royal University in Calgary, Alberta. She received her PhD in Sociology from the University of Alberta (2011), MA in Sociology from McGill University (2002), and BA Honours in Sociology from Queen's University (2001). Caroline is the mother of three young children. Her areas of expertise include: the sociology of motherhood/mothering, gender, family, domestic violence, disasters, social inequality, social policy, and qualitative research methods. She is a contributing author to *Criminalized Mothers, Criminalizing Mothering* (Demeter 2015) and the co-editor of upcoming Demeter Press edited collection book *Mothering in Disasters/Mothering Disasters*. She is currently conducting a three-year study on the impact of disasters on the family (with a focus on mothers and mothering) funded by a SSHRC Partnership Development Grant. She is also conducting a three-year study on children, youth, and family resiliency in post-disaster contexts, funded by an Alberta Innovates Health Solutions CRIO research grant.